bum rush the page

bum rush the page

a def poetry jam

Edited by Tony Medina and Louis Reyes Rivera

THREE RIVERS PRESS

NEW YORK

Published by Three Rivers Press, New York, New York.
Member of the Crown Publishing Group.

Random House, Inc. New York, Toronto, London, Sydney, Auckland
www.randomhouse.com

THREE RIVERS PRESS is a registered trademark and the Three Rivers Press colophon is a trademark of Random House, Inc.

Printed in the United States of America

Design by Paula Kelly

Library of Congress Cataloging-in-Publication Data
Bum rush the page: a def poetry jam / edited by Tony Medina and Louis Reyes Rivera.
    1. American poetry—20th century.   2. Oral interpretation of poetry—Competitions.   3. Poetry—Competitions.   I. Medina, Tony.   II. Rivera, Louis Reyes.
PS615.B86   2001
811'.5408—dc21   2001027783
ISBN 0-609-80840-0

10 9 8 7 6 5 4 3 2

First Edition

The prerequisite for writing

is having something to say.

—*Langston Hughes*

CONTENTS

Open Your Mouth—and Smile

Every Word Must Conjure

Drums Drown Out the Sorrow

contents

i x

When the Definition of Madness Is Love

We Whose Fathers Are Hidden

Seed of Resistance

Beauty Is Moving Us Forward

It Was the Music That Made Us

Children of the Word

contents

FOREWORD

By Sonia Sanchez

What I remember about reading the first time to an audience is that I was stricken at how the words stayed on the page. And how at the same time I remembered the language of my grandmother and the language of my father and jazz musicians, how their language/sounds bounced off paper, went into some sacred space of broken tongues, re-entered the atmosphere at such a pace that their re-entry burned the edges of our souls and our ears as we listened. Went home, again.

When I first heard some of the older poets in the anthology read, their words sped from the paper to our ears and back to their pages. And among those of us who listened, there was a recognition of poems well-done, executed. Poems in keeping with the times, on-time poems, necessary poems, history/herstory poems. I think when they finally heard some of us read, they saw us look at the word, splice it, look up at the word and jazz it up, look backwards at the word and decide to disconnect and reconnect it at the end, stretch it, moan it, groan it, peel it, and then finally, redress the world and say, "See, this is a poem." And I saw other poets, I saw white poets, begin to come and listen to how we read because people didn't read like that, or had not read in that fashion before. And our generation of Black Arts poets began to show poets how to read.

These new poets, these hip-hop poets heard the sound and picked it up. And they did the same thing we did with poetry and sound, they did the sound, the pace, the pace of sound, the swiftness of sound, the discordant way of looking at the world of sound, the blackness of sound, the color of sound, the beat of sound, but above all it was that fast beat. It was what I called the new bebopic beat. Because when the bebop people started to play nobody could keep up with them. It was so fast you couldn't even hear. I would always say to my kids when I first heard hip-hop, "I can't hear it. I don't understand." And the same kind of thing when Dizzy and Max were playing; nobody could play it except them, and nobody could hear it. You had to have a fast ear to hear it cuz otherwise they would play it and done been gone. Same thing that happened with rap. It came at a fast pace and if you turned your head, you missed it. It was gone. The bebop, the bam, and the hip hop.

Each generation brings something new to this thing called craft, to this thing called poetry. What we did when we looked at Margaret Walker and Gwendolyn Brooks, we went back into their herstory and history and pulled back from Langston Hughes, Sterling Brown, Dudley Randall, and Robert Hayden, that whole group. We pulled from them the craft of writing, the discipline of writing and the history and herstory of our people. Then we said,

"Let's bring it to a new sense of history. Let's in a sense 'reword' history, refocus history with these new words and a new way of looking at the world." So we employed what they gave us along with what was going on in the world: the politics of being Black, from civil rights to Black Power, to the new sense of self, to the new sense of who we are/were. And we came up with poems that did similar things that Miss Margaret and Sister Gwen and Brother Sterling Brown did. But we also, I think, began to give it a new modern sound that was part of a twentieth century sound. And I guess what I'm saying is that at some point you had to look and see that their poetry was viable, but it was another sound. It was a different sound. When Baraka, Askia, and I scatted, used the music of Monk, Coltrane, Dizzy, the blues of our people we cut the century in half, re-entered the century with the good news that the Africans were all alive and living in the Diaspora. This is the very modernist way we looked at poetry. The world not ending with a whimper, but being full of ideas and sound and music that challenged everyone.

What we have to learn, it seems to me, in this 21st century, is that we have been history, and we are history. And we have to unearth the history. To me, this 21st century is a serious time to look at ourselves because there's a possibility that some of us will disappear in this 21st century as a significant force in world history. I would not have said that in the 20th century. But because we have not understood our history, we have allowed ourselves to be bought and killed out of history. I mean, there are people who allow us to be bought out of history. So at some point, it is necessary, it is incumbent upon us to look and see as poets still poeting in the 21st century, *how do I go out of my skin and return again with friends who will have something relevant to say*?

It might not be a new discussion, but it's something that comes up time and time again. And each poet has got to respond to it some kind of way. Once when I was teaching, some of the little black kids were being chased home by some of the older white children who were calling them nigger. And so I went home and wrote a poem: "... nigger/ that word ain't shit to me/ don't you know where you at when you call me nigger/ I'll say it slow for you—niiiigggger./ I know I'm black,/ beautiful with meaning nigger, my man/ you way behind the set." Those children memorized that poem and when they were chased again, they stopped the chasers and they turned and said, "That word don't turn me on man/ I know I'm black." And they flaunted their blackness in the streets. And the white kids stopped in their tracks. And this is important: If they could chase someone with just one word, then they have the power, but if you could stop the word's importance by replacing it with something new, then you had the power. I tried to reinvent the word to give them the new power. And that's what you have to do. I empowered those children. They were being chased with a word. They were running. And when they stopped and turned with their interpretation of the word nigger, they were at a new place with themselves. They put the white kids on pause. A safe place to be, lovin' themselves in the middle of the 20th century. And what I feel in this anthology is the love these young people have for language. Their tongues caress the words with humor and irony and love.

INTRODUCTION

Our culture shapes us to compete, to gobble each other up for money and prestige. This is never more apparent than with the current onslaught of sensationalized "reality" television shows like *Survivor* where the objective is to win at all costs. This popularized exhibition of Social Darwinism glues us to the tube while big business parades its endless battering ram of commercials and misinformation across our retinas and into our frontal lobes.

Poetry has taken a similar plunge with the advent of the Slam. The Slam pits poets against one another in gladiator-like scenarios where they compete for chump change and prestige, judged by a select group of audience members (sometimes consisting of other poets; most times not). Too often in this arena poetry is not what matters, but performance—how well one can recite a line or two, no matter how backward or banal. A cat could read the phone book and, if his or her voice hits the right note, their facial expression caught mid-strain in the glare of the spotlight, as if in mid-shit, they just may slam their way to the top of the (dung) heap. Here, poetry is cheap, is cheapened.

A good number of folks running around calling themselves poets care less about poetry than about "blowing up." When I first hit the New York scene running (some twelve-odd years ago), we used the term "blow up" with regard to saying something political or profound, not about seeking some sort of fame or fortune. Poets I ran with talked about "dropping bombs," or "blowing up the spot" like rappers talked about "dropping science"; it was about saying something deep and powerful—and leaving a hole in the stage! It is that same "stage" that haunts us today. Serious poets who also happen to perform well on stage are constantly being called spoken-word artists and are not taken seriously as writers. Poets (especially those of color) who use the word (use language) to effect change are therefore ghettoized by those in the academy and those at the gates as solely (or "simply") oral, urban, or street poets. In other words, they are not *real* writers because they're not busy polishing their poems until they disappear, creating verse to decorate the parlors of the rich and bloodless.

On a similar front, publishers tell us poetry doesn't sell, yet the same old cats are constantly being published. The critics and canon shapers continue to insist that poetry and politics should not mix.

Here, in this strange land, poets are constantly in a dilemma. They are, as Amiri Baraka puts it, "the niggers of literature." But where once there were poets who used their words to burn down Babylon in all its bumba clot madness and confusion, these days everybody and they mama wants to be a poet, but without reason—sometimes without reading. Today, poets who are committed to poetry *and* the people find themselves sandwiched between the mindless circus show of slam sluts—heads running around with microphones in they briefcases like pool sharks—and angst-ridden anglophiliacs in MFA-induced comas who confine their poems—all they have to say—to two and three line stanza breaks. (Why should what you think or feel, what you see and believe, the way you relate to the world, be confined to a neat looking flask or the same old, boring geometric shapes and figures? Since when should every one's poems be an isosceles trapezoid?)

Any poet worth his or her weight in syllables and words uses poetry for certain reasons, be it to define one's self, to defend one's self, or to describe one's environment with accuracy, communicating a clear understanding of what is going on in the world. But what appears in many of the so-called new American poetry anthologies are the usual lot of dry poets shitted out of the bowels of Ivy League schools and other stamp-of-approval institutions designed to stamp out creativity and promote mediocrity. They deliberately exclude socially responsible poetry that speaks for and to a generation that did not benefit from the reforms gained by the Civil Rights Movement or the riches of the so-called New Economy. They ignore poets who could care less about being the kind of poet who in neatly polished poem after neatly polished poem perpetrates a fraud on reality. This book works to counter that trend and bring poetry—relevant, meaningful, provocative poetry—back to the people.

This book exists in a paradox. While it will be closely related to what some are calling the spoken word—that which lives in performance—the poetry gathered here, for the most part, maintains the integrity of the page, of the written word. It proves, as Adrienne Rich put it, that "poetry can be 'about,' can root itself in politics . . . without sacrificing intensity of language." At a time when the prison population has doubled in the span of 10 years (from one million to two million), as a result of the so-called war on drugs, gentrification, racial profiling, and the rise of privatized prisons; where crack and AIDS are as common as talk shows and pollution; where women and children are being incarcerated at alarming rates; where the death penalty threatens to be the next reality show flickering on your TV screen; where globalization threatens to dumb every one and every thing down and suck the life blood of the earth, turning everything nice and shiny and white as an American Standard toilet bowl, these multivarious poets emerge, armed with the word, going from the personal to the political to lay out a broad, sweeping range of aesthetic and social concerns, right (read: write) on time.

As editors our intention was to make this anthology as literary and dynamic as possible. We sought to publish quality poetry of all styles and aesthetic concerns that reflect, for the most part, the last ten to twelve years of this new resurgence in poetry here in the U.S., as well as abroad. Here is a democratic orchestration of voices and visions, poets of all ages, ethnicities, and geographic locations coming together to create a dialogue and to jam—not slam. The poems here work together for a common goal and purpose: to celebrate life, language, and poetry and cut through the mound of concrete and dung attempting to smother us and our sense of outrage, culture, humor, and creativity. Collectively, and individually, this is our mouth on paper, our heart on our sleeves, our refusal to shut the fuck up and swallow our silence. And if you hold the pages of this book up to the light at an angle just so, it's as close to an autopsy on capitalism as you're gonna get, for now.

There are many ways to access this text. Of course, each individual will approach it according to his or her particular process. I myself tend to gravitate towards knocking out the shorter poems first. Perhaps it is my New York state of mind, always on the run, on the move, running from place to place at warp speed time.

But I'm going to be bold enough to suggest, having read the damn thing from cover to cover I don't know how many times, that *you* read it from cover to cover; perhaps consciously skimming past titles, and going straight to the body of the poems (unless a title functions as the necessary first line; though seemingly apparent, one must be cognizant of this technique). If you were to approach it this way, you will begin to get and hear things us editors had the privilege of ruminating over the months we spent racking our brains on the submissions. There is a music that takes place, filled with metaphors and memories, madness and messages. Like being at a poetry reading, or a jam session, each poet and musician approaching the mic individually—and as a whole.

In the time it takes for a punch to be thrown or a rock tossed, a hand to swing in anger or self-defense, a switch blade to jut from the shadows, or a bomb to be dropped on a village of innocent men, women, and children, poems are being built, constructing a world less agonizing, a world that weaves worlds—weaves people—together.

The poets in this book confront head on, with all their lyrical and philosophical depth and swagger, the violence that's imposed upon them here on a daily basis. They force their beauty onto the page (onto the world stage), rage made beautiful, even when they curse and sing, see and celebrate, moving people in ways that they have not been moved—be it through faces and ideas, or words (worlds) strung out of life's mouth like popcorn or webs. They use their work as a force for change. Because they believe, as the Nicaraguans, that we are all born poets; it is the society we live in that takes it away from us; and it is our job to take it back.

The primary goal of the poet, the primary role of poetry, is to humanize. These voices, these visionaries, understand this. This is their mission, their goal. This has been their objective all along. It is that face they see in the mirror, or through their window, that drives them to force the world to keep it real, act like it knows and, ultimately, to recognize their beauty—and their pain.

These are poems that are tough, honest, astute, perceptive, lyrical, blunt, sad, funny, heartbreaking, and true. They shout, they curse, they whisper and sing. But most of all, they tell it like it is. Enjoy the onslaught of feelings and syllables and words! And always remember: Poems are prayers we submit to in our spiritual silence.

And finally, as you read these strong and beautiful pieces, think of our youth, our future, when you consider the words of one of our most important poets, Lucille Clifton, who says:

> Come celebrate with me
> that every day something
> has tried to kill me
> and has failed.

Tony Medina
May 15, 2001
Harlem, USA

DEDICATION

Margaret Walker
July 7, 1915–November 30, 1998

Dudley Randall
January 14, 1914–August 5, 2000

Zizwe Ngafua
March 4, 1938–January 10, 2000

Raymond R. Patterson
December 14, 1929–April 5, 2001

Safiya Henderson-Holmes
December 30, 1950–April 18, 2001

Gwendolyn Brooks
June 7, 1917–December 3, 2000

INVOCATION

Margaret Walker *(Jackson, MS)*
We Have Been Believers

We have been believers believing in the black gods of an old
      land, believing in the secrets of the seeress and the
      magic of the charmers and the power of the devil's evil
      ones.

And in the white gods of a new land we have been believers
      believing in the mercy of our masters and the beauty of
      our brothers, believing in the conjure of the humble
      and the faithful and the pure.

Neither the slaves' whip nor the lynchers' rope nor the
      bayonet could kill our black belief. In our hunger we
      beheld the welcome table and in our nakedness the
      glory of a long white robe. We have been believers in
      the new Jerusalem.

We have been believers feeding greedy grinning gods, like a
      Moloch demanding our sons and our daughters, our
      strength and our wills and our spirits of pain. We have
      been believers, silent and stolid and stubborn and
      strong.

We have been believers yielding substance for the world.
      With our hands have we fed a people and out of our
      strength have they wrung the necessities of a nation.
      Our song has filled the twilight and our hope has
      heralded the dawn.

Now we stand ready for the touch of one fiery iron, for the
      cleansing breath of many molten truths, that the eyes
      of the blind may see and the ears of the deaf may hear
      and the tongues of the people be filled with living fire.

Where are our gods that they leave us asleep? Surely the
      priests and the preachers and the powers will hear.

Surely now that our hands are empty and our hearts too
full to pray they will understand. Surely the sires of
the people will send us a sign.

We have been believers believing in our burdens and our
        demigods too long. Now the needy no longer weep and
        pray; the long-suffering arise, and our fists bleed
        against the bars with a strange insistency.

Dudley Randall *(Detroit)*
A Poet Is Not a Jukebox

A poet is not a jukebox, so don't tell me what to write.
I read a dear friend a poem about love, and she said,
"You're into that bag now, for whatever it's worth,
But why don't you write about the riot in Miami?"

I didn't write about Miami because I didn't know about Miami.
I've been so busy working for the Census, and listening to music all night,
    and making poems
That I've broken my habit of watching TV and reading newspapers.
So it wasn't absence of Black Pride that caused me not to write about Miami,
But simple ignorance.

Telling a Black poet what he ought to write
Is like some Commissar of Culture in Russia telling a poet
He'd better write about the new steel furnaces in the Novobigorsk region,
Or the heroic feats of Soviet labor in digging the trans-Caucausus Canal,
Or the unprecedented achievement of workers in the sugar beet industry
        who exceeded their quota by 400 per cent (it was later discovered to
        be a typist's error).

Maybe the Russian poet is watching his mother die of cancer,
Or is bleeding from an unhappy love affair,
Or is bursting with happiness and wants to sing of wine, roses, and
    nightingales.

I'll bet in a hundred years the poems the Russian people will read,
        sing, and love
Will be the poems about his mother's death, his unfaithful mistress, or his
        wine, roses, and nightingales,
Not the poems about steel furnaces, the trans-Caucausus Canal, or the sugar
        beet industry.
A poet writes about what he feels, what agitates his heart and sets his pen
        in motion.
Not what some apparatchnik dictates, to promote his own career of theories.

Yeah, maybe I'll write about Miami, as I wrote about Birmingham,
But it'll be because I want to write about Miami, not because somebody
        says I ought to.

Yeah, I write about love. What's wrong—with love?
If we had more loving, we'd have more Black babies to become Black brothers
        and sisters and build the Black family.

When people love, they bathe with sweet-smelling soap, splash their bodies
        with perfume or cologne,
Shave, and comb their hair, and put on gleaming silken garments,
Speak softly and kindly and study their beloved to anticipate and satisfy her
        every desire.
After loving they're relaxed and happy and friends with all the world.
What's wrong with love, beauty, joy, or peace?

If Josephine had given Napoleon more loving, he wouldn't have sown the
        meadows of Europe with skulls.
If Hitler had been happy in love, he wouldn't have baked people in ovens.
So don't tell me it's trivial and a cop-out to write about love and not about
        Miami.

A poet is not a jukebox.
A poet is not a jukebox.
I repeat, A poet is not a jukebox for someone to shove a quarter in his ear
        and get the tune they want to hear,
Or to pat on the head and call "a good little Revolutionary,"
Or to give a Kuumba Liberation Award.

A poet is not a *jukebox*.
A poet is *not* a jukebox.
A *poet* is not a jukebox.

So don't tell *me* what to write.

Zizwe Ngafua *(Philly)*
Nommo

Hear this my clarion call . . .
Life Lurks/watching as
Ova
Ellipian child
grizzled warrior/from dust
to dust
smiles at you from shadows
is shadows.

My palms outstretched in the
face of
the
sun
i say to the birds of the
wilderness
        Take what i have
        in my
        hands.

Raymond R. Patterson *(New York)*
No Jive
You've taken my blues and gone.
          —Langston Hughes

You took my cake and you walked,
You took my buck and you danced—
You hardly gave me a chance.

You took my ray and you ran,
You took my swing and you swung—
You nearly stole my fun.

You took my jazz and you jumped,
You took my bop and you blew—
Shame, oh, shame on you!

You took my scat and you skipped,
You took my rap and you ripped—
It's time that you got hipped.

When you took my rock and rolled,
When you took my soul and split,
You didn't get the half of it—
Oh, no! You didn't get the half of it.

Safiya Henderson-Holmes *(New York)*
failure of an invention

i am not any of the faces
you have put on me america

every mask has slipped
i am not any of the names

or sounds you have called me
the tones have nearly

made me deaf
this dark skin, both of us

have tried to bleach
i can smell cancer.

this thick hair, these thick lips
both of us have tried to narrow

begging entrance through
the needle of your eye

some of me broken
in the squeeze

and even as I carry
a bone of yours in my back

your soul america
no matter what we've tried

i've never been able to bear

Gwendolyn Brooks *(Chicago)*
Building

When I see a brave building
straining high, and higher,
hard and bright and sassy in the seasons,
I think of the hands that put that strength together.

The little soft hands. Hands coming away from cold
to take a challenge and mold this definition.

Amazingly, men and women
worked with design and judgment, steel and glass,
to enact this announcement.
Here it stands.

Who can construct such miracle can enact
any consolidation, any fusion.
All little people opening out of themselves,

forging the human spirit that can outwit
big Building boasting in the cityworld.

The Disdirected

Some folk think that poet
is but another word for star
where star don't mean to signify
beyond the glitter & the glimmer
of cold coke
cocktail glasses clicking
up against the hard vein sweat
of who you know
& how that knowledge could get me into bed
with someone who might rub me
if you please

> dust
> rust
> slowly
> solely

nothing else but sheen or shine
making out like substance & sustenance
have no place beyond the deadly force
of cut throat yester-rape
where the mundane shame of pain
looks to them like crusts of shadows
falling into disrepute
but that ain't what a poet is
& stars just seem that way
to those who look
but cannot see
exactly what they checking out . . .
musicians on the run
the people & their sweat
still & slow
who sour
sweetly near romantic pools
neath salt bed seas by curaçao
in the midst of devastated nueva york

> newport
> newark

running toward the edge of hell
at every corner of the road we call

> right here:
> a hemisphere of slaves
> now kept as household maids

with hairnet wet & woven
like the pubic curls
of wombless tubes
got cut & sliced
like the olla or an oven pot
cooled to simmer til it's hot

I said
some would think that there ain't nothing else
but glitter gut
star dust versifying lyricists
who glut the gleam of gotten gain
measured by a gutter cup of
get what's mine or steal what's yours
cocktail sipping
evening gown
hard-on pants of beaded braids
bread with butter
vegetating knitted shawl

Oh, but I paid 600 dollars to have my hair . . .
fixed(!)
like spaded cats that can't create
a child their own
like the studyless who
hawk up on a benevolent phrase
from those who hunt down anything
& once absorbed
call it mine(!)
or like the unstudied undersullied wouldbe
groups of disdirected poets
tuning up on trite like lines
they'd never lived
        never tasted
        never known the pain thereof
lacking keys in tune with insight
vision staling from a beamless search
lacking grace to dig down deep
inside the pit of
constant climbing
elbow rubbing
searching for a coattail pulled
a cocktail lost
but never sit beneath their guiding stars
to question what it was
preceded hate
confused with doubt

unclear &
tearing at the fibers of illusion
like the way some think perhaps they came
upon the earth selfcreated

but they never even read a book
that didn't lie
or steal or con
the sanity & sanctity of breath
& never once have tried to excavate
the question & the meaning
of the dance that comes with song
or use their eyes to see or sense or feel
beyond the question & the meaning
of sparkling rays pulsing to perform
while every throb of thirsting
                    searching
                    thinking being knows
that nommo prophet keeper of a narrative pursuit
means that poet is a struggle for
a glimpse of light
a grope for hope
urging war against deceit
but studyless & wouldbe,
no direction in their dance,
they dis the fact that
star is just another word for sun
imploring heat speeding
past each wave of night imploding
from the energy of dusk
creating rise & giving voice
to one more poet
who ain't no way like elbows
to be rubbed or snubbed
but is in deed a pulsing push
of constant growth & pain
reminding us we're all just flesh
& real enough
to sit beside & ponder.

Louis Reyes Rivera (New York)

bum rush the page

The Way We Move

the way we move, funk groove
beat the rhythm out some pavement,
our elegant violent attitude, quick
slow motion movement in quicksand
in somebody else's shit house shanty town
shingly jingly chains clamped on our neck,
hang to the floor scrape spark and clink
and we make music out of this cool behind dark
shades, taught to fear the sun, hiding in
beauty parlors and bars draggy face with
hatred and ugliness,
                    and it only comes when you don't
accept the natural gifts, the fingerprints of a
higher order of peace and simple logic, what makes us
phenomenal is that we can sleep walk in
harmony, never breaking a sweat 'cept in factories
or bars, prisons we even build systems for, our
own street logic and survival, but this is not where
we're meant to be, not on the operating table of
extinction or at the broken doorstep of finality
stumbling drunk confused scagged out on whiteness
and greed and stupidity into the bleeding face of our
dead father, and we are not supposed to move
this way, slow mumbling suicide in quicksand and defeat
we must refocus, we must see again

Tony Medina (New York)

...And the Saga Continues

for Gary Graham

From Guinea to Haiti to Brooklyn
And back
From Guinea to Haiti to the Bronx
And back
From Brooklyn to the Bronx to LA
And back
From Philly to Haiti to the New Jersey Turnpike
And back

From village to hamlet to Borough
And back
From LA to Orange to Newark to Guinea
And back
From PR to the Bronx Brooklyn Queens Guinea
And back
From Soundview to no view of the anguish of . . .
Mother Mother why have you forsaken me

Bless me father for they are winning
And my mutter is crying
Bless me father for my mutter is crying
At the sight of my dying
Save me Lord from being vanquished
Save my mutter from this anguish

From Harlem to the Bronx to Brooklyn Queens Newark San Juan
and the nation's highways   I languish
In my blood and tears   of my mother's anguish
And back

Call the name . . . Call the names I say
you know them better than I

Shaka Sankofa   Malcolm Ferguson   Patrick Doresmond
Abner Louima   Amadou Diallo   Kevin Cedeno   James Byrd
Matthew Sheppard   Anthony Baez   Michael Stewart
Earl Faison . . . etc. etc. etc.

And the list gets longer week by week
An African got lynched today
Juneteenth 2000

From Texas to Chicago to Watts to Newark
And back
From PR to Cuba to the Dominican Republic
And back

Africa calls from the bottom of the Atlantic
And back
From Ghanaian fields smooth black skin
Turns purplish   under lash   under water
And back

Can you hear them gurgle . . . Abnerrrrr
Can you hear them scream . . . Amadouuuuuuuu
Can you hear the windpipe snap . . . Antonyyyyyyyyap

Blessed be   Blessed be   Blessed be
Dear Lord have mercy   Lord have mercy
Have mercy on me
bless me father for I
have sinned . . .
with my mind I daily will demise
of the western ways and all of its compatriots

Bless me father with a bottle of scuppernog or
Wild Irish Rose to soften the blow
of this monster's breath   upon my neck
And back

in harlem   in havana   in charleston   in Porto Prince
the saga continues . . .
blood   blood I say
blood in the rectum   bullets in the gut
in the head   the chest neck
And back

A rope a nightstick pepper spray
Or a lethal illegal injection
from the State
the state of tex ass   where seldom is heard
an encouraging word and the sky is cloudy
all year
how 'bout florida or new jersey or new york
the city so nice   they kill you twice

Next stop   Ghana   to the Congo   to Zimbabwe
And back

Ted Wilson (Orange, NJ)

blood i say, study our story, sing this song

Bad Times

Our churches are burning
beneath locust black skies.
Empty pews hiss
the names of silent thieves.

Cracking stained windows reflect
the faces of thieves
who haunt the rafters
on rural southern roads.

Shadows bow
like Sunday congregations
to preachers holy-ghosting sermons.

Our churches are burning.
The graveyards' spirits are quiet.
Bats dip and swerve
like flames.

Our churches become charcoal aftermath
and cornfields are full of smoke.

The willows wail and weep.
Ferns fan themselves.
Wind erases footprints
of thieves who stalk by night.

Our churches are burning.
No one searches the woods.
Thieves slip in and out.
No sirens scream, no alarms go wild.

Our churches are burning.
These are bad times
bad times
bad times

Our churches are burning.
The bells do not peal.
The covenant still speaks
to our people's weary hearts.

Lenard D. Moore *(Raleigh, NC)*

How to Do

It embarrasses my niece to think of her mother
Walking the streets with a cart
Picking up empties
For their deposits,

But my sister knows how to do
Which was all our mother asked of us.
She's learned how to do,
Which is both a solution and a test,

So I stand in line with my sister
At the supermarket.
Today's the best day of the week
To bring the bottles in.

It is a poor people's science,
A concept that works until
Someone with power
Notices it works,

And then, it doesn't.
There's at least 15 carts,
At least 10 people in line,

But only one guy
Behind the counter:
Not what's supposed
To happen.

The manager shrugs
His shoulders when asked.
No rules here,

Points to a sign taped
Above our heads
Which, boiled down,
Says wait, behave.

No rules, except for
What's always been:
Do what you gotta do.

And the poor stiff
Whose job it is to sort the clears
From the greens, the plastics
From the cans, who is short
One or two people this shift,

Who flings my sister's
Stumpy treasure
Into the hamper's
Great indifferent mouth,
Temporary chief of staff
Of Lotto,

Who's been instructed to keep
The refunds down to

Twelve dollars worth of
Store credit, no matter
How many empties
Come in,

Maybe he has a favorite song.
Maybe he's a good guy
To have in a pinch.
He's not paid enough to reveal that here.

This, as my mother would say,
Is the way we have to do:
Tired as convicts, we inch along,
Shift our weight
On the black,
Sticky carpet,

Beholden to nobody's luck
But our own.

Cornelius Eady (*New York*)

Like a Dog

heavy gold bracelets
hit my shoulder
free weights
on the pale hand
she raises to caress
my face
dull and overlooked
her mouth reeks
of excesses
rich white woman
at my reading
needing
needing to
touch my outlaw
touch my
needing to touch
my outlaw hair
outlaw hair
                is it real
to touch my out
law hair to touch

hair my hair
only to say
she liked my poem

Cheryl Boyce Taylor (New York)

Lonely Women

we are fatherless daughters
entering womanhood
with only half our selves
worshipping the mystique
of masculinity

naked bodies flying
willingly
over the edge
of countless cliffs
praying the god of gravity
will grant us grace

you see us at parties
getting drunk on emptiness
dancing dirty with strangers
or worse—with men we know

we will do what we don't
to please our lovers
'cause this one could be
the one
our hearts hold
scrap
books full of faded photographs
of the faces of
could have been

we marry money
for security
become servants
in master bedrooms
and wake up in dream homes
turned nightmare insanitoria
where we are ex-wives
wondering when
love disembarked

the journey to death us do part
we are patient predators
in pitiable holding patterns
vultures in friendship's camouflage
who pick the meat from marriages

we are tits and asses
flaunting form
fitted fashions
so when a man comes our way
he can see good reason to stay

we are new and improved
women working out
toning up
slimming down
laying on the hippest beaches
at the hottest getaways
under the sun bright spotlight
praying that some bronze brother
will have cause to pause
long enough to discover that
we can whip up gourmet soul food
help meet the mortgage
watch sports all day on Sunday
and ride him from midnight
to have mercy
and we are women of our word

women with it going on
plenty of papers and props
driving fancy cars to fine homes
that we share with our
parents
children
fantasies
fingertips

we are lonely women
waiting for someone
to want us
wanting someone
to need us
needing
someone

Kysha N. Brown *(New Orleans)*

On the Other Side

for Pearl Cleage

MY lover once informed me that miles davis was a real man 'cause he didn't
    take no shit.
He always knew where his WOMAN was,
underneath
his heel.

So after a while, I began to wonder every time MY lover would beat the shit
    out of ME,
did miles davis beat the shit out of his WIFE?

Did he scream in HER face in restaurants?
Did he kick HER in the stomach or slap HER in the street?
Did he call HER bitch over and over and over . . . ?

Gently he would place the needle on the record
Sketches of Spain, MY lover would play;

Wishing that the songs would end so that I could bleed in peace.

And I wondered, did miles davis beat the shit out of his WIFE while
    recording
Live in Paris: A Return to Romance?

Was SHE frantically packing HER bags for the
last
time
while he composed songs that made jazz cats shiver and say,

Damn, how does he do that?

Was SHE suicidal hiding in HER basement while he joked with the police?

Are they the reason why I don't dial 911 every time MY lover beats the shit
    out of ME?

Is MY lover the reason *Kind of Blue* makes ME vomit because it drags ME
    back to the time that I
needed stitches in the back of MY head and could find no one to take ME to
    the hospital?

I wondered, could miles davis beat the shit out of his WIFE and still be the
    world's greatest
trumpet player?

Could his **WIFE** still be a **WOMAN** of courage and sanity to leave a "genius"
   because **SHE** had
had enough humiliation and embarrassment?

Because **SHE** did not want to be raped by him and his music every
waking
exhausting
agonizing
dawn?

Could **MY** lover still be a man even though he beat the shit out of **ME** and
   promised to kill **ME** if
I left?

I wondered, did miles davis express those same sentiments to his **WIFE**
   while accepting
Grammys, sipping champagne, and playing with Coltrane?

Benin Williams *(Pasadena, CA)*

N

for Enivalda Santana

every day
she tiptoes through a minefield of emotions
ignoring the tremble of her sanity
as it slips down the empty cavern
her chest has become

in the dark
she cries for her body
touches the flaps of skin
masquerading as a belly

bitterness joins her for a drink
and they laugh at the ridiculous photograph:
her thin frame stretched past breaking
bloated with the greedy weight of twins
sprung from seed she doesn't remember
inviting in

beneath the moonlight
she sits at her easel
suppresses the rainbows
begging to burst from her fingertips

paints instead tight colorful squares
stabs in roofs and cobblestone streets
with angry fingers

every canvas is the same
the tourists like it that way

in the morning she will
tote water, cook two meals,
wash three babies, avoid her sister's fists,
rub her knuckles raw on laundry,
refuse to bed foreign men for money
and take deep drags of her cigarette
scowling at the world

Kiini Ibura Salaam (New York)

Her Scream Has Been Stolen

She wouldn't recognize it
if she heard it saw it
read it in print
she imprinted differently

So does she scream?
Does she know herself
what is her life how does she
see the sky what does her
river taste like upstream and
downstream and how does it
make love to her body as she bathes

What does her scream sound
like can she hear it
when it echoes off the leaves or the
cliffs or the streams or the mountain
peaks or canyons gardens marshes
beaches over water and land she
didn't know was hers until she was told
it wasn't?

Did she know
this river could be owned?

Samiya A. Bashir (New York)

Crater Face

is what we called her. The story was
that her father had thrown Drano at her
which was probably true, given the way she slouched
through fifth grade, afraid of the world, recess
especially. She had acne scars
before she had acne—pocks and dips
and bright red patches.
                                    I don't remember
any report in the papers. I don't remember
my father telling me her father had gone to jail.
I never looked close to see the particulars
of Crater Face's scars. She was a blur, a cartoon
melting. Then, when she healed—her face,
a million pebbles set in cement.
                                    Even Comet Boy,
who got his name by being so abrasive,
who made fun of everyone, didn't make fun
of her. She walked over the bridge
with the one other white girl who lived
in her neighborhood. Smoke curled
like Slinkies from the factory stacks
above them.
                    I liked to imagine that Crater Face
went straight home, like I did, to watch Shirley Temple
on channel 56. I liked to imagine that she slipped
into the screen, bumping Shirley with her hip
so that the child actress slid out of frame, into the tubes
and wires that made the TV sputter when I turned it on.
Sometimes when I watched, I'd see Crater Face
tap-dancing with tall black men whose eyes
looked shiny, like the whites of hard-boiled eggs.
I'd try to imagine that her block was full
of friendly folk, with a lighthouse or goats
running in the street. It was my way of praying,
my way of un-imagining the Drano pellets
that must have smacked against her
like a round of mini-bullets,
her whole face as vulnerable as a tongue
wrapped in sizzling pizza cheese.
How she'd come home with homework,
the weight of her books bending her into a wilting plant.
How her father called her slut, bitch, big baby, slob.
The hospital where she was forced to say it was an accident.

Her face palpable as something glowing in a Petri dish.
The bandages over her eyes.

                              In black and white,
with all that make-up, Crater Face almost looked pretty,
sure her MGM father was coming back soon from the war,
seeing whole zoos in her thin orphanage soup.
She looked happiest when she was filmed
from the back, sprinting into the future,
fading into tiny gray dots on UHF.

Denise Duhamel *(Miami)*

susu*

susu we say when women put
they pennies and heads together
time wrap around a dollar
to pay for operation
passage, life and sanctuary
to send a child to freedom

no man to organize endow interest
give air condition building
for our time made gold
labor into paper wings

each month one draws
each month each gives
a circle weave and sing
from our most elder mothers

I explain this and yanki friend say
what if one take
and never give again?
no federal deposit insurance
cop stop take advantage

I pause consider this yanki thought
what strike is not that
such a thing happen
but that this reason not to do the thing at all

perhaps this the tree that grow
from seed surround by weed

*Isusu: Yoruba word for the women's investment circle

orchid in a field of razor grass
black hands labor bathe in bleach

not that we never thief each other
cheat and steal, not that we hands
so free of Queen Victoria whitening
but this ain't stop the susu none, eh

bleakness all the more reason for flamboyant petticoat
silence all the more reason for j'ouvert morning
hunger all the more reason for share stewpot
murderation all the more reason for the children birth
thief all the more reason for open hand

what give must come back
a circle weave and sing

R. Erica Doyle *(New York)*

An Asian Am Anthem

Way back
to the yes yes y'alls
when I tagged bathroom stalls and my brother had new wave posters wall
    to wall

I dreamt of the times they dropped Agent Orange and called it Kool Aid
bound our feet and called it first aid

Woke up into a spirit rotation, a soul inflation: the Asian Persuasion
Asian my orientation, Asian American my nation
wanted to kick specifics about being Asian pacific
but they taxed my syntax/orientalized my oriental eyes
and blinded me with Full Metal Jacketed lies

While overseas/policies/let bygones become icons
on desktops/double click to open windows/into sweatshops
tried to get out but the doors were Jessica McLint-locked

Never the mellow yellow but rather yelled and bellowed
at those white fellows who knocked me down
but I got back the fuck up again
coaxed by folk hymns, dead ringer for the revolution
leaving behind the brainwashed contusions,
red white and blue confusions
in a nation of computer generated illusions

14

They offered fame contracts/complete with blue contacts
assimilationist hot dish/slit skin and split my ancestor's bones for a wish
buried our history under haunted trees
taught self hate by their taunts of Chinese Japanese dirty knees

They want to halt our progress
but we left 'em behind cuz we got more sides than a stop sign
unwind tongues/rewind time/to study our story and sing this song
with sloppy mathematics calculate the ragged ratio
of this yellow braggadocio and blow the speakers to their stereo/types
Hai Ba Trung delegated to a ching chong pantheon
but we castrate and bat around their white balls cuz we the ping pong
    champions
so fuck their Buddha boxes and Bindi kits:
fake ass renditions of our ancient cultural traditions
we reclaim, remind, retwist our minds
for our persistence of resistance
this thing called us/flush/bullshit to flourish/nourish
like rice ciphers/decipher/cropped tongues from here to trife times
with truth rhymes/our wind chime choruses/forming audible life lines/
we recite/overturn/with vocal overtures

Asian American anthem
beyond Suzie Wong and Hop Sing bows
I'm singing for ya'll/so can ya hear me now
this is for my people who got turned down
but refused to yield
for Hawaii sun sweat in sugar cane fields
for sisters pissed at Ling on *Ally McBeal*
for my brothers who stay strong without the steel
for those not on their knees from slipping on their own
banana peels
brainwashed colorblind
pushed aside
for culture pride

They can't evade this Asian American invasion
Yellow Nation
made up of crews rollin in Isuzus
with the buddhist trinkets ya mama gave you
hanging from the rearview
they call us slant-eyed
but we're clear view
and they're see thru
Don't be fooled, ya'll.

When will they learn?
The only time they see the light

blood i say, study our story, sing this song

is when their houses burn
Yellow Nation
time to
get up
wake up
stand up
make up
take up
lash out
strike out
make out
break
out

Thien-bao Thuc Phi (*Minneapolis*)

Scout

for Hank Howard

Look here Boy,
"Scout,"
I've seen your name in newsprint
fake name fake skills
"eight-inch slammer"
ready to pitch into somebody or lead him home,
Slugger.

How it turns them on to hear Parisian French
coming out of a mouth that
looks like God dug a finger into one corner
and pulled
said "Sneer, here."
This mouth's made for sex.
For slamming.

The writing is on the walls—
inked above the roll of industrial tissue—
a new song of the self, plus hourly rates.
You never run out of ways to sell it.

I've seen the offers in the classifieds
(weekday specials),
in the eye or two you send my way, suddenly shy
if shyness works.

Knowing what the Lord gave you is one thing;
making your living off it is another.
But every love requires its documentation.

Baby tow-head with porcelain skin
first birthday: mom with box camera and pedal pushers
dad hopes for baseball and cross-country.

Later,
Scout finds out in the locker room what all that's worth.

That sweet, drawling North Carolina tongue
leaves these Western boys gasping, coming apart
like a lump of hard rock sugar in the rain.

If they uncover your several lives,
do you just let 'em go, or smile that half-moon boy-smile
bent like a fishhook
with a barb that's painless going in
but man oh mother what a fucker coming out.

Wendell Ricketts (Oakland)

This Old Man

The New York Knicks are making front-page news—
Spike carrying on courtside, fragile
old Patrick in his stitches and splints—

I don't even like basketball
but now it's everybody's headline, front-page news. I flip
through six sheets of crime stats and traffic chatter,

pictures of hot kids swimming at the hydrants,
what somebody had to say about our crazy mayor.
Six pages to turn before learning

how one uptown viejo spent his last morning,
before neighbors called police
before police shot the man

63 years old and even crazier than the mayor.
This old man, he was one, didn't even have a gun.
They had pistols: they were two.

They had nightsticks and backup and handcuffs.
They had time to make another choice, but
if a cop crack his trigger back, throw the judge a bone

I find them here on page seven
after taking Poppy out with just one shot.
City cops are learning to destroy us

with minimal firepower: a single bullet
gets a page seven mention, 41
might get you cuffed on the 10 o'clock news,

the dead man is incidental, jet slag
from the undergound urban war.
and this old man ain't going home

This old man was standing on the stairstep in his jockey shorts
waving a rusty machete. Dreaming awake of island greens in need of
    harvest
dreaming the feel of good earth under the naked skin of his feet,

hefting the useless machete as he contemplates the properties of ripeness.
Maybe the two officers say FREEZE. And maybe they say DROP IT.
And maybe they only speak English, so that this old man

never understands the cops or feels the shot that drops him
dead, into his dreams of the field. Dead and buried here on page seven,
because he wasn't nobody's hero, he wasn't nobody's Sprewell,

not this old man, standing on the stairstep in his jockey shorts.
Not this old man, swinging a rusty machete on the stairstep, crazy—
not this . . . disposable . . . old man.

this old man, he was one, didn't even have a gun
if a cop crack his trigger back, throw the judge a bone
this old man ain't going home
if a cop crack his trigger back, throw the judge a bone
this old man ain't going

Jackie Sheeler *(New York)*

Afternoon Train

for Richard A. Rowe

In New York they have banned smoking,
smoking in zoos, smoking in restaurants.
The public has become a court of scrutiny,
where the law's paper eyes hunt for mutiny.
I read the news in a Philly El station,
with the doors open to admit the season
of doleful shoppers. I lean into the heat
coming from under my seat, feel the waves
of electric fire, fire with a pardon's grace.
Into the train come the smooth faces
of young black men with too big pants
and too little time. They bring a din
with the bravado of wearing dark skin.

In the ease of my shoulder in the window,
I find my haggard smile. In a show
one turns on his radio, dares me in a glare.
He believes me to be one of the judges,
but I am a remnant. The soft bass nudges.
I think of my own youth in public transport.
Music was our way of negotiating the port,
life's landing spot, the chasm we name
the hundred names of struggle. Our music
let the world know it did not understand
childhood or adolescence. What hand
can we, the old, give the future of life?

I see courage in these young men,
in their haunting stare. I see my eyes
in their eyes. I see our body ties.
My face emerges in their pupils. I go
on reading, pressed in the window.
I feel the weight of a space packed
with the blackness of black men.
We are all young men for the ride,
even me, their self-appointed captain.

I am leading them to the endless mile
of themselves, suffering with a quiet smile
their silent challenges. An old cat,
I know young cats must feel they can
hassle me if need be. This gives pride
to older men like me as we steadily ride
away. We want the healthy majority

blood i say, study our story, sing this song

to leave us quiet whimpers of seniority.
They know I am not afraid to die, and
my only fear is of my lack of fearing death.
They do not know this truth will one day feel
its way to them, fired from hate's blue steel.

The train launches itself into the city.
I chuckle at the radio playing more softly
than the youngsters know. I would play it
loud enough to halt the train, if I could teach
them all where the train is steadily going.
We are riding to the hell of a war zone
where we are feared and desired at once.
We are riding to the hell of being so full
of mystery and life that our lives are at risk.
We are riding to the hell of not being trusted
by women who so often say they love us.
We are riding to the hell of understanding
why we are cats, given the grace of trickery.
We are riding to the hell of not knowing
America is hell and hell is full of smiles.

The train rides over broken Philadelphia,
with faces too young to understand pity.
Their voices carve rough laughter above
my prayer. *God, give us a field for love.*

Afaa M. Weaver (Boston)

Beginning at the End: Capital/Capitol Punishment

Here I stand in my cell looking out to freedom, Lord, here I stand
Here I stand just thinking 'bout freedom, Lord, here I stand.
I see myself as a living/dying man looking out to freedom all over this land
I'm in my cell and it hurts like hell, Lord, here I stand.

Here I stand, I didn't kill nobody, Lord, but here I stand
I never pulled the trigger but they're going to pull the switch
It may be heaven or hell, only you know which
Here I stand, a miserable son of a—, Lord, here I stand.

I want to scream something like gendercide
That wouldn't be too dignified
Furthermore I'm a man of pride
Rather be silent when he died.

It's gettin quiet now . . . must be time to go, Lord, here I go.
Can you hear my heart, it was beating fast, now it's beating slow
Here I go, now it's all your show, Lord, here I go.

Here I sit, my head is shaved, they strapped me in, my mother just waved
Is there anything I can do to be saved, Lord, here I sit.
There is a grin on his face as he throws the switch
Is he a man or the devil, I can't tell which.

Well here I sit, now I don't give a s—, Lord, here I sit
(Here I sit, I think my heart just quit, Lord, here I sit).

Well, here I lay in my coffin with my new suit on, Lord, here I lay
Here I lay . . . my friends and family go by I can feel some look, I can hear
    some cry
I want to say something but I can't reply. . . . so here I lay
Here I lay and hear my eulogy and find out what this society thought of
    me.

The pallbearers grunt and lift and it's a guarantee no more of me will they
    ever see.
I listen closely, Lord, and heard somebody say, *Aah, he was just one of them*
                        Black poet singers, anyway
I hear the thuds of dirt thrown into my hole, Lord, have mercy on my poor
    Black soul!

It's getting dark down here and so damned cold from beginning to end
I guess my story is told. There's nothing left for me to say except . . .
I'm guilty of being innocent, Lord, and here I lay!
And I believe in John 3:16 all the way

Back to your right hand is where I hope to stay
Our Father who art in heaven, hallowed be thy name . . .
Is it God, Lord, Jehovah, Lord? Yaweh, Lord? Krishna, Lord?
Obatalah, Lord? Wakantonka, Lord? Allah, Lord?

Rich Bartee *(New York)*

blood i say, study our story, sing this song

A Chinese Man in Smyrna

There was always an official to please.
Mine practiced calligraphy.
We would talk for hours about art.
I'd say, *Gracious Efendi, your hand*
is so sure. Your judgment impeccable.
You know, for instance, just where
to leave a white space. Like pure
silence. I'd show him my books
from Shanghai. Unfurl scrolls
my family kept for generations.
Luckily, my daughters
did not interest him.
For all he cared,
they might have come from the moon.
It was Christian girls
he lusted after, Christians
he called pigs and the children
of pigs. I did not interfere.
I did not complain.
I did my job in peace,
which was to teach art.

All those years,
trying to keep balance.
A little extra ginger in my tea.
Practice every morning
with my grandfather's
ceremonial sword. An art object,
poised in air. For health.
For fitness. Then on September 13th,
1922, I heard soldiers yell

Long live Mustafa Kemal! They had taken
my students away. Without thinking,
I grabbed the sword. Rushed out.
The ground cracked open, full of demons.
A crying boy with a bleeding anus,
seven men around him. Four girls being raped.
Get their heads, one soldier said.
He held up the head he had just

sliced off my youngest student. Her eyes wide open.
I saw my official
bend over one girl, his torso
thick as a tree stump. The white space
around him unprotected,

ready for his bayonet, a suffusion
of red for this pretend
artist, patron
of the arts, and I had waited too long
but knew better now,
and took my sword.
Cut off his hand.

Sharon Olinka *(New York)*

450 Years of Selective Memory (Smile)

Smile
Show me that the seeds of your discontent
Have not taken root
Display for me
That sign of eternal,
Internal well-being
Smile

Show me the wisdom of my ways
Your soul unfazed by unreasonable demands
Heated irons held to your skin,
Pain and anger held within
With teeth clench of

Show me twenty-eight ways I haven't done wrong
Leap-year me into a season of self-righteousness
Black-cavalcade me away from nearsightedness
With an intoxicating elixir so strong,
Nectar of a deaf, dumb, and blind nether-god
Antidote to sodium pentathol and leather wrist straps

Just
Give me some of that ole reassurance
Tell me that it ain't so bad
Sing undisguised work songs to me, white as cotton,
Take me back to
Simple days of rules of order
Proper divisions and simple instructions:

Tote, lift, hump and hew
Soft, humming nights and
Busted mouths oozing red on brown

Smile,
Show me all thirty-two,
Lift your tongue to show me no hidden razor blades,
Show your molars hiding no encapsulated cyanide
Show me no incisors sharpened for mortal combat
Let me touch your lips and mouth for familiarity,
Bring me closer to you, the way it once was
Peel back your lips and bless me with your easy fortune

Open your mouth
And
Smile.

Ken McManus *(New York)*

the n-word

i want to write a poem
about the time a little white boy
called me a _____:
but i can't use the word:
it's busy,
busy, i say:
headlining the new civil rights agenda,
bedding down with dictionary editors,
shuffling back and forth between
huck finn and *new jack city:*
oh, it's busy, *busy,*
and i wouldn't want to disturb it.

i want to write a poem
about when i was nine
and a little white boy
whose coat sleeves didn't reach his wrists
called me a _____:
but i can't say the word:
it's busy, i tell you:
black folks got their mouths around it,
chewing, swallowing, regurgitating,
chewing, swallowing again, re-
defining it, they tell me:
they're calling cow-cud

what i thought was bull-shit:
either way, i can't stomach it!
since the word is busy, busy, busy,
i wouldn't want to disturb it.

i want to write a poem
about how this little white boy said it:
wasn't even talking to me:
told his father *wait*—
i wanna play on the pinball machine
soon as the _____ gets through with it.
yeah, we *both* up in woolco
mooching amusement in the toy department:
neither of us could afford the damn thing:
but this little white boy
he called me a _____:
and i still can't say the word:
it's busy,
busy, you hear me,
all tied up with quentin tarantino
and i wouldn't want to disturb it.

you know, i thought i'd write a poem
about the time this little white boy
who could be married to my ex–best friend,
could end up wrapped in a confederate flag,
who could be our next president
the time this little white boy
called me a _____:
but i *won't* use the word:
i'm busy.
deeply involved in self-definition
and world-reconstruction:
busy!
i said i got work to do
and i'm tired of being disturbed.

Evie Shockley (Winston-Salem, NC)

an open letter to the entertainment industry

if there is anyone
in the audience
in the entertainment industry
watching me perform,
i want you to keep in mind

that if you are casting any films
and need a korean grocery store owner,
a computer expert,
or the random thug
of a yakuza gang,
i'm your man.

if you're making jackie chan
knock-off films
and need a stunt double,
that stunt double is me.

if you need a chinese jay-z,
a japanese eminem,
or a vietnamese backstreet boy,
please consider me,
because i am all those things and more.

i come from the house that
step n' fetchit built
and i will broken english my way
to sidekick status
if that's what's expected of me.
make an asian *different strokes.*

i'll walk around on my knees yelling,
ahso, what you talk about wirris?!

because it's been 23 months and 14 days
since my art has done anything for me,
and i would be noble and toil on,
i swear i would.

live for the art and the art alone,
and all that crapass.

but college loans are monthly up my ass,
my salmon teriyaki habit is getting way out of control,
and i want some
motherfucking cable!

so you can understand where i'm coming from
when tight verse
exhibiting dynamics
within the text
falls by the wayside
and our culture

rejoices in its
pretty, packaged, boygroup,
talentless twats
sent from florida
to make me puke.

but i'm not preaching. nome siree, boss.

i cannot stress how ready i am
to sell out,
wear jiggy clothes,
and yell from the top of my lungs
any hook i am told to sing.

if you want the caricature
of a caricature,
then i am that caricature.

if you want an exotic dragon lady
like lucy liu,
who fucks like a kama sutra
come to life,
just tell my ass where ya want it,
and i will bend over.

if you need a voice-over artist,
just tell me
where you want the,
hi-ya's! to go
and i will be there,

because i am all that and more,
i am a pop culture whore,
i am a co-sponsored world tour,
and i am
an appropriated culture at my core.

i've been noticed, acclaimed, and funny

and now all i want
is a beach front house to paint in
and a range rover
to listen to my music in,

cuz struggling fucking sucks hard
after the ninth package of ramen noodle soup.

i'm beau sia.

give me a chance,
and i'll
change the world.

Beau Sia *(Babylon, NY)*

Metropolitan Metaphysics

The back seat of the bus baby!
as any urban wayfarer will tell you
without batting an eye
or quivering a whisker
is where you gotta be at!
Where the nocturnal mysteries of the city
accumulate
like snow flakes in the December horizon
where flying fists sprout
unexpected
like deranged
death blossoms,
Where you can see the witch doctor
in the black overcoat
flash his bus pass
and take his seat
without him seeing you first!
                    And that's just where I'm headed

to the far right seat in the corner,
where all the real nickel slick
ice dudes
are destined to be
(as soon as they step aboard and pay their fare)
It's just metropolitan meditation
in the rear of a rapidly accelerating 54C,
oblivious
to the gun metal grey skies
darkening outside of my window
aware of only the cityscape of passing Pittsburgh
Electric Mosaic of crumbling brick
and Steeler Sunday celebration
drunkards disguised as Slim Coyote
swaying eerily
with stolen tobacco pouches
beside the bus schedules
ghosts of dead jazz musicians
sitting in seats reserved for the elderly

(an old lady, withered hoodooo mama,
call her Cajun Katie,
born between the teeth of a Louisiana lightning storm,
gives me the Evil Eye over her bag of groceries!)
And that bus driver
Whoooooa!
Quite the holy
madman is he,
expertly steering
that zooming stagecoach
through bustling streets,
like Hendrix in heat
a sleek steel bullet speeding
through crosswalk
and traffic light
and stop sign
and universe
at light speed arrow
pedestrians yielding
bums on Liberty
see the comet's tail comin from the tailpipe
and start acting all Orion
'cause
this ain't no ordinary bus
no regular remnant of hulking '80s crap
and patchwork motor is she
chugging
brimming over with rush hour commuters
and misbehaving children
naw,
this bus is a clandestine marriage
of public transportation
and subsonic rocketry,
juju mystified jazz specters,
Indian Gods in ghostly forms,
and most of all
                    Me

James Flint (Pittsburgh)

America Eats Its Young

America's still eating its young,
But I think she need to get slim.
Fast!
Somebody tell that heifer to exorcise her demons,

Stop chewin on black children
& reduce her jail cell ulite.

Ain't nobody want her breast-milk
So she's backed up, chest swollen.
See justice for black folk
is notoriously lactose
intolerant.

Maybe she should get a tummy-tuck,
Cuz her underbelly's showin.
And we see a disproportionate percentage of black boys
Locked up in the belly o' dat beast,
She likes darkies,
Developed a taste for dark meat,
I mean she's been suckin the blood from our marrow
since
Slavery

Too bad most innocent cons
Don't have the Canadi-ons
To clear up the lie—
Po' suction causes a clog in the system
And a lot of black boys get lost in the system.
Inmates studying law to find a clause in the system.
I mean,
they know dey gon' die,
But at least they could try to put some sorta
—Pause—in the system.

4 cops get acquitted.
And Giuliani got the nerve to give
Applause.
For the system.

America's still eating its young
And she's got a mansize hunger
So she eats a snickers
Cuz snickers satisfies you!
Cuz eating these snickers satisfies you!
Eating these snickers satisfies you!

Eating these—niggers
satisfies you.

And she'll do anything to sadist-fy her mansize
hunger.
Sodomize some mother's child,
then pick his broken manhood from
between her teeth
with
toilet
plungers.

Maybe we should staple her mouth shut
41 times.
Or sorry, just shoot the staple gun at her
41 times
And maybe 19 will sting.

It . . . it . . . it was self-defence!
See, we thought lady liberty was holding a torch.
Who knew till after it was just a home-fried chicken wing.
But you understand our dilemma,
I mean the whole world knows

America eats its young.

Jemeni *(Toronto)*

laughin at cha

for a half-ass writer who thinks
langston hughes ain't nothing

you think gasoline extinguishes fires
you think sand quenches thirst
you think you can catch the wind in your hands
you think bessie smith was just whining
you think elvis was the king of rock
you think charlie parker was just tootin around
you think james brown can't dance
you think aretha franklin can't sing
you think castor oil and ear wax taste good
you think the sun ain't hot at night
you think the earth is as square as your head
you think columbus discovered columbus ohio
you think joe louis was a punk
you think liberation is just a state of mind
you think black women ain't beautiful

you think apartheid was just a misunderstanding
you think i'm taking you seriously

hurry now,
i think i just saw the wind
running past you.

Kenneth Carroll (DC)

Rosa's Beauty

it was a ritual
one Saturday a month
storm or shine, broke or not
Mami would drive us to Rosa's Beauty
near la 17 in Santurce
where a barrio's history is the mad work
of knives and men

but there we were on our way to get our hair done
to be called 'chinitas'
straighten out kinks we couldn't correct in our everyday
couldn't make family better, bring fathers back home
but we could look real nice
like real Puerto Rican girls should

it was like walking into your girlfriend's house
Rosa's, with its lime green tile floor,
slippery with black hair clippings
under a forest of high-heeled, flip-flopped women
spitting fire in Dominican Spanish
frying pan hot, *ahí* in each word
room aflame with their lipstick
all talking the same *bochinche*
about who was doing who
and who got deported off the island
and what *puta* cut what cabron

five hours amid smoke and ash
lotions and dyes tinting the air
scissors and mouths moving
to any mambo radio tune
and by then my head was burning alive
with the power of the relaxer
unable to wash it out
for fear of staying black
and we all knew that's what we didn't want

we wanted to shake our hair
(since we couldn't shake our skin)
loosen wool into Chinese silk
smooth flat and fit for feathering
on Antillian days under salt and sun
ruining a girl's reputation for
looking right and good

now I'm thirty
and a box of Dark and Lovely is a stinging
memory of a young girl's addiction
dishonoring the women born of the coastline
mother, grandmother, before even them
women swimming seas, bearing storms, fighting misery
with hair stronger than the ropes that held them.

Jane Alberdeston-Coralín (DC)

Overworked

After we
ovulate
menstruate
gestate
lactate
procreate
and prostrate ourselves to creation . . .

After we
raise children
raise grandchildren
raise men
raise hell
and raise the dead in tribal dance . . .

After we
clean house
clean clothes
clean collard greens
clean people's stores
and clean up the aftermath of wars . . .

After we save souls
save schools
save trees

open your mouth and smile

save whales
and save the world from eternal damnation . . .

After we do
the impossible
the improbable
the unthinkable . . .

Must we also put out the trash?

Lucy Partlow *(Baltimore)*

Nintendo

to Ali and Drew

Men's fascination with Nintendo is
Rivaled only by their fascination with
Women is rivaled only by their
Fascination with cars is rivaled
Only by their fascination with each other
Men hug through Nintendo and
They cry on each other's shoulders
Through cars and
They affirm their masculinity through
Women who
Hug each other, cry on each other's
Actual shoulders
And these facts alone affirm their femininity
Maybe it's one big phallic, sexual thing
Nintendo I mean
Long, black sinewy wires
That enter open and eager
Nintendo boxes
Ejaculating their bits of fragmented
Images to culminate
Into an orgasmic frenzy of
Aw, man's and *Nigger, that's*
What I'm talking about, fool!
A surrogate, though, or rather a
Manly cushion of plastic and wires, and
Computer chips
So instead of mutually identifying with
Each other, they mutually identify with
Alajuwon and *My nigga Jordan.*
And instead of touching, they touch

Their joysticks at the same time
In the same room
And that's just like touching, isn't it?
Well, isn't it?

Treasure Williams (Memphis)

Stealth-Pirates of Cyberia

Far into the amber night of future these first
renegade mentats suffered
from extreme technophilia
with no use or respect for authority.
They compressed their streams
& spoke code so low
their equations made love to machines.
Sold their minds by the hour
but tapped into the power
& reprogrammed lockouts with dreams.
With virtual faith & maximum stealth
but no hint not ever of clatter
they turned virus to health
protonic matter to wealth
as they eavesdropped police band chatter.
These alchemical thieves
for whom no one grieves
give us hope
for the uncertainty principle.
Because the incorporate state
gave no word of their fate
despite an army of speakers.
They'll never find
those young pirates who sailed
wearing nothing but steel-toed sneakers.

Blair Ewing (Clarksville, MD)

The Death of Poetry

You were invited there
You overslept again
What's your excuse this time
You missed the boat/vote/rote/moat/bloat/goat . . . You missed the goat

The book was printed up
The words all ran together
The pages blank with ink
So the faux po's used invisible stink

It was a fluke that you were inside of the coffin as they swung it upon their
    shoulders
On the way to the gravesite
Wasn't it a real nice graveride?
You're finally inside in
Real nice riptide

Woho the Death of Poetry
Mercifully fast
Only lasted a millennium or two
The art of the past

No mo po
Get down to bidness
Po's no show
Ho ho ho—Good riddance

The view was dark/hark/lark/bark/stark . . . The view was stark
The time was passing slo/emotion
The day was crambe repetita, Cabbage leftovers,
April is the cruelest . . . coolest! . . .

The creeps were creeping out
Launching eulogy missiles at the street
The words' worth opposite beat
The drummer's melodizing feet

Typewriters on parade
Walt 'n' Emily rolling grave
Nothing left save to save
The Death of Poetry

It was a computer thing—
A neuter thing
Belligerent knucklehead
Brat art teeth shred
Flesh word battery nozzle
Blue skinny grenade carousal
Itchy mean grouse rasp kiss

Whatta life death is
The Death of Poetry

Bob Holman (New York)

Last Visit to Chestnut Middle School
M-I-N-O-R-I-T-Y

Can one of you kids
Define the word Minority?

Carlos: It means little kids!
Shawanda: It means young people!
Kim: It means small groups!
Ernesto: It means a whole bunch of Minors!

S-T-E-R-E-O-T-Y-P-E-S

Can one of you kids
Define the word
Stereotypes?

Carlos: It means Sony!
Shawanda: It means radio!
Kim: It means FM/AM!

And how about you, Ernesto
Do you have some witty definition?

Ernesto: It means all Puerto Ricans drive foreign small cars and eat rice &
beans too much *pernil* and steal and have roaches and have twenty babies
and are all on welfare and all Black people drive Cadillacs and love fried
chicken and can dance very good and rap and Asians know Kung Fu and
    stink . . .
And I think stereotypes
Also have something to do
With my stereo!
Yep!   Stereotypes
Also have something to do
With my stereo!

Jaime Shaggy Flores (Arlington, VA)

open your mouth and smile

Learning to Drive at 32

I should have learned to do this years ago:
maneuver a car in and out of traffic,
gliding my vehicle swiftly down the highway

as if I'd been doing it all my life, as if
I hadn't been crouched in the back seat
those Sunday afternoons my father tried

to teach my mother to drive: no, woman,
you daft or something, I swear I'll leave
you right here—his voice filling the car

as she fumbled with the wheel, hands clumsy,
car lurching then stopping as she fought
for control. I should have learned before

now, at thirty-two, my driver's ed vehicle
careening into a parked van, my foot
stuck on the accelerator I think is the brake,

hands atrophied on the wheel, my instructor
slamming his foot on the second brake
as we crash, metal on metal, impact

fracturing the van's windshield to a web
of damage. Should have known I'd make
a mess of this—going too fast or too slow,

not looking left and right, wrong foot
on the accelerator, wrong foot on the brake.
I shouldn't have remembered—my father,

still calling her stupid, my mother, head
down, arms folded, not saying anything
except all right, all right, you drive.

Allison Joseph (Carbondale, IL)

Mr. BOOM BOOM Man

Here he comes!
Distorted bass
nearly three blocks away
I wait
at the mercy of the traffic light
waitin
n waitin
for it to change
from red to green
so I won't have to deal
with him . . .
Mr. BOOM BOOM Man.

But my rearview mirror
it doesn't lie
n pumping his system
from my behind
I see his calling card
baby lavender twinkle lights
hugging a chrome-plated license plate
five-digit proclamation:
Double O Bad
coming at me!

A fifty-pound medallion
heaving a hickey-stained neck
closer
to the center of his manhood:
his beeper.
He pulls up slowly . . .
lowered Nissan mini truck
fills the vacancy on my left
n as the automatic tinted window
makes it slow way down,
I start to wonder
Why,
why can't I be like the cool girls
and like the cars that go:
BOOM BA BOOM . . . ?

Dig the way quarters
bounce off vinyl roofs?
Funky, fresh and stoopid
they say.

But then a flash
of gold gilded teeth
blinds my thoughts
n Mr. BOOM BOOM
shouts out:
Hey!
Sen-yo-reeeeta!
mamacita!
You speak English?
Hey . . . YOU
I'm talkin' to you . . .
aaah, you deaf bitch!

And then
I remember.

I wanna yell out,
Yeah, I speak English,
Pig Latin too
so Uckfay Offay
Mr. BOOM BOOM
Take your fade
n f-f-fade away!

But the light has turned green
n I don't have the time
(or the balls, really)
I take off
FAST
leaving behind
Mr. BOOM BOOM
Bu-foon.

Michele Serros (Echo Park, CA)

Road to the Presidency

Inauguration,
Condensation,
Built on fornication
And fabrication.
Exaggeration of communication
Did not have sexual relations
Propagation.
Need renovation,
Not accumulation,

Of corrupted minds set
And deliberations.
Washington admiration,
Adoration,
On the backs of slaves
Aggravation.
Yet preparation,
Gestation,
For another white male
Ejaculation.
Come realization.
Need re-evaluation.
Proclamation all
Represented in legalizations.
Not degradations.
Officials
Accusations
Drug relations,
Pants too low
Discriminations,
No representation.
Yet higher taxation.
Add dark faces to barred damnation.
Tired of the abbreviations, capitalizations,
Cross my T's and dot my I's elaborations.
Correct the manipulation,
Your hesitation,
False dedication.
President for the people?
Assassination.
Accusations.
Fake lamentation,
Arise sick sensations,
And to add to
Democracy's mutilation,
Bush is our new president.

Oneca Hitchman-Britton (New York)

open your mouth and smile

For What It's Worth

to His Excellency Pope John Paul II

Galileo is laughing at you
from on high.
Over a millennium late

your apology is too expensive
and nothing from the Vatican is free.

You want me to take you seriously?
Give me back my language
resurrect the murdered Mythrics
and give them Sunday once more.
Make the Madonna and baby Jesus
look like me again.

Keep your apology
and pawn your golden robes
give your stolen riches to the poor
canonize my martyred culture
remove the bearded white man from my dreams
so I don't spend eternity toiling
in his vineyard.

I wonder if heaven's got a cotton gin
for all those long white robes. The saints
go marching in?

Do I get to sit next to you, Johnny?
Or have you got another prepared apology for me
in heaven when you tell me
take my pyrite bowl of eternal supper
and eat at heaven's back door?

Must I lift holy hands to Hitler, Johnny?
and be marked by you again
cursed, the son of Ham?

Your cross burns Negro spirituals
and changes sacred lyrics too
his yoke is easy
and his burdens are white.

I don't want your apology, Johnny.
Gimme your beanie.
I'll pawn it for Fiestaware
and McDonald's french fries
Or maybe a wrap from The Wrappery on Union Ave.
to break with broken urban realities
living death row fantasies
of cash money rains
burning ghetto tear incense at 2Pac's tomb.

Galileo is laughing at your apology, Johnny.
He's laughing as he pours one out
He's laughing as he pours a 40oz out
for Copernicus' children.

Keep your apology, Johnny.
The Earth is still spinning
and
I am
unmoved.

Benjamin Theolonius Sanders *(Memphis)*

open your mouth and smile

It's Called Kings

I'm angry because I hate to be angry and because I hate to be angry I'm angry angry makes me smoke too much and drink too much and eat too much or not enough binge this and binge that saturate yourself in something or the other to forget the fact that I'm angry I'm angry because I don't like who I am who I become when I'm angry I'm mean and vengeful and vile and acid and ulcers and high blood pressure and headaches and backaches and aches and aches and aches and my head aches when I think how much I ache when I'm angry and how constipated I get when I realize how much I ache because I am so angry I'm so angry I don't want to wake up much less go to bed that's how angry rage rage rage fear pain anger I'm angry because why can't we all be the same not some have too much while others not enough of nothing to eat not enough of a house over our heads not enough of the pain in our hearts that makes us so angry angry angry because don't tell me that that guy sleeping on a stoop down the stoop from where you live doesn't make you angry or the $40 real live trees that smell so good when you go by a whisper in our minds of a time gone by a time when the wind smelled of the sea or of trees a clean clear smell no more long time gone by your need to get out of the city and how many of us get a chance to get out of the city rolling up our pennies those of us who still have any left you know you are poor when you have to count your pennies in America to get high to forget how angry you can get in America in the land of milk and honey brother kills brother for a woman for a life for a piece of the land we shoot each other up day after day after day we shoot each other up because we're so angry we're so angry we break things we throw things we beat we beat each other up even those we love we yell and scream and scream and scream and hurt and cry and cry and rage and scream and cry and want to kill and want to die because we want to kill ourselves most of all because we're so angry one must get very angry to put on a white robe white being the color of virtue of grace and add a white hood covering up the rage from our face and go burn a white cross on somebody's lawn because of their color or creed or else to put on a white robe and stand on a white altar covered with the most exquisite white cotton and lace and hold up a gold chalice filled with red blood in which we submerge a white wafer and eat and drink of another's flesh and blood in the name of the Lord in the name of the Lord this is my land says the conqueror and kills and kills with ease and grace in the name of the Lord whose Lord is my Lord your Lord is my God your God is your God my God do I believe in the Lord and Dukes and Earls and Princes and Pearls and Lords and Knights of the round table around the table of the Lord of the round table who rules above all and tells all the knights who sit around the round table what to do when to jump where to live divine right of kings have divine rights and dukes and earls and princes and pearls and lords the lord of the land and the supreme commander of the armed forces of all the nations and the people the masses of people who believe in the lord homeless wanderers wandering wandering wandering nomads migrating roaming moving constantly moving running from the landlord constantly moving constantly moving because the landlord owns all the land constantly moving in the name of the lord constantly moving constantly moving I'm angry I'm angry I'm angry I'm so angry.

Susana Cabañas *(New York)*

Billy

Jefferson Highway,
Selma Alabama.
I rode the hips of
gas masked storm troopers.
Red necks
under sky-blue hard hats.
Itchy fists
at my throat.

Wallace's boys
stood three deep
across four lanes
Their rebel cry,
Get those goddamned niggers,
curdled my skin.

I ached for those
five-hundred bloodied pilgrims.
Longed for calmer days.
My spirit meek
beneath bark.
Shade for brown bodies

Only shame hangs
from the limb
turned blunt weapon;
billy club

Oktavi Allison *(LA)*

every word must conjure

To Become Unconscious

I read in *Webster's New World Dictionary for Young Readers*
that Black was to become Unconscious
line 21, page 75, copy written in 1979
you can check it out if you like

Now, I took that and take that to mean, with the hidden agenda exposed,
    that White means to
become Conscious, and when I became Black/Conscious I really became
    Unconscious

So let's dispel this shit for what it really is

What is really being said is that when I spent $60 at the salon, for a perm,
    wash and set every
month I was Conscious. Every two weeks at the nail salon, with a check for
    $35, plus 20
for a pedicure, and $10 for a design on two nail, made me real Conscious,
    and when I thought
that *Vanity Fair,* I mean *Fashion Fair,* helped my skin look more satiny
and silky like the White skin on the commercials, I was the most Conscious
    there was.

It wasn't until I realized that 60 + 35 + 20 + 10 =
TOO MUCH GOT DAMN MONEY!

to be spending on artificial beauty, when just being Black was beautiful
    enough,
All I really needed was some Black seed.

When I came to myself and appreciated the curliness of my hair, how it
    symbolized all the power
in me, and the work that needed to get done, couldn't get done with my
    nails that were 1.5 inches
long, when I realized Black was Me and that's all I could be, you right I
    became Unconscious.

Ebony Page (Dallas)

Letter to an Unconceived Son

This is America, son.
Place where you have never been born
because I was never ready to face
that dark-brown-daddy-challenge,

the pull and push of you across
tightroped chasm between
what we've lost
and where we've found ourselves.

This is America.
And last night I had a dream
where a black man shot another
black man in the head and laughed.
It was like a football game to him,
spiking the ball with a bullet
in the concrete end zone,
the crowd's roar
and stomp and heave
roiling in his ears.

This is America, son.
And I am not dreaming.
This is where violence is as casual
as gang signs hurled down 63rd and Western
The land where disappearing brown women's bodies
are just another headline on page 3
of the Metro Section, next to the ads
for deodorant and toothpaste.

This is the place waiting
to grow up so you can grow up.
You are soft prisoner in my flesh,
promise in my loins, secret in my DNA
I keep locked under latex every time
I make love to a woman
that wants me
to love her
into loving you.

I could've been daddy three or four times now;
have wiped the butts and kissed the cheeks
of other men's children,
loved them squalling into my life—
enough to know they were my children, too.

And yesterday,
I sat in a south side kindergarten class
where the ABC blocks and Legos mix colors
like a cauldron of rainbows.
I watched while the children
wrestled on the rug.

I wondered
if you would have Keyshawn's bowlegged walk,
or Diondre's smile that spreads his gap-toothed
mouth wide as his favorite sugar cookie.
I wanna know if you'll have Sedan's wild-eyed
brilliance when he knows the right answer to 3 + 2.
I wanted to know if we would ever be right
for each other, if I would ever pass the test
of your childish faith.

This is me, son. The country called father.
Waiting for the time to be right enough,
knowing there will never be enough right time,
preparing a place in the crook of my arm
for your weight, your solid thump of heartbeat.

This is me, son.
Wondering if I'll ever be strong enough
to hold your hand.

Tyehimba Jess (*Chicago*)

The Usual Suspects

Black Male, 6′2″, 28, wearing drooping baggy jeans,
patterned boxers, tan work boots. May be carrying
a gun

Black Male, 16, dark blue sweats and skullcap. Last seen running
south on Main

Black Male, 30, red Chicago Bulls tank top and matching
shorts. Arrested on the corner with other Black Males ages
32, 27, 19, 12

Black Male, 42, unkempt beard, dirty clothes, no
permanent address. Has not bathed in weeks

Black Male, driving late model car. Reason for detention:
Busted tail light, weaving/unsure driving, possible expired
tags or license, no reason for him to be in this neighborhood
at this hour anyway

Black Male, 19, dreadlocks, oversized clothes
claims to be a "rapper"
Black Male, 30, says he is "a poet." Beat him into
silence. Rap them blind

Black Man, 50, says he is a college professor. See
how well he grades papers handcuffed in a cell

Black Man, 57. Occupation: jazz musician. Has clippings
in pocket as quote-unquote proof. Burn them

Black Man, 39. Protests he has no interest in, would never rape
a woman. Says he's gay. Mention this when throwing him
in cell with other inmates. If not one now, he will be
once they're done

Black Man, height 5'8", 5'7", 4'9", 6'1", 6'3", 6'5", 7'4"—
A 6'9" Senior from the University of North Carolina

Black Man, weight 150, 195, 210, 200, 260, 190, 300—
Weighing in at two twenty-five, pound-for-pound the best
fighter in the world

Black Man, age 27, 32, 48, 73, 16, 17, 18, 8—
aged 13 and 9 respectively, under arrest for attempted murder,
have been charged as adults (charges later dropped)
Black Man   Black Man   Black Man   Black Man   Black Man
Black
Man

Reginald Harris (Baltimore)

Blooming Death . . . Blossoms

The pink blossoms
litter the street and stick
to every car window,
like confetti on Fat Tuesday.
It is the first true rain of Spring,
and it broke like the tension
of my brow.
Some great blast surging towards
the blackest paved earth,
to BOOM, rahhhh!
shake the earth,
atomic blast,
E equals M
C . . . shatters
sending blossom petals, in the explosion,
over everything, the wet, black street, a charcoal mirror,
and cars, like ash from Mt. Saint Helen's.

every word must conjure

Death Blossoms,
falling to the ground like manna.
This bitter nutrition is unsafe for us to eat.
My mind is w/ Mumia
and how his sleep is tormented
with the walk,
how the pensiveness of mortality
rattles his dreamlife.
Raagh!
As he wakes to find his
white nightmarish opus,
a reality
and his heart sinks
and he is sick with anxiety as
demons surround him,
orange suit, in collusion with supremacy,
with the powers that be,
with the powers that be,
with the powers that be killing us . . .
wounding Diallo in the armpit,
in the soles of his feet.
(How many ways are there, that a man can be shot in the feet?)
Walking across a tight rope of bullets
or ka ra tae kick to the oncoming hail of gunfire,
or laying in peace as the soul jettisons
through a James Bond like
escape hatch, leaving the cooling, perforated body,
becoming a corpse.
Dearly beloved we . . . are gathered here to celebrate
*a thing called life . . . **
Life, LIFE, L I F E!
The only true thing we have a right to.
Not to privacy or to speak freely,
or to own land or a gun . . . or to pursue happiness.
These rights are nice but people have lived w/o them
in China, Tibet, Abyssinia and Israel for thousands,
and thousands of years.
But life,
no,
that right has insured that we are here and will be here.
And Mumia,
I cry for you as I do not know the misery
of desperation, and the clacking of shackled feet,
Or the pacing surge of a panicked chest while the scales pen your demise.
Oh Mumia,

*from "Let's Go Crazy," by Prince

It was a . . .
It was a . . .
It was a . . .
ambush in the night,
all guns they aiming at . . .
*you.**

Andre O. Hoilette *(Dayton)*

*from "Ambush in the Night," by Bob Marley

What the Oracle Said

You will leave your home:
nothing will hold you.
You will wear dresses of gold; skins
of silver, copper and bronze.
The sky above you will shift in meaning
each time you think you understand.
You will spend a lifetime chipping away layers
of flesh. The shadow of your scales
will always remain. You will be marked
by sulphur and salt.
You will bathe endlessly in clear streams and fail
to rid yourself of that scent.
Your feet will never be your own.
Stone will be your path.
Storms will follow in your wake,
destroying all those who take you in.
You will desert your children
kill your lovers and devour their flesh.
You will love no one
but the wind and ache of your bones.
Neither will love you in return.
With age, your hair will grow matted and dull,
your skin will gape and hang in long folds,
your eyes will cease to shine.
But nothing will be enough.
The sea will never take you back.

Shara McCallum *(Memphis)*

every word must conjure

The U.S.A. Court of No Appeal

A magazine jury of twelve rounds
A prosecuting trigger

& forefinger judge

A witness box casket on a tombstone stand

The accused found guilty of melanin

In the first degree

A death verdict in a graveyard court—

Injustice sustained;

Objection overruled.

George Edward Tait (New York)

on the state-sanctioned murder of shaka sankofa

they are killing me tonight, they are murdering me tonight.
8:49 pm pronounced dead, with one eye open.

these names i place in my mouth tonight. shaka sankofa, amadou
diallo, and mumia abu-jamal. these names familiar on my tongue. all
african, muslim names. all eastern, all other. until the end of his
breath, shaka sankofa, born gary graham, urged black power. march
on, black people, he said.

dead. and an example, now, to all people. a promise of what is to
come. state-sanctioned killings of innocents. a white towel they
placed on his face, to cover his stare.

i place these names in my mouth, and think of how american the name
shaka tastes. how american mumia sounds. and the names of men we
love who are called after prophets, nations, blood lines, warriors.
the men we love who can never have enough eye witnesses. the state
will turn back even god's eye, and witness murder easily.

if i could talk right now, i'd call my girl, and tell her to keep our
son inside. to shape his head into a bullet-proof crown. i'd
whisper my intimates' names into a secret pot, bury it under a tree,
and pray for strength to grow. i'd at least scream this pain out

into the street. rage at this night. i'd call wbai and say, i don't
know what to say. my sisters are somewhere tonight, broken down one
more time.

and what are we gonna do? shut what down? boycott whom? appeal to
which court?

and a 17-year-old gary graham, criminalized since birth. chose the
name for himself sankofa. a ghanian word, meaning to learn from the
past. transformed himself into a soul outside of bars and skin and
even death.

it is hope they killed.
it is life they ate.

i love you, he said several times. i love you. learn from the past.
george bush jr. is a murderer, as is his father. learn from the
past. we still have mumia. learn from the past. i love you, he
said. one eye open. i love you. sankofa.

62200 10:49pm

Suheir Hammad (New York)

An Epistle to the Revolutionary Bible

meditations on Philemon & Shaka Sankofa/
Gary Graham, a victim of Texas' death row

Dear Shaka,

I have never written to you. I have never spoken to you. Before I left Texas,
hurrying away to the book learning coast of liberalism, you were only another
black man, who just didn't know right from wrong. And I think of you now,
today, and every day as I pass over a bridge in Houston between the halls of
higher education and the brick-barred house of hell called jail. All boarders
glance between the two. All of us only a witness away from making either of
these man-made structures our homes.

Up until the day I glimpsed that simple truth, wedding myself to causes of
self-definition and political prisoners in states other than the Lone Star. Like
most of America and the world, I expected little more than Bushes and green
backs from cotton and oil fields. But denial and ignorance are not rushing
rivers of life. They are the fierce formula, the lascivious liquor concocted for
the death serum they shot into your riotous veins.

I glimpsed the fruits of your will to live from outside the walls. Your strug-
gle reawakened us: *For we have great joy and consolation in thy love, because
the bowels of the saints are refreshed by thee, brother.**

But a quiet quorum failed to see the profit in your freedom and evolution. Instead gatekeepers, prideful leaders began to feed upon you. But your last resistance humbled them. Your last words reawakened the patois of the Fifth Ward streets where you and your brothers yelled, *You better recognize!*

We were witnesses to you that day in June, another Onesimus among us, valued as a slave, not a brother. Onesimus, whose name means useful, was a slave like you. A briefly noted character in the *Book of Life.* He, like you, abandoned his given station, his given name. Stole away from his master. Paul wrote to Philemon from prison concerning Onesimus, a runaway slave, appealing to Philemon out of a higher law, evoking the Old Testament provision: *Thou shalt not deliver unto his master the slave who escaped of his master unto thee. He shall live with you in your midst; you shall not mistreat him.***

We are to honor your spirit: Your worth as a father, a brother, a thinker, a pro-active human, is greater than slave-like utility. Too many see profit in exploitation, reveling in ghetto inhabitants' submission to the temptations of the underground economy that captured you. But your life sired courage in me—I say to the naysayers and accusers, *If he has done any wrong or owes you anything, charge it to me.**** Conscious ones will no longer release broken souls to the Romans. Left to their whims you are "free" labor, a tool.

On June 22nd, you were the number of man, of every man resisting the unnatural masquerading of tradition and ritual as justice. Your words, a potent drum beat, more powerful than the prince of the air for six hours, and we clung to every word you uttered during your last six minutes. Radio, TV, and cyber-ways sent a wave of radical resistance to the planet's six billion. Media punditry called it rambling, but it was a sacred song, the cry of a guerilla from the death gurney, arousing us from politics' poppy fields and wizardry. You became more than utilitarian to the political and Machiavellian.

I know this ink is your blood. All the words I write. Know from the heavens that there are wiser warriors in the midst of the haters. And know (because even revolutionaries are human enough to discuss the weather) that the fat, round summer solstice sun would not sit on your death. We all watched the night fight with the day. Your day, and our day, on a Texas June day hotter than any in July, we all wiped our collective brow, sweating life from once apathetic pores, holding hope in our hands on placards painting love memories of you, witnesses to the illness that leaves us legally blind, the weak legally benign. Yes, they did murder you that night, but the blow did not extinguish your spirit. There are more Onesimuses among us . . .

This epistle to you, brother,
from a sister on the bus,
forever in motion.

Andrea Roberts (Houston)

*,**Philem. 1 African Heritage Study Bible, King James version.
***Philem. 1:18.

Warrior Womb

for all those awaiting liberation, still
for Suheir and Suzan Hammond

Warrior wombs at night
Thrown up towards the bullets
Shoot at Olive Trees
As Palestine gives birth to herself
With the stars that are refugees

Meanwhile
Rich men declare peace in their palm pilots
And the *NY Times* seems concerned that Clinton has not been able to sleep
He has bags under his eyes and awakens with headaches of talks with
   swarthy
men who passionately defend Palestine being born again.
Yet Israel, a close friend, makes the US more prosperous for those who can
afford to talk for hours on their cell phones about the stocks of the latest
nuclear consumer products and cost efficient mind prisons.

Or maybe he cannot sleep
Because there are warrior wombs being thrown
Wombs and wounds everywhere
Palestine screams, pushes and curses asking for some tenderness
To create herself, to love herself

I want to ask you with concern, have you seen the eyes of the children?
They are weary of the pictures of decapitated limbs
Repeat the names of the murdered and murderers
Sing in poems
Sooth a movement with papier-mâché rocks
And hope for a moment when Palestine can rest

They have bags under their eyes
The men, women, and children of Palestine
have bags under their eyes
under the white candlelight of this night
with bags under their eyes
Hold Palestine's hand with a tight grip
Tell her she will be born

As rich men draft peace with poison-tipped ink,
coloring terror, drawing out whispers

We wait patiently watching
for warriors to be born.

Lenina Nadal (New York)

every word must conjure

Cowboynomics

Go home, America
but you may never know exactly where
and home is now a foreign affair;
an alliance with hideous tyrants
and oligarchic dictators
holding peace ransom by treachery
with purple hearts that seduce
the filthy rich marching with the saints
to resurrect the profiteers
and brutally impoverish the noble poor
who worship bold-faced liberation;
as these pot-bellied autocrats
ambush the assassinated dead
by ripping off the tongues of prayers
of widowed mothers and stolen wives
who sleepwalk to sniff or kiss
those demised then embrace
to heal their own wounds;
when there could be no question
the doves that pray by day
turn into bats at night to play
with vultures early morning
and rape virginity before it's born
so they could all withstand
the wild stench of freedom!

Come home, America
shift winds or hit the road
and get off the next exit,
but perhaps you may not be that aware
home is now a foreign affair;

a flea-market where mice and rat patrols
turn amok like scattered shadows
under a drunken moon to plea-bargain
with flies and insects for chopped off
genitals or mutilated breasts,
and the rampaged eyes torn out
of children's faces when
diehard cynics trade aspirations
with rightwing maggots
so they could all scrounge
the Heartland and dance passionately
the tango delta with ravaged nuns
before sucking death from its anus!

Return home, America
and patrol your own heart
but you may never know exactly where
and home is now a foreign affair;
an outward-bound backyard broker
with rattlesnake eyes
set adrift from dusk to dawn
between bamboo skies or plantain trees,
mounting its flag on uprooted winds
passed roadblocks
and sideroads of genocide
that now bewitch the drumbeat
of wardogs who get unscrupulously
drunk on amnesia before asking
the neurotic fascist daughter's hand
with prick diplomacy
so they could all bankroll
the pomp and pride of the elite
in the name of National Security!

So come and shift winds, America
or hit the road and get off
the next exit: return to yourself
and remain to patrol your own heart;
but you may never know exactly where
nor perhaps be that aware
home is now a foreign affair
where American is no longer
spoken anymore

José Angel Figueroa (New York)

every word must conjure

Demockery

teeter totters
on the precipice of our
discontent
put thru the microscope of integrity
coming up deficient of honesty
as the college
elects to misrepresent
the voices crying out for proof
that the constitution is constitutional
not just archaic babble
from centuries past
guarded by gargoyles
on the steps of justice

apathy is the aching tooth of dracula
fangs dripping middle eastern oil
stock market flutter
as fat sam
needs a colonic
five hundred years of lies
backed up in his constitution
constituents tired of
being pregnant with hope
struggle for abortions
feeling voting had no purpose
in this hypocrisy
where the two-headed coin
has two bad signs
and anyway it falls
oppression is

martial law
hiding in the shadows
waiting for the eagle to fall
conspiracy theories ignored
while those that disorder the new world
wait for its delivery
to the gates of hell

Ngoma *(New York)*

Executive Privilege

As of late, the President
of the United States
has been impacting my life
in ways I'd rather he not be.

Last night watching TV news
my 9-year-old son Casey asked,
Daddy, what is oral sex?
It's when a woman kisses
a man's penis, I mumbled bravely.
No, it's when a woman puts
a man's penis in her mouth,
I amended.
Gross, Casey responded,
as a blanket of cowardice
descended over me
and I couldn't
explain further the specifics

of cunnilingus,
or that same sex partners
approach oral sex
with as much lusty gusto
if not more
than do a woman and a man.
I should have told
my son more,
maybe I shouldn't
I don't know,
but I didn't.

This morning I watch Bill Clinton
on television
and he's telling Saddam Hussein
that he's gone too far
over that line in the sand
and the U.S. won't back down
and Saddam better get his shit together
because the smart bombs will drop
like giant turds on the heads of Iraq's people.

I try to remember if people
in the sixties really believed
that man's aggression toward
other men and women was caused
by not enough sex;
if the frustration of untapped release
curdled like milk gone bad
into belligerence and violence.
Which doesn't really explain
Clinton's newest posturing
unless as it said in the *Daily News*
he doesn't consider oral sex
to be sex at all
which seems farfetched
but then again he didn't inhale.

Of course it's not my business
where he sticks his dick
and I shouldn't care, but
I've been married 13 years
and have worked hard to stay
on the straight-and-narrow.

Yes, I'll admit in the name
of poor married bastards
like myself I resent

that the President
gets more coochie
than me.

Next time my children
ask about sex,
I'll tell it correct
to give them a chance
to grow up free
and less hung up
about sex
than me.

2 *(a few months later)*

Dad, did the President lie? asks Casey.
It sure looks that way, son.
If you ever do that I'll be real mad at you.
Don't worry Casey, I'll be good.
Mom says if you had sex with Monica Lewinsky
she'd divorce you.
I don't think that'll ever happen, don't worry.
Then you'd be fired, or you'd have to resign
as our father, adds six-year-old Levi.
I will always be your father Levi, no matter what,
I add authoritatively.
Like Darth Vader is Luke Skywalker's father.
I realize this conversation is going nowhere so I try
to change the topic, but Casey interrupts:
Dad, do I have semen?
Not yet, but you will in a few years.
Will it ruin my clothes?
No, don't worry about that.
Dad, why did Monica Lewinsky have semen on her dress?
I don't know.
Is Bill Clinton going to get fired?
I don't think so.
Do you think he should get fired, Dad?
No, I don't.
What happens if you don't let the semen out?
I don't know.
Do your balls explode?
Don't worry about that.
Dad?
Yeah, Levi.
Do you think I would make a good President?
Sure, maybe, I guess.

Danny Shot *(Hoboken)*

Question

*A brother offended is harder to be won than a strong city,
and their contentions are like the bars of a castle.*
—Proverbs 18:19

What up, brother? the white teen with dreadlocks
    and a confederate flag tattoo on his arm asks,
and the black man to whom the question is addressed
    seems pensive: He may teach college or fix cars,

but right now he's a philosopher weighing an answer;
    he's survived his first year in the south, but he always
expected love and hate to speak clearer
    on red soil. Dreadlocks and a confederate flag?

What message crossed in the mind of this young man?
    Did he start to listen to reggae after the tattoo?
The nanosecond freezes before they pass each other
    on this street corner in downtown Asheville, North

Carolina, which allows enough time for him to remember
    the last time he had seen a confederate flag
so out of place. He was driving a Uhaul truck
    down I-71 in Ohio when, to his surprise, as he approached

Cincinnati, he saw the largest confederate flag of his life painted
    on the roof of a barn. In Ohio, where slaves escaped to find
freedom, a confederate flag? A flag of secession, of blood and bone,
    of black against white, of homeland fighting homeland, of fear

of unity; the belief that blacks lacked spirit and heart; the grief
    of loss and longing; fear of shackle and whip; hatred so deep
that it pitted him against his own brother; hatred so deep it made
    him gnaw off his own white hand; turned lovers into soldiers,

into wielders of guns and bayonets and bottles and stones—
    this flag, this birthmark of an endless struggle to conquer
and enslave and betray—to betray himself—yet holds, for all its
    pain, something worth pride in his white mind? The black wonders

if dreadlocks can make a white boy a minority in his own country.
    What up, brother? Of that abrupt question—from salutation
to spitting in each other's face, to looking into each other's eyes,
    to not shaking each other's hand, to weeping at each other's

history, to killing and forgiving and loving and enduring and enduring,
    of that abrupt question, and these transitions, and that electric

current sent to the brain and the heart and the tongue and the spine
　　　and the bowels, raising up one more remnant of history—nothing

remains as clear as the laughing wind that brushes his face when
　　　he hears brother slip from between the teeth of a contemporary
confederate. *What up, brother?* The white asks the black, who
　　　decides to say nothing, verbally, but stands and stares into these blue

eyes, as if he were the one who asked the question, like a sphinx
　　　tripping up a fool with the wrong answer to another tragic riddle.

A. Van Jordan *(Asheville, NC)*

georgia avenue, washington d.c.

for Kenneth Carroll

explain this to me as i conjure images of
rosa parks boarding the bus. i am on the back
of the bus georgia avenue, brightwood bump along
bottle of southern comfort in my
lap, taking shots not gulps
and this world, the only world i have
always thought was authentic and
trustworthy is completely safe.

explain this to me as i take another
hit. i am on the back of the bus. every
black man who enters the bus comes
to the back. we like it here in the back
i guess. the back of the bus is where we
are told to go. love the back. sweetback
fine lady this back of the bus.

on the back of the bus we smoke pot
drink wine
talk bad about the gov't
in the back of the bus, we tell
each other that the white man is
the devil.

on the back of the bus, we own the world
no one who comes to the back of the bus
does not use more cuss words than english.

on the back of the bus i meet 1 million malcolm x's
8 million michael jordans, 4 million eddie murphys

on the back of the bus, i feel safe.
funky funky safe. george clinton funky.
bootsy collins funky.
radio loud violating the local
ordinance funky. the back of the bus is
a rowdy rowdy negro.

the back of the bus is crowded. many of
us are standing. no one is getting off.
we are going up and down the avenue,
passing the wine, smoking the dope,
shooting the shit, and no one wants to
ever get off.

the bus driver is an uncle tom. the ads on
the walls are propaganda. we are an afrikan
people and where in the ads does it say,
afrikan people are beautiful. i want to tear down
the ads. i want to get off the bus but the bells
do not work. i have been on the bus too long.
the bus will not stop and the driver is
an uncle tom. he cannot hear us yelling that
we want to get off.
the wine is wined, the dope is doped
the shit is shot, it is time to get off
because we have seen this shit before.
get the driver, tell him, let him know
he is a black man and the black man is
a beautiful person.

he stops at last. we are no longer reading
the ads. we get up from the back and head for
the front door. but we go out the back; the
front of the bus is scarier than the back.

we get off and stand on corners now and do not
board the bus. we have wine and dope and funky
funky music. the bus comes up and it is full of
young black boys younger than us who used
to see us doing what we used to do on the back
of the bus. they are doing it now.

the bus driver is an uncle tom and will not
stop for them. the ads are still there. the young boys
talk bad about the gov't and tell each other that
the white man is the devil. i, with southern comfort
in my lap, conjure images of rosa parks boarding the bus.
i sit down on the corner and start to drink my liquor.

i look around and there is no one around. my friends
are all gone. *this is for the brothers who ain't here,*
i say to myself.

then i pour out some whiskey on the sidewalk as the
young boys riding on the back of the bus stare at me
and wonder why

Brian Gilmore *(Tacoma Park, MD)*

A Palace of Mourners

I've tried to store away
and refrain memories from surfacing,
but miniature Houdinis escaped
from opaque brain cells
that harbored a palace of mourners
from the country of my birth
where nightsticks have swung from Columbus
to modern avarice leaders whose draconian
passions have cooked fear into our psyche.

After nights of past memories
poking needles in my sleep,
floods of images breached the silence
of my pen. Joseph, a 26-year-old journalist,
arrested in August of '92, demanded to speak.
My head became an echo-chamber
where the tales of the dead
and the brutalized reverberated.
Their screams, exploding
the coral of memories, forming
an enormous tapestry of narratives
and brutal images: like Joseph's blistered buttocks,
broken right knee, and cicatrice head.

The army wanted to teach his tongue
the language of silence.
Thin, glowing wires
turned his tongue into an eel,
slapping words to incomprehension.
Still, he did not swallow fear
and confess.
His tongue trumpeted justice
despite his scars and inability to move bowels.

In light of this carnival
of nightsticks and stench,
I've desperately tried to write
about the movement of clouds
and pastoral images, but the screams
and agonies of a valley of Haitians
ferociously migrating to the center
of my pastoral scenes
have torn up the white lilies
and the dandelions.
Instead of flowers,
my pen bleeds an agonizing nation.

Patrick Sylvain (*Boston*)

Palestine

I am not an Arab, I am not a Jew
Abraham is not my father, Palestine is not my home
But I would fight any man
Who kicked me out of my house
To dwell in a tent
I would fight
To the ends of the earth
Someone who said to me
I want your house
Because my father lived here
Two thousand years ago
I want your land
Because my father lived here
Two thousand years ago.
Jets would not stop me
From returning to my home
Uncle Toms would not stop me
Cluster bombs would not stop me
Bullets I would defy.
No man can take the house of another
And expect to live in peace
There is no peace for thieves
There is no peace for those who murder
For myths and ancient rituals
Wail at the wall
Settle in "Judea" and "Samaria"
But fate awaits you
You will never sleep with peace
You will never walk without listening.
I shall cross the River Jordan

With Justice in my hand
I shall return to Jerusalem
And establish my house of peace,
Thus said the Lord.

Marvin X (San Francisco, CA)

The Road from Khartoum

I have heard their groans and sighs,
And seen their tears, and I would give every
Drop of blood in my veins to free them.
—Harriet Tubman

In the day
sand rains
down on us
coarse as camel
hair against
blistered thighs
advancing
from the vast bases
of the Sahara.

In the night
the wind rolls the
grains back
like broken promises
flinging
them through the air
lethal missiles
to settle upon
the hard backs
of this geography:

Aluel Mawien
(girl, age unknown)

Alei Nun Akok
(boy, 14 years old)

Achok Chang Angora
(girl, 2 years old)

Elizabeth Ading Deng
(mother, 25 years)

no longer Mrs. but missing
and presumed dead
one of many thousands gone
and yet
no one speaks
of murder of rape

the desert strangles
more than words
Allah Akbar!
God is Great!
armed men
on horses
have no need
for translators

our names
do not represent
women and children
whether
Christian, Muslim, or Ancestral Other
we are all *abd*
slaves

we are the spoils of a celestial war
and such acts are
the accident of history
celebrated in mosaic structures
jihads old
steeped in memories
   of an eye
      for an eye
     a tooth
        for a tooth
        and 35 US dollars a head

what this journey has taught us:
that foreign policy is UNclean
teeth biting down
on black throats, ripe as dates
that pain is fragrant
as the oiled skin of concubines
that truth can be stolen
hidden in oil drums shipped to Canada
that following the north star will not lead us to freedom
that some Talismans do not protect but exploit
that excuses are ubiquitous

every word must conjure

as cheap
and as plentiful
expendable
as human labor

These truths the sun reflects
illuminating the harsh tender
moments in this, our third republic
demanding that every word must conjure
while the sands of rains
pour down on us
paving the road from Khartoum
to freedom.

Sheree Renée Thomas (New York)

A Modern Love Poem

for a love in progress

1619: exhausted, you appeared—
spear broken and body bloodied
and I became the Nile for you,
bathed you in my fluidity,
me, weaving through your toes, resting in your navel,
tickling your ears and caressing your soul

And then came *Jesús* . . .

to take you from me
whole, the sun rested atop the brush—
briefly, a smiling face,
Raw, it seemed, lifting you from my waters
to sail on others.

It took seven lives to find again
that color of the sun
never quite understanding why—
until now—the haze of a setting sun
was my joy
            and my melancholy.

Jesús was yours and *Mercy* was mine.

Candice Nicole Love (Chapel Hill, NC)

In Praise of the Seattle Coalition

They came from around the globe to change the shape of the globe
They formed a human chain and sidewalks declared their support
They led labor down unpaved roads and mountain ranges from all sides
    tipped their peaks in salute
They wore turtle caps and the Pacific roared its approval
They chanted *This is what democracy looks like* so that we who could
    not be in Seattle could watch TV & see what democracy looks like
They called for human rights and were gassed with inhuman chemicals
They insisted the food be kept clean of genetic experiment and were shot
    with rubber bullet pellet red meat welts
They demanded an end to worldwide sweatshops and were treated
    to the best nightsticks multinational business could buy
It was a coalition for the ages, of all ages, of all stages, of varying
    degrees of calm and rages
After curfew, the skies lit up & birds flew across continents to celebrate
Ancient redwood trees shook their leaves to prevent WTO delegates
    from being received
The town salmon agreed to wear union windbreakers for the week
When the mayor outlawed public gasmasks, the air sucked up to help out
It was the audible applause of the quantum that drove the police chief mad
A dog ran across the road to dispose of pepper spray containers
Stampeding cops were stopped by dolphins swimming in mid-street
    I saw this every hour on the hour behind the CNN lens
In a thousand tongues, even the internet logged on the side of the young
O friends, you have jumpstarted this nation and revealed an America
    with a million human faces
Of course the corporations were defeated, any objective observer
    could see they were outmatched from the opening bell
Now come the subtle somersaults and the internationalist flips
Now the courageous maneuvers that follow a win
Now the flexible glue to keep a coalition together
Now spreading the fun so that more can participate
Now there will be more democracy and then even more democracy
Now you are welcomed heroic at the dawn of a century

Eliot Katz (New York)

Blood Is the Argument

All he wanted
For Christmas
Was a fly girl
In a red dress,
Forty ounces &
A blunt,

Rap music
Coming out
The side of
His mouth,
A smile across
His dark face.

He was Tupac,
Biggie Smalls.
A legend
In his own mind.
End & means,
Product of all
The wrong things
Done by all
The wrong people
At all the
Wrong times.
He was blood
In the argument,
Lesson of what
A generation
Forgot to teach.

Fred Hampton
Murdered in
A Chicago
Rooming house,
Bobby Seale
Hog-tied in
The name of justice,
Assata running
For her life,
Geronimo Pratt
Thirty years
In the penal colony,
Huey mind drugged,
Strung out,
Dead on a
Revolution that
Was more rhetoric
Than action.

Somehow
We have
Forgotten the
Lessons of our

Past, fine
Line between
Thought & deed,
Preaching to
Congregations,
Half-stepping
Their way
To oblivion,
The twenty-first century,
The dead & dying
Among us call out
For more than
A whisper,
a rap line
Throw over
Home girls
Weighted down
By the size
Of their earrings.

Ghosts &
Murderers
Are the sum
Of our memory.
They stumble over us
As dead men
Pressed between
the pages of a book
& those not crushed
are born again,
waiting on Jesus
for the last revolution.

Small pockets
Of resistance
Left over
From the sixties
Still plot
Insurrection
Yet know we talk
A good game,
That we've
Been played
& are still
Our best, worst enemy.
The nightmare
Of our lives

Is to live
Each day
Remembering
Talk is cheap,
Life a fragile
Commodity on
History's shore,
Reminiscing:

. . . if you hear any noise
it's just me and the boys
making like revolution.

Gary Johnston *(New York)*

drums drown out the sorrow

Amadou Diallo
from Guinea to the Bronx
Dead on Arrival

Bang Bang Bang
Forty-one shots
Forty-one shots

Did we get him?
Did we get that animal?
Did we get that black animal?

We only needed nineteen shots!

Every second of every minute
Every hour of each day
from Los Angeles to Chicago to New York to Toronto
to Philadelphia to Vancouver to Detroit to Newark to Hartford
unarmed men—and women—die under the hands
of the trigger happy Death Squad Unit

I am not a hired killer
I am not a member of the KKK
White Aryan Brotherhood
or the Church of Creation
I'm only doing my job.

The countless cries of

No Justice No Peace
No Justice No Peace

I hear the sound of the human cry
from the soul through the heart
I hear the cries of brothers and sisters
of human love loss
above the blue horizon skies

And if I dream on a dark night
my love guides the sound of unity
before we will perish under the
KKK US Nazi Aryan Brotherhood

We ain't gonna be stopped
and we are gonna move
before words will mean nothing
and death will fall on us all

I hear the cry of

Backward Never
Forward Forever

I hear the cries of mothers and fathers
I hear the rhythm of the bata drum calling us

Justice Now Justice Now Justice Now

Carlos Raul Dufflar *(New York)*

Another Scream

The Young Man
Amadou was always fascinated
by the glitter
in the films and magazines.
The lure of white smiles
and prosperous rainbow people.
The glass and brick buildings
that seemed to tower above
the african skyscrapers in his capital city.

He sat at the feet of his big brothers
Who came home with tales of
Wealth and women
And endless opportunity
In the Promised Land
The city of gold and glamour
The insomniac's heaven.
The sleepless one with many dreams yearned for this place.
So he came to claim his space
And make his fortune.

The Mother
She was too devastated to cry.
As the contained scream

Was the mute ululating wail
That moved her forward
To the plane
Through the crowds
Past the flashing cameras
She thought only of his fascination for this place.

It was garbage day
In New York
The debris and stench filled the air
And her lungs.
She marveled at the magnet pull
This place of concrete and contempt had on her son
Who used to lean West
even as he faced east in prayer.

Allah is Great!—she affirmed
as her legs threatened to fail her

She wanted to bury herself
In the mountains of trash
And join her son in Paradise
Where his body would not
Be riddled with nineteen bullets
Or his ears filled with the sound
Of forty-one shots
But radiantly black in white robes.

Allah is Great!
She thought as she watched
The man who ran the city
Condone this massacre
In his eyes of ice
That looked past her
At the uniformed men
With pasty skin and broad shoulders
Standing tall in their murderous hearts
and murder-mangled hands.

The Murder/Poets Bearing Witness

After the police rained a storm of bullets
At this young African man
Whose dreams of a new millennium of opportunity
were shot down
Forty-one times

drums drown out the sorrow

The poets gathered
On the way to a well of words.
Among them a sister of questionable origins
Posing as a queen
Who met a bearded brother with bombs bursting
In his metaphor-filled brain
Who walked lock step with a man closer than kin
Who stayed close to the ground and recorded the cadence of concrete
While he loomed above the giraffe people.
They all shared a bowl of beliefs and conviction
under the umbrella of minor celebrity and promised glory.
They came trying to destroy the scream
They shared
One octave captured
in each of their throats
one scream echoing
forty-one times

Malkia M'Buzi Moore (Atlanta)

A Well-Bred Woman

She leaps to her feet
condemning the cops
who shot her son.

She turns into something
primitive screaming
the American word for

a man who sleeps with
his mother, whose mother
is a female dog.

She puts her hand over
her mouth as she hears
the keys rattle and they

are let out to walk free
on the green grass outside
the courthouse where

no lion is waiting
to eat them though she
prayed for one, no owl

hooting at the noonday
sun, no calamity like a
building waiting to fall

on the black sedan
that drives away
down the highway.

The reporters ask and
she tells them Amadou
is a common name

in her country, it is
like stones on the road
and there are many

fathers named Diallo.
They all rush out when
they hear the drums

saying *your son*
your son your son
Amadou they look

everywhere in the home
in the compound
in the cassava fields

down by the riverbanks
where the crocodiles
steal the goats

They search until
they remember the one
who went to America

Then they hug
the remaining Amadous
and weep

Mervyn Taylor (New York)

drums drown out the sorrow

Amadou

Each night, as I step beyond the four
walls of my apartment, the wind awaits
and wails like a mother delivering her
child to auction blocks on Southern
courthouse steps.
Your name has become a cry falling
upon stone ears of justice, who remains
unbalanced and unyielding in deferred
silence and truth.

The world heard the New York night ex-
plode into 41 pieces of bone and bullet,
scattering dreams and family bonds over
oceanic tides, your spirit caught up
with those of the ancestors, leaving
bruised flesh crumbled on vestibule floors,
its carpet insatiable like a sponge.

Now what will halt the anger of demanding
feet, who shall wipe away pain streaking
our cheeks, where will our screams go that
become entangled among the clouds, when will
the Constitution no longer be antiquated
words on mildewed paper, how am I to sing
America's song when lamentations are
lodged within my throat?

I must move on. The sun has fallen
into the earth. I have become a mere shadow,
standing here my wallet is way too black.
And with each step I take, the wind howls,
Amadou, Amadou,
Amadou.

James E. Cherry *(Jackson, TN)*

BLS

I heard it on the radio today
that Betty Shabazz is dead   that she died
yesterday   at 3 p.m.   in the Bronx

I'm walking in a city where it's news
that Betty Shabazz is dead   that she died
yesterday   and I'm talking to the woman

behind the sandwich counter   she is Black
we say   I didn't know   I heard the news
on the radio this morning   we mourn

the dead woman   we don't know   what it means
that Betty Shabazz is dead   that she died
yesterday   one paper summed up her life

as Malcolm X's widow   . . . only woman
I ever thought about loving   he said
a quote more than thirty-two years old now

Betty Shabazz survived twenty-two days
with burns over three-quarters of her body
Betty Shabazz survived thirty-two years

without the great rebellious Mister X
Betty Shabazz survived Hoover and Nixon
Reagan and Bush   Betty Shabazz survived

five of Ed Koch and Rudy Giuliani's
campaigns for a brighter whiter New York
Betty Shabazz survived all that   and death

has not stilled her   Betty Shabazz is shouting
They are killing   they are killing   my husband
it's her voice on the radio   she's crying

phone calls flood the station   people are grieving
that Betty Shabazz is dead   that she died
yesterday
            it's all over   the radio

G. E. Patterson (Minneapolis)

drums drown out the sorrow

after diana died

we would meet in secret under
pretense in pairs, sometimes
in threes but that was not so often.

i had been the first to say it that
her death saddened me, i whispered this to
a woman who was black

like me, political and proud
we knew, both of us did, that this death
was not ours to mourn,

this was why we qualified it the way
we did. first we talked about all the other
deaths, the genocide in Rwanda

the boys killed by police in harlem and brooklyn, the ones
with their backs turned, with their hands in the air, we
agreed those deaths were the true details of sadness

still there was something about that woman
adorned with stolen gold, a silly title and dyed
blonde hair that pulled at us, we remembered

the time she was interviewed on tv, the things
she said, that it didn't matter how the world perceived her
she could still be found on her knees

with two fingers down her throat trying
to force herself out of herself, trying to flush
her own self down the toilet. that image

connected us to her forever
this is what we said to each other.
after that we cried and after that, nothing.

asha bandele *(New York)*

Dudley Randall
(1914–2000)

He left us a library
of books and archives,
poems starring Booker T
and Pushkin, starring W.E.B.
and the blues

He willed us a library
in the middle of the 'hood,
on the front porch of our family tree,
full of chapters from histories
known and unknown, full up
with cityslick ways and country sayings

in his last will
and testament, He
deeded us his 40 acres,
his mule, his pages
of a lifetime spent turning

the pages of a book of knowledge,
a book spelled out in the minutes
of a poet, and the hours
of a Blackman born in the 20th century

born with the windows of a poem
and the doors of a pioneer,
dressed in some blues

He dressed up in the pages
of his generation,
and after the killings that battles bring,
after the war of words, the riot
coming loose at the end
of the story

He left us a library
which never closes,
not even at the end of a long day,
or the end of a lifetime
filled with wide-open creative doors
and handwritten pages.

Ahmos Zu-Bolton II (New Orleans)

Hoodoo Whisper

for Quincy Troupe

Say it in sheets of sound
power of language with big fists of teeth
singing secrets from the crossroads
saying secrets from the hoodoo
way up in East St. Louis soil
the groove of alphabets
in the blues of a new atlas
way up in a silent way
like the sho enuf shaman man you am

Say it because
the pact was sealed in the other world
There are some
who could claim the word for hisself
who would wrap it red cloth
could caress it along fire
like the marriage between flame & light
who dip it in a repique of thunder

drums drown out the sorrow

make yr head flicker with the spirit of rhythm rhythm of spirit
as if Shangó hisself
had weaved you a red kufi

And there are some
who trap the ódu way up in them bones
who spill the past & therefore future
between blood & honey
divine what ain't nobody seen
And this here is an oríki
in praise of the possibility of
ká-ká-kì-ták tún of tongue
in praise of those
claiming their language
tonal y todo
with a hoodoo whisper
like Miles Dewey Davis III
like the sho enuf shaman man you am
sho enuf shaman man you am

Repique: Spanish. Drum solo, drum roll usually on a conga drum.
Shangó: Yoruba/Afro-Cuban deity of thunder, fire, drums, male virility.
Ódu: Yoruba divination verse, as in Ódu Ifá. Also the spirit embodied in a divination
    verse.
Oríki: Yoruba praise poem. Reserved for praise of deities, important people, family.

Adrian Castro (Miami)

Sammy Davis, Jr.

who can make the sun rise?
sprinkle it with dew . . .

she awakened me with tears
    get up baby / get up & pack
    martin luther king, jr. has been shot & killed
    you & i baby / we're goin to
    atlanta

mom & i flew there to pay
our respects
say goodbye to a man & hello
to his dream
    i have a dream
    that one day . . .

we crashed a hotel segregated
high rise tower on peachtree street
with white valets
& nervous executives
eager to appease they sorta
welcomed our presence kinda
treated us proper like
tellin us 'bout all the amenities this four star
had to offer
so many things but i only heard
   the pool / the pool
    we have such a lovely pool

so first things first
i went to swim
lap after lap
back 'n' forth
like esther mae williams come down outta da hood
oblivious
to the scavengers & piranha
angry white men pointin / disgusted
flustered white women in high heels / appalled
   there's a NEGRO in our pool
   a COLORED girl, i tell you
   mommy, will she hurt the water
       we can't go in til she comes out

i executed my backstroke
eyes climbin high towards heaven
& fixed upon hip black man stridin balcony tough
jumpin / projectin
non-containin himself
      you stay in that water, girl
      you swim & swim some more
      dontcha pay no mind to those circlin sharks
      look up / see God / & swim girl swim

sammy took us out to lunch
said what i had done was no different
than martin or rosa or harriet even

cuz that is how we swim this meet
just livin life as we choose to live

one backstroke at a time

Jacqueline Jones LaMon (Lancaster, CA)

drums drown out the sorrow

Glad All Over

I saw Julian Bond in 1965 at a SNCC rally,
just outside this shack on the side of town where
I was not supposed to be.
It was even poorer than where I lived.
I was curious. Everyone was curious.
This was about organizing. But were we ready?
As ready as Black folk in West Memphis, Marianna,
Helena. Up and down the Delta. Was it so bad
that there could be no turning back?

In a mythic retelling, I could say I joined SNCC,
attended every meeting, rallied all my friends,
marched every march.
But mothers have eyes and ears everywhere in small towns
and mine found out.
She wanted change as bad as she wanted the schools integrated,
hot running water in our house, a car loan paid off,
and a husband who did more than scream at her daily
before he went to wherever he worked. But first
things first. I, eldest daughter. She, working mother.
No contest. At home I had to watch my brother and sister.
Tend to the house falling down. Some of my classmates marched
to the center of the city, were jailed. A boycott began.
It seemed as if it failed, this boycott.
But downtown was dying since Black folk weren't buying.
The Chamber of Commerce refused to say it was so.

It seemed as if nothing changed. For a while, I stood
on the sidelines as those becoming mythic figures of history
crashed by. Until the day Arkansas state troopers stood
in the front of my mother's house, high-powered rifles aimed
at the people on my street—my childhood in gunsight.
This after our neighbors—a father and two sons—were arrested
by the corrupt sheriff, taken to jail, then released to the waiting

Klan. They got out alive, but only after broken collarbones, broken
legs, hemorrhages, bruises, contusions, stomped-on dreams.
I see my mother, who until that day could not say *shit*,
go up to one of the troopers and politely, quietly demand:
"Sir, see these children. Please lower your rifle."
He did.

Later that night, every house in my neighborhood stood ready.
The only lights visible were street lamps.
My brother and a friend sat on our front porch,
loaded shotguns in their laps. Waiting, waiting for any white man

to come down Division Street. Inside our house, my mother prayed,
and I started this poem that returns every twelve years
like a labor that must be done
if I am to ever grasp my mother's feat,
our family's ordinary courage.

It's hard to see children in T-shirts that read "Any Means Necessary"
and know that they have not sat as my brother
sat on a porch with a rifle waiting, just waiting to kill
any white man fool enough
to be a member of the Klan.

So, yes, we did not all meet the firehoses in Birmingham,
or face down Chicago police in a battle for the hearts and minds
of suburbanites fearful that Fred Hampton, George Jackson, even
the dead Martin Luther King would disturb their manicured lawns
"Glad all over" bubbles up, the secret joy beneath grim turbulence
of a decade now known as much for the pursuit of pleasure as for
political assassination, a war broadcast nightly, lawless police,
ritual murder and hard, harsh truths. Getting harder.

Patricia Spears Jones (New York)

Dancing after Sanchez

it's like God calling me out
from a dream
rhythmic beats pounding my skull
goose bumped into a reality
not my own
vagina creaming
body moving
   and i am still
beats of the protector i cannot see
if only i can dance to answer the call
if my head would only jerk in response to my feet
thighs tantalizing my wet dreams
if i would only release
desires to rise answering you
the call to wholeness
to dance on drums
dance on drums

this is my song to you

Staci Lightburn (New York)

drums drown out the sorrow

The 13th Letter

i've been blues travelin/ through mississippi streets
scat chanting/ chant scatting
mississippi beats
to the rhythm of the belt/ squeezing around Raynard Johnson's neck
i got hell in me
knowledge and rage/ tap dance/ like mr. bojangles doing a soft shoe in my
chest/ and the best i can do is sit/ in mississippi/ looking out of my
window as i write this poem/ the tree in my backyard has grown/ and i hear it
moan and wail telling me of its kindred and the pain they feel

this shit
has me twisted
like the belt around Raynard's neck

each tree/ speaks to me/ and i see blood raining from mississippi skies/
falling on white magnolias/ as the killers of my people/ live out the great
white lie

it use to be/ Menelik and me/ i was his queen
it use to be/ Marcus and me/ i sailed the sea back to an African identity
it use to be/ Medgar and me/ i heard the bullets roll around in his body
it use to be/ Malcolm and me/ i still see his blood on my hands
it use to be/ Martin and me/ i heard the thump of his body when it hit the
balcony even though i was still in my mama's womb when this cowardice
    system
shot him down
it use to be/ Marley and me/ i use to sing but now i speak
it use to be/ Mandela and me/ my fist is clenched even in my sleep

it use to be Mary (the whore) Mary (the virgin) Maat, Makeda, Black Moses,
Mother Parks, Mary McLeod Bethune, Maya, Martha, Margaret Walker,
    Myrlie, Mama,
Mystery Mother Earth and Me

now it's just me and . . . me and . . . me and . . .

mississippi

Jolivette Anderson (Jackson, MS)

In Black Churches

in Black Churches
i saw what the WORD could do
make cripples walk

make others talk in strange tongues
get old arthritic grandmothers
out they seats to dance
give dirty low down sinners another chance
give some folks the strength of twenty men

in Black Churches
i saw what the WORD could do
witnessed testifying
heard gospel from African souls

in Black Churches
i was chiseled
into speech and thunder

Lamont B. Steptoe *(Philly)*

For Gwendolyn Brooks

I

twelve years ago, i met
chitown with $25, two suitcases
and a folder of poems, in search
of myself. you, haki, and malcolm
had knocked enough red dirt
from my eyes to see black.

II

i have seen your words
change rural fourth graders
into southside pool toughs
hustling corner pocket,
jazz in june.

III

in class, you ignited riots
watched us loot and ransack

IV

at dinner, your mortality
stiffened me. forced to consider
this in your absence, sobered
by the bone of your words.

Quraysh Ali Lansana (New York)

tonal embryology
for nwenna kai

> the spirits move mountains
> when you call them out
> and the songs sleep inside you
> until you call them out
> —Cassandra Wilson, *resurrected blues*

you are the scorpion whose affinities reveal past lives
and you've got the bends of women in your hair
and you've got simone's spirit in your throaty giggle
on december's new moon—bestir the voice
scatting through the thoroughfares of your dreams
cause the spirits move mountains
when you call them out

on january's new moon walk into the chamber of songs
'cause there's a conjure woman leaning on your larynx
and you've got billy's spirit in your diaphragm
and you've got white nights beaming in your irises
and there are tonal embryos waiting to be born

folade mondisa speaks (Chicago)

Zizwe
January 10, 2000

For each year of service
there was thirty dollars
and a dime waiting for me
Reward for submitting to
ten years of moving in the
same space and never
moving ahead

It came right after I
learned that you had passed
over
No fanfare, no confetti,
no whistles blowing, bells clanging,
lectures or toe-stomping, heart-holding
dissertation on foibles and fractures
beneath the system's structure
You left, sitting upright and poised
in intellectual repose
as if just having finished the refrain,
the composition, a final thesis
You left without telling anyone
time had come
You merely bridged the parallel
And I didn't hear a sound
which was the strangest thing of all
because I took comfort in your
elucidating noise, your razor-edged
cutting, perceptive and stinging noise—
A sound so big, I cannot sleep complacently
the sleep of one who settles for
thirty dollars and a dime for each year
submitted

Tanya Tyler (*Newark*)

Ali, Bomaye*

*"Me, We." Poem delivered by Muhammed Ali
at Harvard University Commencement*

Right hand lead pure
    disrespect sends
Foreman into
    rage swinging fists
motor swinging
    anger like a
son trying to
    chop huge father
lynching tree down.
    Ali raises
fists on ropes blocks
    punch after punch
after punch, four
    rounds Foreman tires

Ali pounces
        from the corner
swinging knowledge
        boxing knowledge
swinging boom! boom!

George Foreman falls.

Ali circles
        cat eyes watching
wounded victim
        struggle, artist
contemplating
        the canvas "Big
George" is crumpling
        to, he is one
more victim full
        filled prophecy
of Muhammed
        then Monsoons pour
stadium on
        to roads jumping
chanting strong in
        early morning
Ali riding
        past Zaire past
faces shining
        in rain Ali
watching Zaire
        standing so tall.

*"Ali, kill him!"

Hayes Davis (Silver Spring, MD)

Phyllis

It's strange
I know exactly what killed phyllis hyman.
Perennial yearning for love deeply felt,
grounded with tenderness
real is what she craved.
Bound and caught
like a slave to a manic nightmare,
she learned to sing her way out of

and through the blues
bearing a body too large to hold.
A body too large to hold up.
Big, diva lady, a woman so beautiful
how could she live on
part time, half time, in-between,
co-wife, liaison, piece-meal kinda love.

Perhaps she would have gladly given
up her song, midnight, all day
snacks and the food for a whole love,
deep like soft wood of cypress
fresh and earnest as first birds of spring.
She would have gladly given up
her death for a full hearted,
straight ahead love all her own.

Jacqueline Johnson *(New York)*

Timbalero

Homage to Tito Puente

Timbalero—if you don't know
what it means—where
on earth have you been?

Tun, tun, tun, Timbalero
—onomatopoeic beat—
strike those skins
without mercy . . .

The thick blood rising to the temples,
the coarse hair raising on its ends,
swing those hips in wild gyrations,
sweat and breathe the archetypal
rhythms of the tropics, lose yourself
in the trance of just becoming
—becoming one with the beat—
primeval instinct and luscious mood.

Tun, tun, tun, Timbalero
—onomatopoeic beat—
strike those skins
without mercy . . .

drums drown out the sorrow

The voluptuous metronome
of the races rising from the Carib Sea,
let us dance in abandoned frenzy
to your dark indigo moods,
those deep blue thuds
and blood-red resonance
—exotic staccato on burnished flesh—
a rain of syncopation drops unto
the fertile earth, a crop of multihued
intonations rise above exploding skies:
Tun, Tun! Bang, bang! Click, click!
Red, white, blue and black!

Timbalero, strike that hot-iron beat
again and again and again—
be wild, do not contain yourself.

Timbalero, ashanti blood throbs
deeply at the throat, my insides
feel the rushing pulse of countless
drumming hands who nameless
traversed the Atlantic bound—
that fluid bridge that links
the darkness and the light.
Iron shackles resonate their
cold-metallic counterpoints
to the searing heat that
cannot escape my soul.

Tun, tun, tun, Timbalero
—onomatopoeic beat—
strike those skins
without mercy
'til the four trumpets ring:
the end of all time . . .

Tim, tim, tim, Timbalero
—Oh! Rise again—
Shaman-king of the Beat!
Tim, tim, tim, Timbalero,
Orisha, Ayé!

Julia Maier (New York)

Puente

for Tito Puente

Let's not talk of subway series
Or dead birds or mosquitoes or robust crops of pollen

Let's not talk of air raids and naval assaults eroding Vieques
We both know the fish will not return to feed the young curb of hungry
    stomachs

The stalking barracuda is oblivious to our pain

So let's not frown or slip into moods when the empty spotlight appears on
    the bandstand
Where he stood   face brimming with that enigmatic grin
Navigating him through the business

The cosmos welcomes him
As we file past his coffin

It is my understanding   according to the flute player*
That all he sought out of life was a standing ovation

Américo Casiano, Jr. (New York)

*A reference to Mr. David Valentin, flutist and musical director
of the Tito Puente Latin Jazz All Stars.

drums drown out the sorrow

Somalia

Military	Given time	Liquid assets
in a hurry	Ignorance	Different facets
Time to scurry	Laziness	Of a leash
onto shore	Television	So to cease
To restore	Stomp the mission	Origins
It's a chore	To envision	Of our kin
Years of damage	Our control	Darkened skins
U.S. manage	Stop patrols	James Baldwin
To create	Of our souls	Tito Puente
Then escape	Neighborhoods	Palmieri
Anarchy	Welfare goods	Leonard Jeffreys
Starving pleas	Manipulate	Will not stand
Charity	Our innate	Give up command
Misery	Driven state	To the man's
Bigotry	To be free	Masterplan
Crown Heights	Peacefully	To disguise

L.A. rights
Black/white
To death fight
Missing flights
Into space
Shuttle craft
As they laugh
In our face
We're fooled
Out of school
Drugs are tools
To exclude
Original
Man
From the plan
To withstand
Our demise

Live as one
Daughters, sons
Fathers, mothers
Sisters, brothers
Earth and sky
Animals
Never stalked
Never game
Just the same
For all time
Human kind
Use our minds
Make connections
No such thing
As elections
Earth runs on
Stocks and bonds

All our pride
Banish us
Into dust
Will not be
We'll not flee
Historically
Cherokee
Apache
Incas
Mayans
Arawaks
Kings & Queens
Of the sun
Of all men
This the plan
We Will Stand!

Nancy Mercado *(New York)*

epitaph for Etheridge Knight

you lunged
at this square toed
beast,
this condor convexed
inside your chest,
stared it straight
in the eye
and read
poetry.

this decree
to defy
the endless suicides,
the deaths and dyings
from addictions
to dope and drink
in the fields of
cigarette screams,
chased you
into the streets
to steal from
mothers and elders
only to return
as the unborn

to unlove the
beautiful eyes
of your daughters
and future sons
riding bicycles
and portable radios
into the black
anger of America
into the confrontation
without armor
leaving them
bleeding like
ulcers at the altars
of patriotic citizens
cheering the TV
video war
after the football
scores of 100,000
human beings
incinerating
on the highways
of Iraq
off camera
out of focus
in the flat,
white light
colliding inside
aluminum
houses in
Indiana
of no Indians
or anything sacred
but the religion
of basketball
stealing the souls
of brothers
migrating to
Philly and Detroit
or other
marked spaces
to rise on the
physics of
invisible air
above corporate
closets where tongues
were traded with
thieves who chained

drums drown out the sorrow

your grandchildren
to Dutch slave ships
and sodomized them
to relieve the
boredom of the ocean
voyage with no
forwarding address
or postage
except in the
margins of
the library
where the academy
applauded absurdity
and complicated
the simple truth
beyond recognition
to avoid the amber
in your eyes
and your dismembered
voice repeating
in this spiral
of descent
like an answering
machine receiving
an obscene
phone call.

the devil resented
this poetry
of resistance,
this insistence
to remain sane
when the rest
of you
went crazy
with escape,
this art of
resurrection
rose above "the
blood and mud
and shit"
of memory
to sing your
belly songs
of love.

Melba Joyce Boyd (*Detroit*)

Farewell Queen Mother Moore

Moving swiftly from car
Along Harlem street
To Malcolm X/Lenox Ave
Drum beats quicken my pace even more
Wanting to march from Coptic to Baptist church
Drum beats stronger
And liberation flags and Ethiopian banners wave
In the morning breeze
Colors splash
Familiar faces appear
Serious and respectful
In a sea of African progressives
And I enter the church
Stately and impressive
Ceiling with design and color
This former museum now the house of the lord welcomes
the diverse African gathering
and I take my place and stand in aisle
as the procession enters the church
the drummers and flute players lead Ethiopian orthodox
coptic priests and bishops followed by Ashanti kings and
Queen mothers in funeral black and red, followed by
Yoruba white and red, black & green & kufis & Batakaris
& Oshogbas bow ties & geles & crowns & leopard hats
& combat boots and all of those that have fought and resisted
and have not forgotten our motherland
who follow our mother our Queen Mother of the African diaspora
as she makes her final journey, her return to the village
she who has worked with and influenced all of us those who dare to
    challenge
those who dare to challenge those who dare to declare our love for
    Mother Africa
And we bow our heads in prayer
As the bishops and priests of Ethiopian Coptic Church
Lead us in Prayer
As the Okyeme of the Ashanti pours libation to God and the ancestors
Oyakupon Kwane Ama Owia
Oyakupon Kwane Ama Ami
Yaa Assae
And multiple words from many lips speak for her greatness
Her commitment
Her steadfastness
Her loyalty to the race
And songs are sung
Poems herald her life

drums drown out the sorrow

drummers and dancers praise her spirit
and the procession exits the house of the lord
as white doves fly
and drums drown out the sorrow
and bring in the promise of tomorrow
as the hearse and cars move slowly
Queen Mother smiles down on us
With Garvey at her side
As they watch their cubs follow in their path
Oyakupon Kwame Ama Owia
Oyakupon Kwame Ama Ami

John Watusi Branch (New York)

Palenque Queen by Habana's Shores
to Assata in Exile

Maroon Woman, feisty and sensual with Oshun beauty;
the fierce, blue Gulf waters wash daily over your shadow,
as you mingle with fragrant palms and tropical peoples. . . .
Political Exile. Twenty years have passed since the blast
of your Great Escape created havoc for the Empire;
now safe in an African palenque: *Afro-Cuba*, child
of Maceo and Martí, whose guerrilla blood stains
the Caribbean proletarian red. But red is equally spiritual,
being Shango's color and that of mystic Olokun. Both
Yoruba orishas, African deities blessing the untamed,
warrior-spirit. Sista-woman; the years have calmed and
refined your spirit, deepened your eyes, broadened your
smile, unleashed your regal beauty. Maturity becomes you.
Blessed by Oya's rainbow, we behold the flamingo
embodied in the fledgling. A most captivating bird!
spreading her wings over her people's joyous Future.

Of course, 666 and Its minions blockade and spew death-
threats at the insurgent Isle. New Jersey's mini-skirted
Barbie doll threatens Fidel, even the Pope, demanding
your recapture. You see, Oya's rainbow-radiance spreads joy
among our African captives; and even New Jersey stands in
danger of creating young Assatas to come. So Barbie,
the governor, masquerades as Reagan's parrot, Bush's
puppet, tongue-kissing Jesse Helms in a Kodak Moment,
by demanding your head. But we, Thirty Million strong,
Million Man and Woman marchers, say:

Hands off Assata, Republican witch! This Sista you won't
kill or turn into Oprah, going down on Uncle Sam.
She is ours; this Oya Woman, this Liberation Fighter,
this Warrior-Queen, this child of Harriet Tubman,
is ours—the Black Nation's Champion; and we will
collectively Burn Down Babylon, if she is harmed in any
way (you do remember Rodney King?) . . . So, nights
in Habana are rhythmic with Afro-Cubano accents,
and friendships diminish Time's tyranny. O how
we wish your brilliant strategies could lead us, but
realize that only revolution will bring you home.
So bless us, Sista-Woman; keep us in your heart, sing
victories at Bembes & strategy sessions, while we
Carry the Tradition, as militants
raise New African banners
over Babylon, chanting your name & your song,
while we liberate this wretched land!

Comrade Askia M. Touré *(Boston)*

drums drown out the sorrow

when the definition of madness is love

January Hangover

To be with you is my desire
To stay away from you is my ambition
The magic of your great moments
Awakens the superior inspiration
Responsible for perfect compliments
We have many things to talk about
And we have nothing to talk about
The religion of the sleepless candle
Detaining the discovery of daylight
When the definition of madness is love
Was lit by your knowledge of darkness
Your comfort corrects all the mistakes
I was born to make in this world
You are a very simple person
With a very complicated personality
Uninvited visitors with visions
Of watering your plants everyday
Commit suicide to write poems about you
It is impossible to love you madly
Without actually loving you madly
For the best results of your secrets
Of summer I will sacrifice my sanity
And become brilliantly absentminded
To remember how much I adore you

Pedro Pietri (New York)

the hardest part about love

the fallen cross beneath my belly
is the most difficult part of love

i use eight fingers
to part the pink and brown
run one thumb across the slit

and begin
it is the hardest part
the opening
that is the hardest part about love

it is not fucking
fucking is easy
easy to forget tomorrow
and my last name
when a purple and brown dick
is rubbing the in of me
like a wet thumb on a djimbe
cumming and breathing together like that

the hardest part hides behind the space
before cumming after the stories, the funk, the fat
and those bumps on my inner thigh
it is near that part

it is the part
forgetting my father's face in my lap
the part that swallowed the promised wedding ring
that let a dreaded preacher in
and licked prayers into me
like he really meant it

it is the part that keeps my hands in back pockets
the day after i touch
'cause i do not want anyone to know

it is the hardest part
the nexus of nightmares
the power place
the daily news
the place where i cry
the place where i sleep
the color of lipstick
the itch on the bus
the squirm at meetings
the cough of a red, red blood
the place where i count lovers
the darkest hair on my body
my most sincere muscle
the sweet nutmeg sister that humps away memory
the brown bottom drawer where i store promises
the dimple at the foot of my bed

my brightest smile
my constellation of tears

it is the hardest part about love
the opening part
the trusting muscle
the metaphor of my story
the pink pocket of dreams

Imani Tolliver *(LA)*

Lies We Tell Ourselves

There's nothing wrong with
two people agreeing to
use each other but
let's call it what it is.

"Sensual pleasure" sounds good, sounds up-
standing, sounds so very self-evolved.
A good shit gives me sensual pleasure but
it's still a shit

so let's call it what it is.
Let's stop this euphemistic twist
of tongue, let's stop this tryst of
word tricks in the back

seat of your joystick joy ride,
high-speed hot rod coming to a grinding
halt. Turn off your triple-A lip service,
that two-timing sliming out of both

sides of your spinning orb of mouth around
some cockamamie cock-a-doodle
doo doo. You you you you you
stop wheeling your spun-out

deals stuck in the burnt-orange mud
of second-chakra ruts in my road
rage; save your Judas kisses
for some other ass's cheek.

Really, let's call it what it is.
"Sensual pleasure" ain't no

tantric trance when you're frantically
banging your yang against yin;

it's a fancy phrase you chant,
you coo when a coup d'étwat
is your master plan, a booby trap,
your trojan-horse maneuver

to move her to *Yes, yes, yes*
you're the best at your con-
sensual party for one. Yes,
do honor her, serve her

a stiff cocktail straight up,
let her drink your vintage crème de
dink, dunk her cookie in it.
You sure know how to work a room

done up with gorgeous rugs covering
floorboards weakened by the wood
workers who came before you.
You sure know how to tame a

caged pussy, so hurt, so hungry it purrrrs
under your slippery-fingered touch.
So let's stop this cat-o'-nine-tales
whip of self-actual-lies.

let's call it what it is:
—Fucking—
and fucking you by any other name
is just bad fiction.

Marj Hahne (Philly)

8 ways of looking at pussy

1.

enter here and find your home
your bathwater run already
the sun setting in the distance
heat on the horizon of your clit

2.

swollen pussy
all laid out and relaxed
says to everyone in the room
I have been to mecca and back
and it ain't nuthin compared to what you
done did

3.

when you're wet and waiting
I could be lost six
universes away without a map
and sniff my way home

4.

baby, baby, hold still
my dreads are underneath
your thigh

5.

with those three brown fingers inside,
you impregnate me with desire
I grow wide and wild
my water breaks,
this dam gives and we are tossing on the rapids
tossing on the rapids
overturning canoes
water races out and over your arm
warm cum shoots out
races up your
arm, you put
your mouth
over this geyser

6.

I love like the ocean at first light
the waves coming in to meet the edges
of earth; rushing up and back like tiny orgasms
high tide the explosion
of you
on my
tongue

7.

my teeth on your nipple tastes sweet
I clench harder bite down on sensations
like acupuncture—I feel energy rising
connecting from
one hand/nearly elbow deep in your pussy
one hand over your mouth
your sister and my boy cousin
so close they can smell but
they snore instead. you giggle
I bite harder taste past skin
you giggle again.

8.

venus flytrap
eats me alive
everytime

Letta Neely (*Boston*)

Temporary Insanity

You enter the door
Meet my eyes
And breathe a billowy breeze
Across my head
Beads of sweat on your brow
Your hands pillow my ears
Your fingers clasp my neck
And bring your lips to mine
You grab the collar of your
Shirt on my back
And kiss so deep
The muzzle on my heart
Is released and allowed to beat
Freely as you press
Your flesh
Against mine so hard
You straighten the kinks in my back
You bend your knees
To nuzzle the creases of my breasts
Push one of my happy hips to the wall
Spreading me wide like valleys low
You kiss the peaceful lilies to my soul.

Hungry for your watering
I bend my emotions and
Pull support from behind you
Only to carry us to a place
Called temporary insanity—
Temporarily in sanity

And just as I regain consciousness
You send sunshine inside
Your sunshine revives me
And gives my body rhythm
And grooves
Your sunshine oozes
Into my soul
Through my valley
Beneath my peaceful lily
And causes my earth to shake
My earth quakes
From the sunshine and grooves
Rhythm and blues
And we
Embracing
Against the wall
Psalms in heated palms
And we breathe in deep
Each other's humanity
And share temporary insanity.

Tanai Sanders (Baltimore)

alone in belize

so smooth does the sun enter me
quietly, with all his fingers
garafuna breath
cautiously dusting
my urchin skin into
the color of cloth he is used to before
he beds me
i stand barefoot at the center of the world
the end of time
tasting the ruined salt of mexico's
gulf, watching ix chel's dampened hair
cascade into a silver mane
as columbian drug boats
slip their silk poison into the sea

squatting on the goat-heal shore
unable to hear my own breathing
sand flies create a strawberry patch
of my body
i am being eaten alive by insects smaller than
the pores on my fingernails

as I push their full bellies open
they drink my sweat
calling it rain

what makes me think of you now

the crystal gaze of the water
a promise of jelly-fish tonguing
my navel, fingering me under
the burnt waves
the flagrantly cool lick of seaweed

the sea's coral eyes

watching me following me

the only god
brave enough to taste me twice

Shonda Buchanan *(Playa Del Rey, CA)*

footprints

it's not always easy
knowing this day
of time, pulling near
and drawing. from behind,
i hear suction swallowing
day into day. clinging
doesn't stop another dawn
from peeping just now and
night is always a timed space,
sandwiched between day and day.
once more, i hear gone
walking this way. i smell
new season in this going.
how can i prepare for already?
school has no courses to teach
goodbye or farewells of no

return pulling a lot out of sodom
or a messiah into jerusalem,
where rejection was killed
once and for all. where acceptance
was born and began its journey into
this very moment, where even i
know how to rise and leave
with endnotes citing all
last last known addresses.
one comes, still, and visits
with a face i once wore.
now, same face you draw.
yet, i honor your need
and insist on your absence.
you are not the only one
i called or needed to know
what happened after everafter.
nor are you the only one i loved.
there were many i touched and left.
i remember one from one and pray
for all. only you. you. only, only
you could return with this same
picture of now, life-sized,
recognizable, in a reflection
where i sit, still at the door,
waiting for hinges to creak and
wind to blow whistling
kisses . . . shhhhhh.
i hear the sound of
approaching history
and god's foot is
all over this place.

esther louise (New York)

Big World Look Out

Big God
Big Mind
Big Money
Proud Big Gerl
Big Feet & Altogether Complete/Undeniably Elite
That Proud Big Gerl
6'0 And Definitely Not Petite

Big Breasts
Big Gutt
Proud Gerl With/That Big Ole Butt
Sittin On It Strong
Lovin Every Inch—Proud of Every Pinch
That Beautiful Proud Big Gerl

You're Lovin My Big Thighs
I'm Batten My Big Eyes
Proud Big Gerl Standin Strong

I'm in this Big World
Movin Big, Groovin Big
Big Gerl in this
Big Ole World

Big Time
Big Life
Big Money

Proud Big Gerl Succulent as Honey
Proud Big Gerl
Gone move this Big World
Gone Groove It
Build It Up . . . to Break it Down
and Soooth It

Big Ole Mind
Big Ole Dreams

Gone Groove It

Big Ole' Butt
gone Mooooove It

With all My Bigness
Gone Be a Big Woman
Gone Stand Strong

Singing My Song

Proud Big Black Gerl livin in this Big Ole
Fucked-up WORLD

Jeneanne Collins (Baltimore)

when the definition of madness is love

Bullet Hole Man

A Love Poem

i lay in the dark, with him by my side
the first time here, i remember i cried
i caressed his body, and i wept from the soul
when my hand first touched my man's bullet holes
i learned in the schools while he learned on the street
i read in my books, while he read the street beats
this man that i love is strong and so Black
got scars on his chin, knife wounds on his back
got three bullet holes that decorate his chest
they're medals, he says, *for the work i do best*
i sneak now to see him, he lives underground
i love a street man though i'm college bound
i know why he shoots i know why he kills
the hype is not true, he gets no sweet thrills
he cries here at night, but he can't go free
his passion is strong when he makes love to me
i've seen his gun room, i know his boyz well
it boggles my mind this heaven and hell
that i'm living between, two worlds that collided
the secrets i have cannot be provided
for the boys that do follow in unmarked cars
i see them on campus, i see them in bars
they think i will tell, 'cause i'm just too damn smart
to love this Black man they believe has no heart
they try to intimidate, they try to degrade
they've called me a ho and a stupid street maid
they don't understand, they just don't know
my love for this man continues to grow
i lay here beside him, his boyz are on guard
some nights it's so easy, while some are so hard
to think that they could just bust through the door
and end both our lives—i cannot ignore
these thoughts that i have, and he realizes too
the dangers that make up this love that is true
he's my bullet hole man, and i will not deny
i could walk away now, but why should i try
his kisses are heated, his hands are such pleasure
his love making 000000000 i cannot quite measure
i'd drop this degree and pick up a gun
if there ever came time that he'd have to run
i lay here beside him, i know each hole well
this man who is both my heaven and hell
    may the bullets never make it to his heart.

Nancy D. Tolson *(Bloomington, IL)*

Dreadlocks
for Billy

He lets me bury fingers in the lion's mane
longer, thicker than brown, tame waves around my face
delicate ropes spiraled from the same coiled, dark genes
sleeping in my recessive traits

Black, spongy tendrils
mimic shafts of light filtering
onto his back as sun bleached auburn

A man's hair never fell around my shoulders
and shielded me from city light clutter
never arched its tiny antennas in my direction
yanked a yelp from his head if I failed
to watch where my hands rested as I slept

Now, I want to count these boneless fingers
bending to tickle my cheeks and neck
I want to gather these battalions of thick delight
between my knuckles
grab each of these arms holding me close
and give every one its name.

Tara Betts (Chicago)

Roots

I search for your hair like gold in the rain.
You shock me
with the ecclesiastical ecstasy
my nose finds dipped
in the coffee beans secluded
between your crop of braids.

Sage burns around the
trails of sugarcane
my fingers make near your crown.

I caress the soil and soul of you in a storm
of locks and find you
to kiss the silent lightning near your ear.

I find you, to discover a mist of roots brushing
my cheeks.

I smell the beeswax perfumed water of your
garden of tresses and I begin
to grow again.

Arthur Ade Amaker (Chicago)

Six Minutes Writing

That first day
was the longest,
the day after you left.
I spent
six hours sleeping
six hours reading
six hours eating
six hours sitting

six minutes writing

fighting
every inclination in me
to convince the
holiday company that
I was too ill to stay

away, from you.

I wasn't homesick,
Just yousick
which annoyed me.

Until today I didn't believe
that it's not where you are
but who you're with
that makes the difference between
being content and being happy.

Kadija Sesay (London)

Diner

My eggs will never be dry
when I am with you
and no matter how much

I am told to be professional,
when your lips stare at me
like they are hungry
for what is finally real,
and your eyes speak to me as if
they see millennium,
I am the butter
melting on your toast.

RoByn Baron *(Boston)*

Fullness

The warmest kiss
I ever received
Came from Lisa

A dining room
Turned social club
She hired me to dance
For the night

Lisa spun phonographs
For stylish debutantes and gents
Heard "Fly Like an Eagle"

For the first time
It moved like the aftertaste
Of stale lip gloss.

Unnerving. Pleasant.
Conjuring. Lisa smiles
at the shock she paints

Her skin, savory. Posner
Foundation, almost. Rusty

Colombian ponchos.
She lives immanent behind
Her turntables perched on
Glass tables.

She was a Betty Davis album cover
Could have easily been married to Miles

Music goes *dundada/dundudu/*
dondada/dundu . . . dundada/dondududadat!

Lisa's lips—
balloons of fashion

> Fair vibrancy
> *Jet* magazine monthly
> Beauties. Liquor store

Calendars.

Wow . . . she's beautiful, I say
No one hears me.

> No one knows what's
> Happening.

Wanna dance for me next week?
she asks—accept the request with
No utterance.

Her lips, good enough
Payment. Music made it better

My platform
My window
Adoring her

> The full bloom of her
> Hair. A halo around
> Those pouty creations,

Those nail polished cushions.
Those Mary Kay perfections
Flawless arrangements.

My . . .
My
Music goes *dundada/dundudu/*
dondada/dundu . . . dundada/dondududadat!
dondududadat!/dundundundundat!/dondundundundat!

Latasha Natasha Diggs *(New York)*

Wet Dream

I

Sprinkles of rain
caressed my mouth

Thinking it was your love
I swallowed

Only to wake up
and realize
I left the windows
open

II

Calm
like the eye of a hurricane
you lay silent and wait
to destroy my life.

Carlos Omar Gardinet *(New York)*

foursomes

I

so who you be now
is the only one i know
only one i love

II

when music and you close by
i have to shut my eyes remembering
which one of you i'm dancing with
and which one of you i'm dancing to

III

like blood let
it come up blessed
thick this ritual re-opening

of this same wound
this same ground
you return to where you come from

IV

their love
solid as the rock
they smoke

Marvin K. White *(LA)*

Wishing You

I am the lover you have never seen
A shadow behind your smile
Searching your eyes for recognition
Traveling through your body
Like a sensuous serpent
Bent on finding a home
A love complete
I am the lover you don't know
Drifting as I do
In the air around you
Almost touching you breathlessly
With gossamer fingertips
Which refuse to disturb
The sacredness of your wondrous body

I am the lover you cannot touch
A part of you
That you don't quite know but
Sometimes
When you feel a soft warmth on your cheeks
A comfort surrounding you as you sleep
A sweetness in your special places
Just imagine me
Bring me to life
And know you are loved

C. D. Grant *(New York)*

Shunning an Imperative

She plays Miles, roles another joint
strikes a Mary J. Blige misbegotten beguiled pose

trying to get to that city where
Parker's mathematical equations
hide in some obscenity
    The
jonquils and primrose planted in a bed of
bloodstone and aquamarine bushes are still with us—
but
I am Belial . . .
Nostrils wide open, veins hungry, mouthing
incantations to *Spanish Key* on trumpet
reading Faust out loud
drunk on Moett
    Goddamned Miles
swings some shit, and she's
laughing at my explanations
doing leg extensions
with Chick Corea and John Mclaughlin
by the light of a chiffon draped lamp shade
brushing cigarette ashes off the page
and destroying the shapes they make
Dave Holland eggs her on
then
baby powder spills
toothpaste glass shatters
towels are tangled up and twisted
    When the perfume falls around us—
healing bruised lips
and soaking wet
the final ember of handrolled illusions—
I take her body down
shoulders sharp
against the face, a keen reaction
shaking a final applause
from a forced kiss—

May I now have permission
to set fire to this house we've made—

Tomorrow we'll both become unfinished again
(only at certain intervals)
but tonight
Miles plays *Sanctuary*
and we sleep a holy slumber
rained on.

Carl Hancock Rux (New York)

when the definition of madness is love

January 8, 1996

He
left her
a small bunch of
dead flowers—
not dried
and mauve
in color
but
newly
dead
and in varied
stages
of wilt.
He left her
a small bunch
of dead flowers
and a card
on her night
stand
by the bed.
The symbolism
profound.
When
he
left her
with that small
bunch
of dead flowers,
the card read
something about
"special persons"—
ambiguous enough
to make her cry.
When he left her
with a small bunch
of dead flowers
and a card,
he signed his name
and affiliation
then,
post-scripted a lie
to make up for
time forgot
and sealed
their demise

with the same ease
that he closed
the envelope.
He left her
a small bunch
of dead flowers
and a card
on the night stand
by her bed,
patted her
sleeping head—
rattling dreams
of happy endings,
awake;
kissed an innocently
flung hand
with the guise
of knighted charm
and then
he left her.

Kimmika L. H. Williams (Philly)

A Poem for You

in my two hands
I'm holding a book on the life of Jacques Roumain
your breathing lifts your breast
It's your beauty that moves
and there's a painful human hope
protecting tomorrow from today's hell
I dream I dream of Guernica
I embrace you I embrace you
and may the voice of Lorca live on
the breathless wind stretches itself out upon the sea

exact like the sword of clarity
o raging poetry from all the jungles forged
a shadow is terrified by the torch of Césaire
and the word of Paul Eluard
cutting the knot of evil
confers on the dignity of art
the evidence of crystal

I blend you with all I hold dear
you are blood in the flesh

you are saddened and smile in the eyes of the peasants
and there's oxygen in the air
when your look wears the light
of our grandest summer skies

I think about the man I used to be
gone with the waves of life
I'm reborn in the root of your desire
don't say I'm raving
we will pass through the Manchurian border
be it in Vietnam or in the Congo
Madrid or Santo Domingo
be it in Harlem or in Cap-Haïtien

everywhere sadness is like a yeast
our anger swells
o thunder of thunder
we'll be carrying the axe and the flame

your lips is my wound
red of the first dawn
where gold merchants are dying
and the people's blood quietly burns
like water's heart at its source
but when the river begins to flow
nothing can stop the proletarian march
a new sun is lighting up the earth

Paul Laraque (New York)

Throbs for the Instructress

I learned it all from my Eve,
The warm, dumb wisdom;
She's a quicker instructress than years;
She has quickened my pulse to receive
Strange throbs, beyond laughter and tears.
                    —D. H. Lawrence

Let the throbs commence
and everything else
while my words upon your body rest.

Let this ink calm your thirst
and everything else
while reason glorifies the flesh.

In the wind we'll find a ledge
and everything else
while memories digress.

Let my soul be the surge
and everything else
while incantations converse.

I shall assume your scent
and everything else
while the thicket overwhelms the pen.

Only you can be the zest
and everything else
well beyond the caress.

Let me into the depths
and everything else
so as to proclaim our stealth

And if you deny your breast
and everything else
let my gradual return to earth profess

in non-words fallen deaf
and everything else
how poets often squander their verve

following your other self
and everything else
all for the love of love within the spell.

Pedro López-Adorno *(New York)*

when the definition of madness is love

At the Frenchman's

The woman at the table beside mine is crying,
painted mouth a round, wet O, soundlessly
howling, back held stiff against all comfort.
I sip Mexican beer cold from the cooler,
rub cubes of ice between my breasts, smile
a distant smile. I am too hot to be bothered

with anything but the dream on the dance floor.
Thigh high skirts and cowboy boots,
skin tight jeans, vaquero belts,

the dip and swirl, swing out, snap back,
to the chucka-chucka, chucka-chucka
rub-board beat. *Voulez-vous dansez, douce cher?*

You bet your sweet ass, cowboy. But it's so hot—
the Frenchman's AC broke down
by the heat from so much flesh, the steam
within the stuccoed walls like the heat without
rising from the bayou, too thick, laden
with a perfume of things too ripe, too sweet.

Seems like hours since I've danced
and I want to hear you say it, cowboy—
save me from that sad song, mad song place, that
what does it cost me to know you don't want me place
where you're not waiting and I'm left all alone,
where every word is an unripe persimmon

and the lump in my throat heavier than stone.
But you don't, you won't, and that woman
goes buck wild, strikes away the hands of her friends,
lurches toward the pool tables, the fluorescent-lit tableau
of tattooed arms holding someone else. Again.
I mark her progress by the snags in the smooth circling

of the dancers, her shrill counterpoint to Beau Jocque's
baritone, the pool cue held high, the smashed glass,
the laughter . . . I'd laugh, too, if it weren't for the memory
of burning the dolls you gave me in the sink.
Made so much smoke I scared the dog. Wild night
that was of mezcal down to the worm,

a Lady Schick hammered to its thin blue tongue
of steel. That night I swore if I lived till dawn,
I'd never. Never again. But I still love to dance—
especially at the Frenchman's. The thigh high skirts,
vaquero boots, the horses, the Harleys, the sport
trucks out back. Yes, I love the Frenchman's

despite knowing myself far too well in these women—
Hypocrite danseur in my flat-brimmed hat.
Night after night finds me here, trembling.
This body's not a wart I can just burn
off my soul, so won't you dance with me, cowboy,
just once with me tonight?

Kendra Hamilton *(Charlottesville, VA)*

Mata Hari Blues or Why I Will Never Be a Spy

I'm certain you saw these ample breasts lift and catch in a sigh
When I caught you staring
First from the corner of your eye
Then full on and lips smacking.

And though I am a card-carrying-contemporary woman:
Strong, dark sister #091870, sir
Fully prepared to take no shit
Or prisoners,

You noticed the goofy grin and downcast eyes your big-toothed brilliant
    smile elicited.
Still-highly trained and in top condition,
My finely tuned senses were alerted
As you sidled up and took my hands in yours.

You did feel my body shift and warm when you introduced yourself?

The enthusiastic smile and the way I squeezed your hand
Only served to conceal the fact that I am awaiting
The cleverly coded message you'll pass on
Armed
With a sharp-shooting, heart-seeking,
Bullshit detector
Cleverly disguised
As a pen.
Armed and dangerous
Skeptical and coy
Stealthily advancing
Licensed to destroy
And always protected
By my playa-proof vest.
Yes?

The Sapphire's smooth like butter
And
The stone rolls in the gutter
And just like that
We've passed each other's tests.

I relinquish the coordinates you have come for.

Preferred outcome #1:
Ideal if there are conversations
Secret midnight meditations
Meetings of the mind

Vision rearranged
Meetings of the body
Intimacies exchanged
And agreements reached with very few casualties.

Possible outcome #2:
Well, sometimes a missin's just a mission
And
Ya gotta do what you gotta do.
And that's okay
If all the spies play fair

But if you are a double agent
Sent to finally do me in,
I might just let you blind me
With your platinum-plated grin.
Or smother me with lies
Behind those honey drippin eyes
And hands which swallow mine
Warm and soothing, by design.
And in spite of all my armor
Self-control and self-esteem,
I trust you
All the while denying any plots or schemes
And when I'm finally rescued by some top-secret device,
The world has almost ended.
My armor's reconstructed for a heart that's been distended.
And my brand new shield so strong
That when an ally comes along.
I cannot be detected.

Jewell M. Handy (New York)

Yellah

Licorice lips noosed around Her neck as he drooled in Her ear that he
    always did like
Yellah
gals like her . . .
Her response
blinked blindin caution seconds from stop at the intersection of rage
and disgust

was he referrin to
the rays that seeped thru Her eyes from the dawn in Her belly

Her intellect oozin satin
                    PARKAAAAAAY . . .
or could he smell the twang of lemon She left snarled in conversation and
    sheets?

Her laughter's yolk was heavy and golden
vibration hummin in the key of saffron
and sometimes
she did practice an antique
jaundiced kind of grace

Her sallow past—none of his damned bizness.

see
She wuz sposed to feel
privileged
cuz he had a taste for gals same color as the legal pads She battered
    w/incoherent
            poems abt
this same
asininity
Did he really think She would bid him nest in Her hive
swarm Her w/ignorance
embezzle the pollen Her honey left on sleepin lips?

and though She did not envy his ignorance
the blues he strummed across Her yellah
swirled in Her a vomitous green
did he mean
he would still want Her
were She black
like a plantain
hidin all dat sweet yellah
under Her skin?

Lisa Pegram *(DC)*

Extremes Ain't My Thing As Salaam Alaikum

I ain't no baby making machine
where you input yo seed
and out comes miniature men
with bean pies and bow ties in hand

My womb ain't no fast food burger joint
where I stand silent all veiled up

and you give me your orders
and I let you have things your way

I have no tolerance for totalitarians
Who used to be named Tyrone
Taking up my time talking about
The Teachings and how women are to behave

I ain't no neanderthal woman
So, don't think you gone be bustin me
upside my head with a stick
talking about what the Prophet said

I dare you to try to take my daughter
To some serial killer who murders her
innocence by cutting off her clitoris
and tries to convince her to be proud she's mutilated

Don't talk to me about being civilized
while you sit your funky barefooted behind
on the floor talking with your mouth full
and eating with your fingers

I will not listen to your migrant store owners
who mention that you are happy that
"My people" decided to accept "your true religion"
As you sell big jars of pickled pig feet in pink water to poor people

Get away from asking me about
wearing all white on Sundays
when I know that if I did I would
look like some Baptist church usher

So, As Salaam Alaikum . . . my brother!

Tufara Waller Muhammad (Little Rock)

13

you cannot fall
in love with a man
who has HIV
she said
you cannot fall
you cannot fall

you cannot fall
in love
and statistics
and statistics say
he is doomed
but
he has been positive
13 years
he is 32
he is covered in tattoos
and when he moves
he looks
like a living painting
he looks
like a chunk of the Sistine Chapel
he burns like shrapnel
through threads of my skin
and HIV and HIV is
fatal
and so is cancer and I
am in remission and it
could come back
and kill me
and life
is also fatal and you
could be hit by a taxi
or my fist
flying across this
heap of vegetables
and he could be alive
for another
13
years

Jennifer Murphy (New York)

when the definition of madness is love

rock candy

i'm like
rock candy baby
i'm sweet
but i can be real hard
said i'm like
rock candy baby
real sweet

but i can be real hard
if you're looking for a cotton candy kiddy baby
your hand's in the wrong woman's sweetenin jar

i can take you
a "take time" daddy
give your clock a good jump start
but don't come if you ain't ready
and you can't finish what you start
cause i'm like hmmmm

rock candy baby
i'm sweet
but know how to be real hard
i'm just like
rock candy baby
rub me wrong n i can be real hard
so if all you've got is soda cracker loving daddy
you're the wrong rooster for my barnyard

i can warm you in the mornin
with honey huggin ease
introduce you to the forest
n make you wanna
rename all the trees
said i'm like hmmmm

rock candy baby
i'm sweet but known to be real hard
said i'm like
rock candy baby
sweet
but known to be real hard
but if you're a popcorn and salt preferrin papa
don't come 'round here creepin
n don't come round here peepin
don't waste none uh your time peepin
all up in my
double-dipped/chocolate chip/minty ice/oh so nice
i said my honey-dipped/sweetly chipped/sugar'd ice/so very nice
don't waste your n my time peepin
all up in my
said all up in my
candy jar
          don't waste my time now!

A. Wanjiku H. Reynolds (New York)

Love Jam

It was that rainy summer night
when Brother B. was playing
at The Pub.
He took out his horn,
did his thang,
and poured blue
milk into her ear.

She leaned near
and whispered to me.
It was the vaporous voice
of sax.

We picked up on the jam
and danced home
to do it to death:
a duet to Life.

We sang all songs.
We danced all dances
until dawn came

up like song
on Sunday.

Dawn had a rainbow
wrapped around its waist,
and the pot
at the end of the rainbow
spilled over with

the alto rain of sax
and the baritone love-moan
of a saxophone:

sweet baked apple dappled
cinnamon speckled
nutmeg freckled peach brandy
and amber wine woman
WOW
with your piping hot finger
popping black african pepper pot
not stopping steaming coffee flowing
creaming brown sugar growing cane candy
coming cocoa going crazy 'bout

brown sugar teases
GOOD GOD
and pleases
SWEET JESUS
that honey stained soul trained
slow molasses ass
HOTDAM
candied yam and sweet potato pie thighs
and raisin-tipped coconuts raising cane sugar
stone ground brown sugar bowl belly
to the bone to the bone

Everett Hoagland *(New Bedford, MA)*

Cocaine Mad-Scream Article #33 LoveSong

Inside the vessels of too many women I've hid from myself far too many times when I lacked the courage to be alone. You see, I cannot afford to spend another day as a cooperator in a conspiracy against myself. I just wanna be a man. Just wanna be the man that I am and nothing else. Just me, just God.

At this time, I want to draw your attention to the text of Cocaine Mad-Scream Article #33 LoveSong and I want you to read with me where it says: You know, the difference between reality and dream is very subtle. And whether we flow between one or the other, we assume that this is what is really going on. The feeling that we have when coke is inside us or scotch is inside us, or the feeling that we have after three hours of rolling around on the floor and speaking in tongues. That feeling is not the same, not the same as when we wake up to a sober head and an empty bed and realize that the one we love doesn't love us anymore and that this time they're gone, and they're gone for good, and we're clear about that. And then we look in the cupboard. Y'all know where the cupboard is. And the cupboard is bare! And we're clear about that, too. Ah, the way in which we see ourselves at such moments is quite different: we feel dumb, frightened and depressed as all hell. A panic sets in like a child who just lost its mother to a raging storm. The world is no longer seen through the twisted eye of a cold freeze that coke can give ya, no longer moves with the pleasant numbness of scotch and soda, for in that moment of loneliness and fear, the world has a clarity all its own, and it's then that you understand just how important it is to have just twenty dollars in your pocket and somebody to hold you and say, *Baby, you all right with me.* I mean, if you could just have the activities of your limbs that twenty dollars could give you, to take a cab somewhere and receive the affirmation of somebody that you love say that you're OK, then perhaps the burden of that moment will pass from you, but what you fail to understand, what you fail to understand is that that moment can never pass, never pass, as long as you fail to know the deep and sustaining power of your own worth as a person. Oh, you'll get you another twenty dollars like you had it yesterday. I said, you'll get you another fool to tell you how sweet you are, but you won't be worth a dime until you understand: You are the most important person in the world, and there's nobody, NOBODY, nobody who can really love you until you love yourself! Who's gonna take that weight if you ain't? Who's gonna lift you if you won't? Who's gonna deliver you if you don't? Who's gonna write your name? I said, who's gonna call your name in the echo of the rain? My brothers and sisters, if it ain't you, it ain't nobody. 'Cause you see, there's only two kinds of people in this world, now ain't that right? Huh? Somebody who knows how to love and somebody who knows how to receive that love. And when you can love you and receive that love, I mean when those two people can exist in the same person, I mean when the idea of believing in yourself no longer presents itself as a monster image that makes you want to run away, wreck your mind, sabotage your person and hide from the power of yourself, then, my friend, you are truly blessed amongst all mankind and the kingdom of the world is yours!

May the words from my mouth, the meditation of my heart, be acceptable in thy sight and the sight of all things holy, whether present or gone before us, in the orchestra of song, in the collection of ourselves, as we continue our journey on into the night, grappling with this river we call life, a mighty river that flows around and through us all, this holy gathering, right here, wherever we are in this time and space. My, my, my, my, my . . . WHAT IT IS?!

Gylan Kain (*Amsterdam*)

when the definition of madness is love

The Elders Are Gods

In my hometown, there is rust
And shine and kinfolk
Who use the privilege of age
To guarantee their ear of corn.
The old folks say that
If you eat fish-heads, or
Drink coconut juice, you would
Turn stupid. But the elders
Eat everything and
Get wiser everyday.
They set ambiguous rules.
They wall us from corn-filled places.
They say sex is bad for children;
Yet do it in the dark confines
Of their isolated bedrooms.
They say that courtesy is
Good for youth, and palm wine
Bad for their livers.
    The elders are gods.
They sit on top of everything.
They tell us that farm work
Is a good discipline for youth,
That dragging ignorant sheep flocks
To the meandering wind fields
And tying them on the guava-stumps
Is a good endurance-test.
    The elders are gods.
They sit on top of the branches.
They have eyes wide as owls'.
They rotate them to every corner.
They want us to follow
Their bygone norms.
They want us never
To put up a fight.
    The elders are gods.
They sit on top of everything.

Tijan M. Sallah (Potomac, MD)

What the Dead Do

My ancestors arose from graves
cemetery trawlers they rifled the dead's living room
tromping over framed photographs
and wilted floral arrangements.
And they dug, too,
deeper down into the earth
where memory's black corpse
a black satin corpse,
lay huddled with descendants of languages lost.

My name is dead
a slave name, graves.
At night I lie alert
deciphering darkened silence
and polyrhythmic pinch and prick.
Ornery, these dead.
Night rumbles forward
and grave folk preach
You are my people
why can't you speak?

Jackie Graves (Oakland)

creation is a cycle
for Mom

and
i was Born.
i imagine mama smiled and cried
at the woes and joys of bearing female fruit.
her tears fell into my mind like rain,
watered the seeds she planted—
pain,
pride,
beauty,
wisdom . . .
i know she loved me some strong,
cuz
i evolved into the next version of her.
her smile warms the fibers of my being,
where cotton grows in my guilty memory,
stained with strains of indigo.
that sunshine reflected in her eyes

shines on my soul,
making me more alive
and
as i grow older
i am Born
again and again.

Empress *(Forestville, MD)*

Birth

*for mama, daddy, Larry Nolan, Amadou Diallo,
James Byrd, and the rest of us*

sometimes
i close my eyes
n see her six months gone
runnin through the streets
raisin hell
            Please do not share this tale

hot Detroit July 67
I lie in mama's womb
while the national guard rolls by
we sit on the porch
wishin Daddy would hurry home
cuz after curfew
he could get killed in the chaos

again n again
I hear about stolen TVs
n the undercounted dead
but only once
do I hear his name

I like to envision her
six months gone
runnin through the streets
raisin hell
            Please do not share this tale

Before ya daddy
I had a boyfriend
who looked like Marvin Gaye
at sixteen,
Detroit police

picked him/plucked him
from the wrong side of town
n beat him/yes
they spread his legs
n beat him in between
after that
not only could   he no longer
make love
he could not
make war
n at age 24
hung himself
in an abandoned building
during wintertime
        I ran screaming through my mama's house

I see her
runnin/raisin hell
six months gone
        Please do not share this tale
        I have not spoken his name in years

but mama
that hot july
Detroit 67 you protected me
while angry blood ran thick
to save blacklife
you held me/warm/still
in your womb
when I know you wanted to throw
a brick through a window
beat a brutal white cop between the legs
with his own damn billy club
you stayed home amidst
that orgy of rage
to save me
and now
I must tell this story
our story
whisper his name in my prayers
cuz it ain't over

the tightening noose
hangs from a tree/the
beheaded fruit drags full speed
down a dark country road
n lies in an inner city doorway
shot through 41 times

n we .
we still wait
to be born

Kelly Elaine Navies *(Durham, NC)*

Daughter-to-Father Talk

I missed sharing your birthday by hours
and have been yours ever since.
You carried me until your back protested;
we both got teary in that moment.

Mama said once when I was toddler,
you let me splash your afro with
canary and lime green barrettes while you watched
the Jets vs. the Packers on TV.
You only missed two games out of my
four-year high school basketball career.
Your love has always been louder than those barrettes,
the cheers from the stands,
but where does the anger go?

How did it feel when the new office manager
was someone you trained?
When Grandaddy passed on?
Seeing mama in her bra with one side flat
for the first time?

Aside from those rare shuttles of brief entry
into your emotional atmosphere—
candid car conversations where
your contrite profile is most strong,
most beautiful,
you cordon off your soul,
choosing to preserve the hero and not risk
rejection of the man.
We who love you surmise,
volley endless theories
in matches that net nothing.

I am told that I move through this life
With your quiet, yet affecting presence,
and I know how anger and pain
have fed on my insides . . .

bum rush the page

Daddy,
I don't want
a heart attack
to finally tell us
how you felt.

Kamilah Aisha Moon (Kansas City, MO)

Tattooing the Motherline

I am possessed by Eros,
leaning back in a black leather armchair
that squeaks when I move.

A steady-hand girl
who shares my zodiac
penetrates the freshly shorn

thin brown skin of my upper arm
with an ebony ink dipped needle,
sharp as the arrow of Cupid.

She and I talk shop
over the low humming,
the tiny pricking and dragging

of her stylus fingertip
engraving me with the names
of three generations of women

who walked the long path
to get me here.
When her moving hand becomes uncomfortable,

I flex my toes to feel
the slapping of my sandal
against the sole of my right foot,

and lose myself in the funk
of the Ohio Players thumping
from the small gray speakers

that rest on a table
in the far corner
of the white room.

When she is done,
we admire the elegance
of my angry, scripted bicep

slick with Vaseline,
and step outside
for a smoke.

Krista Franklin *(Dayton)*

Our Fathers

We, whose fathers are hidden
Locked in cells/away far
Missing piece/un whole
Dusty dream they stole

Who console when all are lost?
Cracked, broken, shattered, tossed
Where perfect petals don't exist
Some persist, others resist

We, whose fathers' eyes reek mysterious lullabies
Our cries continue still
Staring through that window sill

He almost came
Bore the label of radiant shame
Missing piece/un hole
Dusty dream it stole

Long lullaby ringing through his hidden eye
Permanent cry from vicious voice
Can't feel a worthwhile choice

We, whose fathers' treasure trapped
Forced to draw forbidden map
Sang sweet lullaby, now locked in cell
Can't hear our cry
Or the story they tell

Ta'Lease Niche Cleveland *(DC)*

Mama's Magic

My Mama is Magic!
Always was and always will be.
There is one phrase that constantly bubbled
from the lips of her five children, *My mama can do it.*
We thought my momma knew everything.
Believed she did, as if she were born full grown from the *Encyclopaedia
Britannica.*
I could tell you stories.
How she transformed a run down paint peeled shack into a home.
How she heated us with tin tub baths from a kettle on a stove.
Poured it over in there like an elixir.

We were my mama's favorite recipe.
She whipped us up from a big brown bowl, supported by her big brown
arms.
We were homemade children.
Stitched together with homemade love.
We didn't get everything we ever wanted
but lacked for nothing.

My mama's love was protection!
Like those quilts her mother used to make.
She tucked us in with patches of cut out history all around us.
We found we could walk anywhere in this world and not feel alone.

My mama never whispered the shame of poverty in our ears.
She taught us to dance to our own shadows.
Pay no attention to those grand parties on the other side of the track.
Make your own music, she'd say
as she walked, as she cleaned
the sagging floorboards of that place.
You'll get there. You'll get there,
her broom seemed to say with every wisp. We looked at the stars in my
mama's eyes, they told us we owned the world.
We walked like kings and queens even on midnight trips to the outhouse.
We were under her spell. My mama didn't study at no Harvard or no Yale.

But the things she knew
you couldn't learn in no book!
Like how to make your life sing like sweet potato pie sweetness
out of an open window.
How to make anybody feel at home.
How at just the right moment be silent,
be silent, then with her eyes say, *Everything's gonna be alright,
chile, everything is gonna be alright.*

How she tended to our sickness.
How she raised our spirits.
How she kept flowers living
on our dilapidated porch
in the midst of family chaos.
My mama raised children like it was her business in life.
Put us on her hip and kept moving.
Keeping that house Pine-Sol clean. Yeah, my mama is magic.
   Always was and
always will be.
Her magic. How to stay steady and sure in this fast-paced world
Now when people look at me
with my head held high.
My back erect and say,
Who does she think she is?
I just keep walking
with the assurance inside.
I am Black Magic.
And I am Jeanette Redmond's child.

Glenis Redmond (Asheville, NC)

Father's Day

Little boys ride their bikes
Through cement gardens
Looking—
Searching for the manhood in their fathers' faces
Finding full-length mirrors on street corners in dice games
You will find them watching you underneath black hoodies
Pulled over rows of braided hair.
They love like quiet storms.
Their smiles make brief appearances.
And the women who have them, keeping their secrets
Tucked deeply behind whispers between kisses.

Aarian Pope (New York)

Momma in Red

They said
that the only reason
my momma wore a red
dress to her daddy's funeral
was because she hated him
and was just being sassy

I know she wore it
because it was
the only one she had!

Nichole L. Shields (Chicago)

Wildlife

When an African Wild Dog is cut off
those who once knew it lose its
scent, turn on it for prey when they see it.

When approaching my father
after the divorce
I become the three monkeys
sitting on their motionless hinds:
ears, mouths and lips topped off
like liquor poured into a long forgotten drink,
feelings stuffed to the bottom of the gullet
by a hand secretly revealing
it hates the comfort food of the wild:
coconuts, mango, fresh, keen cassava.
The hand, bittersweet, sticky, must stuff and stuff,
eat Darwinian truth of the wild,
lope across the veldt craftily as an
African Wild Dog runs down its prey,
works its putrid, sweating spell,
its diminutive white-tipped tail as it crams
Impala and Dik Dik down its thick, dark gullet,
later regurgitates the glittering food stuffs,
wefts of bloody hair, crush of teeth,
finely slivered antler bone, the wild ball of deadness,
the mad whirl of transition into the wide waiting mouth
of one of its pups. I imagine myself,
wobbly, little palpitating stomach,
vulnerable, mewing, moaning like it,
wrapped in the wicked stench of wildlife,
prick-eared lust, as it waits for its parents to come off the hunt,
if angry with one another to nuzzle soft tummies.
One parent is not enough.

Karen Williams (Detroit)

we whose fathers are hidden

Chicago on the Day Brother Increases His Chances of Reaching Age 21

Mayor Harold Washington has been dead
for 8 years and I have become an old lady
harvesting spearmint gum
in my purse   offering pieces
exchanging them for others' approval

maroon robes rage suburban green grasses
empty buses   cross interim intersections
and we are among the few here

momma
daddy
sisters
granny

a force of habit, I count the Cullen faces graduating
noticing 2 finishing that which started with 6
4   years   ago

a shot
a gun
a stick
a hit

1 gone for love
1 gone walking on the way
1 gone trying to catch a ride
the last 1 gone just fucked

the ceremony ends
I   am   young no   longer dispensing   gum
grandmother   is   happy
she mentally marvels ingredients of a sock-it-to-me
cake she will serve
set   on   survival

4 eggs
1 stick of butter
1 cup of sugar
6 ounces of sour cream

We head east on 95th   just passing
Chicago's   Mason-Dixon   Line

Cicero
Pulaski
Western
King Drive　　　no　　　Cottage Grove

Finally, brother,　　　we are south　　east
home　　　　you　　　　are　　　　graduated
and our father the Chicago police officer
with　　　　　your　　　　　same　　　　　　name
knows　　　his　　　gun　　　is　　　for　　　real

Taiyon J. Coleman (Chicago)

Lest We Forget

My heart sits back and wonders
Which eye has cried the most
The eye dangling from the rope
The eye choking from the smoke
The eye dancing to the fire
Or the eye fixed on Cavalry

Was it my father or
My great grandson who declared
I shall not be moved!
Only to wake up on the other side of
"The Dream"

But still
My soul sings and
My mind marches
To tunes of the century past
With melodies and symphonies
Tingling in my toes

Patricia A. Holt Abner (Philly)

The African Burial Ground called Tribeca

The kid had walked these streets before
surrounded by the rivers that meet
Upper New York Bay at the tip of Manhattan
China blue pants and bohemian tweed
Mayakovsky hat the color of kief
never knowing his footfalls often echoed
in the forgotten graves of his ancestors

the old produce market was absent of trucks on Sunday
Five Points as it was called way before then
solemn city hall slightly south
where the seat of new york city government lies
upon the graves of the African dead
those who would be american by decree
beside the landfill of the old Collect Pond
now the Courthouse Site, now Chinatown, now Tribeca

the Dutch West India Company's
chain of "New World" trading posts
working their way by trial and error
through the ethics of forced labor
to give way to the "Articles of Capitulation"
of the English and then the Royal African Company's
docking priority for its slave ships in 1665
the Duke of York's inevitable jackpot payoff:
1711 when the slave market became
the biggest business on Wall Street

Sara Penn's "Knobkerry" on Franklin and West Broadway
Black woman humble in a museum disguised as a shop
among the rare treasures of Africa, Asia, South America
offering healings for free from the powers of antiquity
in the late 20th century Knobkerry once among the lofts
of Tribeca demigods Robert DeNiro and Robert Kennedy Jr.
now disappeared like the African dead
to reappear as relentless as the force of Africa
that built the infrastructure of this metropolis of empires.

David Henderson *(New York)*

fatherless townships

there:
township music of Soweto reverberates
   on roads where Biko walked
and time stood still
for little boys and girls who clung to their mothers' aprons,
waiting for their fathers to arrive
after ten months a year of serving paid time in diamond mines.

anxious to the point of exhaustion
they trek for miles on dusty paths
   across sand-strewn flatlands
their tears making mudpies

as trucks carrying their fathers arrived
    at the crossroads.
they felt the vibrations of rubber to gravel in their dreams

here:
we wait for our fathers in malls, town squares, and bullet-riddled corners
where the smoke in the air from SUV exhaust pipes, bonfires, and gunfire
    is more easily extinguished than the
yearning, burning
    in our hearts
because
our fathers never come.

like Nomzamo Winnie Mandela
for us, waiting month to month
    seems like years on end.
crowd chants of
    Amandla!
    Awethu!
make us feel powerless instead.

we must beat our chests
    like djembe drums
take pride in the strides
    we have made
in our solo journeys.
how is it then that
    we are orphans?
when our fathers walk on graves
    where we find
    buried their souls
broken promises
    cut deeper into hearts
prematurely broken by
    absence at birth rituals
our fathers' double-shift jobs shifting focus
    from paycheck to paycheck
lost in moats surrounding
    human services
far from humane
our fathers exist
    only as a number
    ready for deposit
not a name
    (a burden we bear)
    and will remember

printing
    each letter painfully
jabbing
    the pen into the paper until
we feel
they feel the curse it has given us.

fatherless means mothermore
and is why we present our mothers with
    flowers in May
    and
    tool-belts in June.

we sit on overturned cardboard boxes
    that used to hold the
    contents of our lives
hold remains of incomplete birthday party favors
    that were never beneficial to us
because
his flesh
    they did not touch.

Abiyah *(Cincinnati)*

Waiting for the Results of a Pregnancy Test

At forty-one, I am uncertain of more things
than I could have imagined twenty years ago.

Your existence or non-existence
hovers over me today. The voices
of the world my friends, the liberated
women who are close to me, cry
abort abort abort in unison.

Yet the voice inside me shouts
               No

shows my selfishness in its mirror
my soul's dark intent.

This newt, this merging of tiny cells
makes an explosion like comets
colliding in my ordered universe.

I want to say: I'm too old, too tired,
too caught up in trying wings so long unused,

but that voice will not be silent. It beats
in my bones with its primitive insistence.

Little life, floating in your boat of cells,
I will carry you under my heart
though the arithmetic is against us both.

Today I bypass the baby departments,
the thousand reminders that come to me now.
The young women wheeling strollers through
Bradlees, the girl in the maternity shirt
which proclaims: "I'm not lonely anymore."

I want to scream, we are all born lonely,
and the child beating under our hearts
does not change that. I want to lie down
on the ugly pebbled floor of Bradlees and kick
my feet and pound my fists and make this intruder
in my life vanish.

As I stand at the checkout line, I see our years unroll:

the bottles
midnight feedings
tinker toys
baseball games
PTA meetings

are boulders in my path, a mountain
of boulders I will have to climb
for you. I walk into the spring sunlight
while my life snaps closed around me and my fear.

My friends are all my age, their children in high school
as mine are. I will be alone with you.
You will be born with a scowl on your face,
your hands shaking, having taken from the marrow
of my bones my own quaking.

We will rock together in this leaky boat and
I will love you, I know; it is only in these first
moments, while I alter the picture of my life
I had painted with such sure strokes, only in these
moments that I wish you were not there.

Maria Mazziotti Gillan (Paterson, NJ)

Sitting in the Doctor's Office the Next Day

Sitting in the
doctor's office
the next day,
I notice
pieces
of blue soap
from your bathroom
wedged into
the edge of
my wedding band.
I bend to
kiss the soap
and leave it
concealing the baguettes.
Lying on the examining table,
my son stares
at the window washer
outside, hanging
thirteen floors
over Central Park South.
Unlike me, he balances
gravity with a flick
of his sponge,
risking tomorrow
like I risked mine
yesterday
with you.

Laura Boss *(Montclair, NJ)*

Circa

our children
   stand and stare
      disco/nected in wide-eyed wonder
   stand and stare at the edge of our pit
where we dance and grunt
   bump and grind
      twist and shout
         dysfunctional
dysfunctional and drugged
         in glassy-eyed trance
they unaware of the hour
         we unaware of the day

both of us
        for the moment
                unconcerned.
the wise ones said:
    history
        is a teacher
            of those who would listen
        and a knowledge acquired too late
            by those who would not:
three decades ago
        skirt hemlines rose
                    higher and swifter
            than word or deed or contraband thought:
    we long on stroke
        but short on memory
    got good ideas
        but poor execution:
            we are losing our children.
invite them to partake in our failure
    and they come
                chantin death raps and tossin bones:
bettin against life crappin out
                    before we come to our senses
            bettin against life pickin up then goin home
        before we can recover all we have lost here but
                lost innocence can never be regained:
            we are losing our children:
send them off to school on potato chips and reefer
        send them out to play in needle parks and dead-end streets
send them
        out of our arms and away from us:
            two generations into the future are being laid to rest
        stillborn
        in a past they may never know:
we are killing our children
        the old ones said:
            there will come the day
                that the young shall devour the flesh of their elders
                as there will be a poverty of spirit
                    and a forsaking of the soul
    and now,
            as our babies run down well-worn, angel-dusted alleys
                in search of an escape hatch,
                callin it god, callin it self, callin it somethin, anything
                    before their number lights up on the big board
it is difficult to look future in the eye as prophesy becomes truth:
            our children are killing us.

like kamikazes from our celluloid heroics
          and distorted reality
come at us with questions we will not answer
          with attitudes we cannot turn back
     life, like death, has no impact
                    in the face of self-destruction at high noon
     so we turn to neon salvation
          make like every day
               is a Saturday night
                    rolled up in a blunt
                         and wearing a red dress
here, in the forest of our frustration
     in the shadow of a light now dimmed
          we are losing ourselves
and our children
          we are losing our children.

Tom Mitchelson *(New York)*

seed of resistance

Cooking

Melting her candy on the radiator
she was playing "cooking"
she ironed her clothes at seven years old
straightened her hair as best she could
iron burns on her wrist and belly
scars, scars, scars
from playing "mother"
scrubbing and washing Carolina rice
over the kitchen sink
stood in a chair to reach the stove
to cook the rice
that they all ate
and then she sat down
to read the Bible and then to pray,
Please God, I wanna play like a child

Ayin Adams (Maui)

Ben Hur

This is the part where
Charlton Heston's sister
gets cured of leprosy
                    I'm sitting on the couch
It's late
          Charlton cries
I swallow a fig newton

Last time I saw Ben Hur
I was twelve years old
My parents were still alive
Moths swarmed around the porch light,
Refrigerators hummed,
We were safe
          Now I'm thirty
Rocky and Clare
                    in a grave
I start to cry
          because Charlton
is hugging his sister

and he's home
and I'm not
and it's raining
inside the movie
                and out
Outside, the smell of wet dirt
and soggy garbage
                wafts through my window
Shit!
        If I had a girlfriend
we'd screw till the moon was cheese
we'd create our own epic:
thighs, breasts, mole hairs, freckles,
all the noises peculiar to coupling
hips rounding into air, hands palming
flesh, fresh so smooth and rough and sweaty
and . . .

The theme music flares
I know it's a corny flick
I've read Rimbaud
but I'm sad and full of fig newtons
it's late and my hairline's receding
outside the rain keeps falling
looks like a thousand needles
falling under the streetlight's glare,
piercing space
and I wish I were dead or in the arms of a girl
I hear the soft incessant hum of a refrigerator,
the soft incessant hum of me
falling through space, falling asleep
with my hand between my legs

Joe Weil *(Elizabeth, NJ)*

in 5th grade

I

in 5th grade social studies class we
watched roots on tv and i alone matched the darkened classroom
felt white pupils' black pupils
move to corners closest to mine
yet furthest away

and i not knowing where to move
instinct saying "you identify"
(an illogical thought;
its roundness foreign to my square mind. i rejected it. it didn't fit.

II

root—
thick-trunked tree in grandpa's backyard
with raised strong dark limbs stretching up to infinite blue sk(eyes)
and dark red buds
reminiscent of thick blood-filled blisters on my grandpa's hands
—the fruit of his labor
he told me the roots of this tree ran deep beneath the earth
—but i didn't believe. i couldn't see them.

III

on the screen my grandpa and their grandpa
cavorted in an obscene dance of bowing shuffling and
arms raised in anger
proper southern misses swooning
and i
and they concealed tears—both
of shame
i longed to jump up to twirl madly about the room telling of my home with
its high beamed ceilings and thick dark carpeting and smooth heavy polished
mahogany furniture and matching grandfather clock which chimed
     every quarter
hour without fail. my home so much like the ones the house niggers
     spent the
slow leisured southern summer afternoons cleaning.
Shame.
A damned shame.

IV

once on the front lawn i asked my father why
the flowers we planted kept falling over
—their roots are not deep enough—he responded.
as he puttered with the spade in vain trying to restore
fallen buds in shallow soil i looked at his hands
he had inherited the blood-filled blisters of his father. i stared
critically at my own hands.
they were soft and smooth.
(i felt somehow guilty)

seed of resistance

V

one day i woke
stumbled to the
mirror. through refreshed eyes i
looked at my hair. it had been
chemically straightened
(poisoned)
and hung in long limp strands around my head with its regal neck ripened
lips brilliant eyes
pronounced cheekbones that
signified a sensual maturity:
it did not match.
as if in a dream i reached for the shears. as i lifted them towards my head
they grew heavy
and a
few doubts
(niggerboogienightfighterjunglebunnyapemancoonspade)
presented themselves like maggots from the corpse of a rotting animal
i brushed them away
strengthened by the resolve gained from a glance
at my firm jawline and high proud forehead.
snip—and 18 years of disillusionment
fell to my shoulders and onto the
floor

Valerie Caesar *(Stony Brook, NY)*

Complected

What the fine rain does not hide and cannot wash away
are coal fingers shrugging slicker strings tighter,
protecting just-straightened hair. The humidity

is deadly to this delicate process,
and can nap the nape along the kitchen instantly,
reverting to the natural curl she dreads.

The girl beside her wears no slicker but has a ponytail
like Barbie's and is just as fair. The pubescent boys stare.
She's an urban Venus, impossibly waiting for the same bus.

The hooded girl is not Venus. Dark brown is not beauty
darker still a death sentence if you are young, waiting
for a bus, a long appreciative glance, even catcalls, "hey redbone"—love.

The hooded girl hopes the Korean store up the street
will have a sale soon on fading cream and human hair,
because, beauty here is serious business.

Teri Ellen Cross (Silver Spring, MD)

Broken Ends Broken Promises

*for my twin sister Melissa,
who endured it with me*

Braids twist and tie
constrain baby naps never to be free
braids twist and tie
contain / hold in the shame
of not having long black silky strands
to run my fingers through.

Moñus* y bobby pins
twist and wrap
Please forgive me for the sin
of not inheriting Papi's "good hair"
Moñus y bobby pins
twist and wrap
restrain kinky naps
dying to be free
but not the pain
of not having a long black silky mane
to run my fingers through.

Clips and ribbons
to hold back and tie
oppressing baby naps
never to be free
clips and ribbons
to hold back and tie
imprisoning baby naps
never to have the dignity to be.

Chemical relaxers
broken ends / broken promises
activator and cream
mixed in with bitterness
mix well
the ritual of combing / parting / sectioning

*hair buns

the greasing of the scalp / the neck / the forehead / the ears
the process / and then the burning / the burning
It hurts to be beautiful,
my mother tells me.
Pero, Mami, me pica! It burns!
and then the running / the running to water / to salvation
to neutralizer / to broken ends and broken promises . . .

Graduating from Carefree Curl
to Kitty Curl / to Revlon / to super duper Fabulaxer
different boxes offering us broken ends and broken promises
We've come a long way since Dixie Peach,
my mother tells me as I sit at the kitchen table.

Chemical Relaxers to melt away the shame
until new growth reminds us
that it is time once again
for the ritual and the fear of
scalp burns and hair loss
and the welcoming
of broken ends
and broken
promises.

Mariposa *(New York)*

My Name's Not Rodriguez

It is a sigh of climbing feet,
the lather of gold lust,
the slave master's religion
with crippled hands gripping greed's tail.
My name's not Rodriguez.
It's an Indian mother's noiseless cry,
a warrior's saliva on arrow tip, a jaguar's claw,
a woman's enticing contours on volcanic rock.
My real name's the ash of memory from burned trees.
It's the three-year-old child wandering in the plain
and shot by U.S. Calvary in the Sand Creek massacre.
I'm a Geronimo yell into the canyons of the old ones.
I'm the Comanche scout; the Raramuri shaman
in soiled bandanna running in the wretched rain.
I'm called Rodriguez and my tears leave rivers of salt.
I'm Rodriguez and my skin dries on the bones.
I'm Rodriguez and a diseased laughter enters the pores.
I'm Rodriguez and my father's insanity

blocks every passageway,
scorching the walls of every dwelling.
My name's not Rodriquez; it's a fiber in the wind,
it's what oceans have immersed,
it's what graceful and sublime over the top of peaks,
what grows red in desert sands.
It's the crawling life, the watery breaths between ledges.
It's taut drum and peyote dance.
It's the brew from fermented heartaches.
Don't call me Rodriguez unless you mean peon and sod carrier,
unless you mean slayer of truths and deep-sixer of hopes.
Unless you mean forget and then die.
My name's the black-hooded 9mm-wielding child in all our alleys.
I'm death row monk. The eight-year-old gum seller
in city bars and taco shops.
I'm unlicensed, uninsured, unregulated and unforgiven.
I'm free and therefore hungry.
I'm seed of resistance in pod of domesticity.
Call me Rodriguez and bleed in shame.
Call me Rodriguez and forget your own name.
Call me Rodriguez and see if I whisper in your ear,
mouth stained with bitter wine.

Luis J. Rodriguez (San Fernando, CA)

seed of resistance

Water from the Well

for Duriel Fannie Pilgrim Gault

I have your name: wholly holy, Hebrew,
resonance softened by slur of introduction:
of the light of God. Angel warrior. Celebration.

They called you Dura. Mama Beulah named you after a cousin:
D U R I E L, Durle. Letters lazy in field heat. Holler through hills.
What southern tongues twisted with slow indifference, my mother coaxed
upright to give to me: Duriel. Annointing. Chubby brown girlchild
born into memory's bold revision. Now I am a woman
whose dreams extend backward into shadows: I feel my way through
language to arrive at a border town where nothing is taken for granted.

You are my grandmother. You are on the other side: that's how I came
to have your name. This is all I know.

Someone tells me you are my guardian angel, that we are two souls in one
   body,
that you will come to me in my sleep if I call to you.

So I sprinkle rosewater on my pillow and go to bed, wanting
to hear the timbre of your voice, wanting to smell the line-dry linen
of your dresses. I go to bed listening for porch boards' creak, trying to
    imagine
the smell of peach tree blossoms and the earth flavor of red clay dirt.

One night you step from the other side
into my room, which becomes a stretch of ripe cotton rows.
I see you across the way. Your apron, dusted with flour.
We are up on the mountain, in granddaddy's fields. I am skipping
barelegged in a yellow dress balancing an empty tin wash tub on my hip.
Now we're nearer the house. I'm squeeze-yanking cow udders
but there's nothing to catch the milk so it spills into dirt.
I'm in the front room; you are water-waving your hair.
Now it's winter and my chest is tight as cold molasses. I'm in bed
under a handmade quilt, shivering. Goose grease popping on the stove.
You are wringing supper's chicken necks, hands soft white from wash
    water.
You are singing pillowcases from flour sacks. You are teaching the stitch
with your eyes closed. Colored Cherokee woman. I am sweeping ashes near
    the wood stove,
humming quartet songs and "Mississippi Po' Boy." I am sent giggling to
    the well for water.
When I return, I am carrying nothing
but your name
and you are gone.

Duriel E. Harris (Chicago)

The Tragic Mulatto Is Neither

Triple Great Grandpa
desert black born from both
rising from the cradle to fly the soul line
to breathe life into more black children

Stretch that line Granddaddy
Stretch that line

Caramel coated
he caught sweet chocolate
she bore more brown
let the soul line trickle down

generations.

My cousin's flavor
mixed like mine
some kind of swirl Cherokee on top
fudge all over and deep inside

Color vision stays practical
politically we practically black
same shade as the first baby slave
born off the boat

History and family
keep onyx in the mind
Suburbs and brie cheese
cloud the issue

nothing tragic in the mix
no mules to carry esoteric burdens
tragedy falls on leisure time
when sticking assumptions on a Velcro self

culture is deeper than most waters
wallow in the bottom mud
you'll grow gills in time
we all grow gills in time.

Michael C. Ladd (New York)

seed of resistance

I'm Sayin Though

The flavor
 of funk
 is leather
 is thigh flesh wrapped
in gray clouds.

The taste of green wood
 is soft
and neck like.

   Your Bantu is moving me forward.

   The silhouette of your head rolls against brilliant afternoons
while false-ologists doctor your intelligence and make lies
 to ill your reputation.

You invent
 cuneiform for unearthly worlds.

I taste gray cloud on my mind. I
salivate over green wood. Your
Bantu evokes my re-
luctant teeth.

Your brilliant silhouette clutches my eye.

Marco Villalobos (New York)

beauty rituals 2000

just no comb/toe rings/titty rings/rings for the clitoris too/unfinished
poems on the inside thigh/tea tree shampoo/conditioner from the swiss
alps/extra virgin olive oil/shea butter for the roots/maybe maple brown lip
gloss open-toed shoes/cypress leaves/arabian rose/cranberry nail
polish/some henna to lighten the hair/oranges and lemons for the pores/hot
steaming water/kundalini exhalation/God

Nwenna Kai (Chicago)

Medusa

Head full of fragrant vines
I step out of the shower, steam billows behind me.
Hair washing is not casual it is ritual, ceremony of
herbs, oils, sweets essences
a rainforest journey
a shedding

　　　As a plaited girl
　　　I was stung by the word "Medusa"

me and my friends covered cornrows with towels
and slips to toss and flip, to pretend
we were sexy

　　　seduction looked like bustiers, tight jeans
　　　short skirts, high heels—
　　　tresses fingers eased through

hair talks back
swings moods
giggles and hisses
goes toe-to-toe with a hot comb
hair does not lay down—
it caresses is 1,000 spiraling waists
　　　beckoning brown hand

　　　As a plaited girl
　　　I was stung by the word "Medusa"
　　　As a woman
　　　I am unafraid to turn men to stone

Mariahadessa Ekere Tallie (New York)

Starlette

I long for critical acclaim
like those middle American girls
on New York buses bound for fame
who save mini fortunes under mattresses
only to exchange Dairy Queen uniforms
for Best Supporting Bitch performances
in Manhattan cafés

Crave the spotlight like
sun-worshippers chasing rays

bestowing praises on the golden orb
in the sky
oiling milky white skins
until they caramelize &
become shades & colours
that can't be categorized
by nation

Covet media attention
the way Munchausen sufferers
need to inflict pain—
or better yet, the sufferers by proxy
who drive others insane
but wanna keep their bodies intact

I need to act—
require the drama
like a junkie needs hits
deserve a fan club
like Britney Spears' tits

I desire applause like Santa Claus
fiends for his mince pies
need idolatry
the way OJ needed alibis

I am dramatizing now—
if the truth be told

I want to be loved like ladies
who fear old age and spinsterhood so much
they start injecting cowjuice into lips,
fine tuning physiques
with tucks and nips
then position themselves at bar corners
and slip phone numbers into teenagers' pockets

When I enter a room
I don't just want red carpet
I need a trumpet fanfare

It's okay to stop and stare
want to be noticed
like those models that starve themselves
until they disappear—

Ain't no reality here—
I'm living in wonderland

was aiming for Hollywood
but my parents just didn't understand

So I boarded the bus anyway
had saved pennies for a rainy day
hadn't figured on monsoon season

Now I give my best performances
in the twilight hours
when shape shifters dance dreams
through sleeping silhouettes
and my mind is perfecting
Prima Donna pirouettes—

This is when I am truly at my finest
for $25
I'll be your Starlette

Chioma Okereke (London)

exceptions

i before e
except after c

    the world is flat
    the moon is made of brie

or when sounded like a
as in neighbor or weigh

    lie to yourself
    long enough
    you will believe anything
    you say

parallel lines never intersect
    the police are here to serve and protect
when in doubt, go with your first guess
    father knows best
forgive and forget

are you convinced
of the lies
that you've told yourself,
yet?

there is
no tooth fairy
no
easter
bunny
no
santa
claus

planting a flag
on the moon
doesn't make it
yours

makes
a hole
in the
moon

everything comes back.

baby,
come back soon
from whatever trip
it is you are on

while you are gone
write often
send postcards

i will wait
i have been waiting

waiting up nights
waiting for the jackson 5 to reunite
waiting for black girls to be in style

i may be waiting for a while
but everything comes back

afros,
bell-bottoms,
platform shoes,
you
will be
back soon

(i am not so sure
who's lying to who
anymore)

parallel lines
curved and in motion
can meet

that is a tenet
of hyperbolic geometry

e comes before i
sometimes

in words like
meiosis and poltergeist
where there is no c
or sound of a

this is not for you
in the same way
that funerals
are not for the dead

they are for the living
to wail and moan
mourn a spirit
gone home

in that way
this is not for you

it is for
all of the rules
we accepted
in our youth

unquestioned
myths masquerading
as truth

the train comes
the minute you stop
looking for it

$e = mc^2$
    columbus discovered america
we hurt each other because we care

beauty is moving us forward

i before e
    everything comes back

except after c
    there is no tooth fairy

or when sounded like a
    an apple a day
as in neighbor or weigh
    if you have nothing nice to say . . .
lie.

lie to yourself
lie to yourself long enough
and you will believe anything
you say

but it is going to take
a lot more
for you
to convince
me

Felice Belle (*New York*)

What the deal, son?

Will those dreams
I had as a child come
to pass Will I fall
through the sky
landing in a pit
of purple rats as
the apocalypse
loosens its belt
and beats the
pavement until
welts the size of
africa's left nostril
quakes my puny
bones leaving
me levitating
in pork as I
scramble beneath
my folding bed the

darkness so prison-like
that even my mother
southern warrior
that she is cannot
scrape the tinted
windows off that
child's imagination Will
I die the day that I am
born the gunshot residue
of my mother's two failed
abortions black boy richard
wright detested himself
and me twin negroes
who dream too damn
much about death 'cept
we a living death and
a living lie because ma
said the truth shall set
you free and a lie will
leave you dead as the
bleached lips mister littlejohn
would brush with
the stories snared between
his gangrene tongue and that vaseline
they call bacardi I had a dream
about old man littlejohn
and his bacardi dreamt
he was trying to set
the world on fire and ain't
had no matches so he
poured that bacardi all
over his body until
him smelled like baby
powder with a 72-year-
old butt infection and
well Will you understand
when I say mister
littlejohn died the day
he recognized his back
had been a throw rug
longer than it took that
bacardi to burn the corns
from his feet he dead
dead like a ghetto baby
slurping the dust from
his crack mother's nipples
dead dead like the drug

dealer harvesting crops
on this concrete plantation
dead dead like the black
leader whose chicken-greased
oratory sounds like the slave
master's booted foot caving
in my skull dead dead as I felt
in church every Sunday
as reverend right on
stretched forth his mighty
pockets and emptied hell
into my lap its fiery flesh
heated like a jigga who
thought this kiss of the
glass straw would be the one
to put him in orbit without
the space shuttle bringing
him nearer god to me
bow-legged black boy
who became an insomniac
as a man so terrified of sleeping
'cause, like nas said, sleep
is the cousin of death 'cept
death ain't got no cousins
so sleep must be death
and dreaming must be
god usurping salvador
dali's juice and bypassing
the most fundamental
question of a dreamer Will
you mind if I tell you I
believe in god but it
just might not be the
god you believe in

Kevin Powell (New York)

Plain Ole Brother Blues

I concluded years ago
That if I could learn to sing
In an Isley-like falsetto
Or perhaps like Reverend Green
Wouldn't be no woman here nor there
with the strength to turn away

Wouldn't be no woman anywhere
My pretty voice couldn't sway.

Oh to do what Denzel did in *Glory*
When they whipped him on his back.
He let one tear roll down his cheek
But he called the others back.
And the women screamed and hollered
and cried out Denzel's name.
Figure all I need is tear control
And they'd love me just the same.

If I had hair like Maxwell
I wouldn't have to be 'bout shit
No, if I had hair like that Negro
The hard-to-get could quit
Pretending they don't want me
'cause how could they say no
to the not-quite-nappy nappiness
of my cool bohemian 'fro?

But I'm just a plain ole brother
With no gimmicks to his name.
Just a ordinary black man
Who ain't never had no game.
But I know that with a bag of tricks
I wouldn't be so lame.
Just a bag of tricks and they'd let me in
The lover's hall of fame.

Jarvis Q. DeBerry (New Orleans)

Why I Be a Goddess

I be a Goddess 'cause
I be God manifest in woman flesh.
I be righteous of heart,
Quick witted of spirit,
Sexy as the day is long,
With heart mind and body that's strong.

I be a Goddess 'cause
All your names don't suit me,
Can't hold me,
Represent me,
Speak to me
Nor impress me.

I be a Goddess 'cause
I can hear the heavens sing,
Feel the earth cry
And smell revolution coming a mile away.

I be a Goddess 'cause
I hold ancient wisdom,
Untold secrets,
And powerful mystics.

I be a Goddess 'cause
Every time I part my lips,
You hear the creator speak.

Rising two and a half inches above all the bullshit,
I be a Goddess in the midst:

In the midst of sadness,
I be a Goddess.
In the midst of confusion, fake funktified illusion,
I be a Goddess.
In the midst of the New World Order
ain't a damn thing changed old school slaughter,
I be a Goddess
Surrounded by urban underground games
that got your mind with nothing to show
for it,
I be a Goddess.
Flocked by seekers of the American dream,
who be dead men walking,
I be a Goddess.

And I maintain my domain.
Exercise my brain.
Drive bullshit out the frame.
Make all call me by my name: GODDESS.
I be a Goddess,
Why?
'Cause I said so!

Rha Goddess *(New York)*

I'm the Man

I don't have to live large to know I'm in charge
I know where I stand. I have a plan
So I say, *Hey, I'm the man.*

I don't mean I like women
Or I have to act rough,
I like to get pretty and strut my stuff.
But I know where I stand . . . with a purpose and a plan.
So I say, *Hey, I'm the man.*

I have not gone insane. Woman is my name.
But I won't give up my control
Or place dignity on hold.
I will take a stand and get what I demand
There is no *I can't,* just *I can.*
So I say, *Hey, I'm the man.*

I'm definitely a she
But I see beyond the gender of me.
I'm not on your case.
I don't want to take your place.
But I've made a decision
To elevate my position
I have the power . . . This is my hour
I'm in control . . . So design me a role
I'm not playing a game,
So don't call me out my name.
It's about me and the Higher Authority.
We walk hand in hand.
So I say, *Hey, I'm the man.*

But it's not just about me. It's about we.
We have the power . . . This is our hour
To take control of our mind, body, and soul
Together we stand with our purpose and a plan.
Then we be . . . the man, yeah. We be the man, yeah!

Lindamichellebaron (Hempstead, NY)

Dare to Be Different

Wear my colored stripes
polker dot ribbons streaming

Raise my left hand in a right handed world
breath when they say, *Blow*

Walkin down scattered streets
talking to Me

So I'm crazy?
Ask to be individual
I ask questions when I don't know where I'm going

Or where you're from
                    Can I come?

Can I pray out loud in a crowd
            of empty souls?
Will they watch
                    stare
lend an ear
share a single tear for my misfortune?

—I don't think so—

So does it matter
if I choose laughter instead of pain
help a brotherman who doesn't understand
we're the same

If my color's a little lighter
am I whiter
than the other
brothers and sisters
fighting for the cause?

No
it's just a matter of taste

So spicy ain't my flavor, soul ain't my food
I still like greasin

I may be a bit country
but I don't do rock
although I do roll
on occasion

If I ask
will you pass compassion
or am I qualified to be denied
just 'cause my house is across town

Or will you come around every now and then
share a cup of tea, drink from me

Maybe you'll see you're a lot like me
If not, that's cool

Be true to you
I'm down with that too

Venus Harris (*New York*)

Thoughts from a Bar Stool

With butterflies in my stomach, flowers in my hair
Rich color on my lips and perfume on my skin
Remembering what never was
Anticipating what will never be

Rich color on my lips and perfume on my skin
Legs crossed tight, cold hands folded
Anticipating what will never be
Wanting, wasting, waiting . . .

Legs crossed tight, cold hands folded
My mind's eye squints to recognize you
Wanting, waiting, wasting . . .
Rich color fading, skin wrinkling under stale perfume

Deirdre May (*New York*)

A Blue Black Pearl

*In appreciation of Patty,
who I heard loudly*

Forty years,
forty years of
   hurt
climbed into my
   walls.
A cut-out doll
trampled on
spread
eagle style
fallen angel
wings clipped.
Forty years,
forty years of
   hurt

dangled its ugly
   head.
A strayed
   peacock with
plucked feathers.
Who am I?
Forty years
hollering and
   screaming
stopping
   deadened pain
with bitten lips.
A sucked-up
   sponge

of evil talks
of death traps
set
by mind
torture.
Forty years, I,
a blue black pearl
stood waiting
for freedom
as teardrops
rained on my
unsheltered
   hands
For forty years,

a scar so
bright it
   twinkled
in darkness.
For forty years,
I sung over hills
yonder
(where I ought
to be)
as the
whipping belt
flashed
across
my swollen eye,

a blackened
  sushi,
a closed-out sale.
Forty years,
my braided hair
cut and
burned and
pulled, and
somehow
bruising
seemed easier.
Forty years
dragged
through
muddy waters
swishing back
strokes
of human terror.
Swinging
my high heels
walking
clicking
clacking
running
jumping
hallelujahing
backed up/
moved forward
fell down
got up
with no pain.
  Dead.
Walking
dead
for forty years
and counting.
Broken chains
unyielding.
Oil grease gauge
on empty. Forty
  years
was too soon,
my next life
I'll be a light
shining through
the morning
  stars

while the moon's
crescent
  descends.
My blues
turns to
red thumps.
My station
an impending
destination
on a high wire
unbalanced rope.
Judge not
my prosecutor,
but my executor
of pain.
She inflicted
She battered
She a wild-
ass dream.
(Hear me!)
For forty years,
kicked back
and rode the
mockingbird
singing a
jaybird's
chord.
For forty years,
I sang
a blue black
  pearl
toe-jamming
  song.
For forty years,
hurt me,
  Mother,
and I release,
release a
  butterfly
in Bermudan
crystallized
blue water
drifting across
those smashed
memories
opening
like a new box

of Kleenex
  tissues
stopping a
red truck
of singed lines.
Mama,
Oh! Sweet
  Mama,
flesh squeezed
into a two-fisted
walnut crunch,
a mixed-up
nutty bread.
Swinging and
  swaying
a preacher's
  gospel,
Jump back,
I done found
the glory train,
Mama said.
Jump back,
I done found
the glory train!
Mama crooned
out of her
  broken
twisted mouth.
A hypnotic beat
devoid and
sanitized
of truth serum
of God's
  retribution
hands.
Forty years
forty years of
  hurt
itching a scratch
that can't be
  fingered
in my scarred
bruised
heals open
from my rib to
  rib.
Stomped on and

kicked-up to my
  navel
with craved
  initials
of razor blade
  cuts
driven so deeply
only nightly
  cries
of beast-eyed
monster-sized
screams awaited
my sweet
  dreams
of repeated
purgatory.
For forty years,
let me go
pain.
For forty years,
let me go
pain.
Unshelved. My
thoughts
live soul deep
infesting awak-
  ened
moments.
My body recoils
like a snake
lurching
with precision
sharp fangs
of deadly
  gashes.
My adulthood
marred by
self-sold
highest bidders.
I've pimped
and prostituted
only to run
further inside
holding on
to that spotlight
left that aches
across my chest

making room
for my heart's
tiny seedling
of growth
   roots.
Growing like a
   new
forty-year-old
   heart
renewed
of self-worth
of life
of care. Mama,
for forty years,
   Mama,
you've crushed
this blue black
   pearl.
I, a transitional
house guest,
a volunteer
   witness
of your reservoir
of evilness
perched against
a broken
   mirror.
Mama, I've
   swung
to and fro
for forty years!
Re-winding,
Mama, just
   rewinding,
the beat downs
of kaleidoscopic
swirls of reds,
blues, greens,
orange, and
   black
looking for the
   white
space to hold
   on.
(Cut encircled
   glass
blocks the pieces
from unity.)
I sit on my bed's
unmade corner
rocking the
unblossomed
blue black
   battered-
pearl. I sit
   crossed
as arms warmly
embrace
my recaptured
fallen spirit.
My love
begins
for us.

Clairesa Clay *(New York)*

runnin

yesterday
i was runnin
from myself
goin so fast
had dust and
fear like death
comin
caught all in
my conscious
going so fast
sanity got left
7 miles
back
3 revolutions ago
runnin from myself
runnin from my
self
runnin from
my
self
was goin
so fast
head tryin ta
catch my tail
tongue tryin ta
catch my mind

mind tryin ta
catch my soul
wasn't gonna happen
though
not yesterday
not any day
had to slow my
self
down
catch hold of
breath and
reason
had to slow my
self
down
claw my way
to answers
and truth
had to slow
my
self
down
rebuild
strength and
dignity yesterday
was runnin
from my self
was goin too
fast
this day
findin my
self whole
once more
faith and
determination
alive in my palm

Jamila Z. Wade (Boston)

conversations in the struggle
for Kamaria

you swim afro cuban cadences
into the ear of this middle passage creaking,
dance samba upon the wooden deck,

cook paella from high noon's mouth
as we devour it with our fingers
and it is a calm moment for us—
un-sick, very well,
moving and blessing
these swift river days

i need to know
that we get stronger,
hew new masks
from the stone, wood and fire,
our palms full of unuttered dreams.

we line up promises to ourselves:
to remember this thin crack of time,
remember us laughing and smiling—
African women
cowrie and bone intact,
moving homeward,
carving our old ones aloud.

Pamela Plummer *(Atlanta)*

Harvest: A Line Drawing

A body of thirst will stand in morning rain
Testing faith like a safety net; two hands
Side by side collecting drops like so many
Walendas fallen from a tight rope. The trolley,
Cresting the hill, progresses haltingly toward
This corner with shy cries of disc and rail,

Arriving here like a shower curtain
On a power line. This corner near
The place where Ben Franklin built his school
(That lover of women and storms fishing
The seamless night for what breaks—he thought
Light is dark with a crack in it, fisted the stuff

Like a Roman god). If this were a moment,
It would pass. The body would raise a wrist
To confirm itself against a chaos of tangents;
A geometry of possibilities concatenated like
Christmas lights—luminous and interdependent,
Simultaneous flux the way destination

Is a constant *am*. The gutter is a glut
Of leaf and needle and the world is coming down.
But what resists water more than death
Or a good watch? Nietzsche said, *All that's ripe*
Wants to die. Think of the women who do not
Survive childbirth. Bearers of fruit

and pall and the heroic ambivalence of life
I am the way to the city of woe. What a way to go:
Plunging into flesh and dust, both directions
At once. And what of the days before medicine
Learned to ease them from the vine?
Picture them: mother and child at respective brinks

And all that they have in common.
While seasons work to gully
Earth's inventory, this body, despite alternatives, will
Board and stand, reaching in the air with excuses and move
To hold the metal rail and hang; solder and sinew,
Thick with wet, the heaviest fruit, as if it *came* natural.

Gregory Pardlo (New York)

joseph speaks to gericault in the studio
after theodore gericault's portrait study

search the length of your eyes
to find how you judge me. crucified
up
side
down
on your iris. inverted hologram
captured in your acrylic
embrace.

this is how you like me.
still
as the hangman's poplar tree
when the kicking has ceased.
silent.
a mute victim of french
imagination. i make the fatal
segue from subject to object.

you know me not.

i am more than santo domingo
mythologies
exoticized in oil.

the things you sketch into my eyes. bequeath
the borrowed blues
of others, their minor chord pupils.
my sockets are pallbearers
wailing eulogies
for the dead dreams they carry.

someone else's pain is
buried in the sarcophagus
of my face. the life sentence of salon sight.
penalty served
in number of hard stares.
a man is not meant to have
such a close reading of his face.

under the festering
gaze of museum patrons
i become an abject thermometer.
mercury as curiosity. peppery skin tingling
nostrils raw.
scalding is my name.

wear my eyes and see
if you can bear the heat
of revulsion
in the casual glance of pedestrians.
The heat of terror in a child's
shudder
at your smile.
the gravity of not being able to find
beauty
in a mirror.

no you can't touch my hair. its natty
roots will not lead you
to the primitive
innocence
you assume I possess. you cannot access
your past through me
only your uncouth shame.

i am steps removed from being a friend. you paint
my naked body
but I know none of your secrets.

fabricated amnesia:
france has not forgotten
storming the bastille
declaring the rights of man.
she has forgotten
that nappy heads hold souls
that pine for justice too.
beloved homeland hispañiola.
colonial whore.
bedwarmer for the city of lights.
you ravish our sugar
cane, tobacco leaves
and young girls.
make them come
in the name of napoleon.
i can still hear the sweet
resistance
of their guilty moans.

i seek retribution
in the wombs of french
women. burn inside
their solvent fascination.

an acrobat's torment
cannot be captured in water
colors. it leaks out the frame
into a ring of fire. the viscous twists of his life
require a medium
with more texture. something you can rub
between your fingers, squeeze into your mouth.

what is the degree of difficulty
to double somersault
a soul
inside out?

the pernicious whispers i have heard
meditating on museum walls
could shake a nun's faith.
niggers hang in the permanent collection
because we have practiced on tree limbs.

a sacred text
rescued me from the raft
of the medusa:
the holy book of strategies for surviving oil-based quicksand

can be found
on the papyrus of osiris.
i read it by candlelight.
it recites itself
as i sit still for a living.

a man should narrate
his own psalm. that way nothing
gets lost in the translation
between self & easel.
i sell my soul, my body. i cannot
get them back. they are dried
on the edges of brushes.
joseph is my name.
i am a man
no matter how much oil
you spill in my eyes.

Michael Datcher (LA)

Entrancielo

eyes whistling in the dark
mountain strips from mayhem
this borrowed night from devil knees, at the door
a gift, grazing this room as wide
as all failing   . . . it's my eyes that listen
                    as I whistle in the dark

this room will serve as another memory is all
this heart will strafe a thousand hearts - her every
will all - and I, will her
    . . . and our traffic
is ours - and never still
    . . . and all I mention
is understood   . . . and no more invention
in this tongue, there is
                . . . no more invention in this tongue, there is
                . . . no more invention in this tongue
                    . . . and this room
and where this room came from
                    . . . on this ship
            . . . which whistles presents for the dark

                    . . . where
                no one's eyes - are

no one's eyes - and
no one's door is
           no one's door - and
sound is a connecting suite
through walls, this wall - my sleep . . . is a chamber
wench
a robber titus, manding band - I might not
wake
      I might
            not I . . .
                  I might just stay
inside this coward's inspiration - there is nothing
else
to work from, everything has been used

                  to gain some insight
from your end - what a carousel . . . a merriment of voice

what pleasing disfigurement of sense and reason . . . how
blank
this might be - the prettiest place along the canal
                        is this a night ship
for wasted boys to claim incomplete sonatas
and fractured hips
            where is the legacy
of a bitter fool when sleep lies flat - this beat -
this wretch
this dusted liquid heat, whose envy
circles baby revolution on bony seas
                  what a wavy hull
there is in sleepless time - this night - where I
can't go
not yet . . . don't take me
                  not in some bed which isn't mine - this
night . . .

Edwin Torres (New York)

New York Seizures
for Raymond R. Patterson

#1

I sit in a glass submarine
Watching contortion consume beauty:

as flesh inches toward dust and oblivion,
. . . *a-what-a-ya-wanna, eh!? a-what-a-ya-wanna!*
As flesh inches toward the next corner of tumult—
To where wrinkled octogenerians,
Spontaneous in their gloom,
Stagger-stab the grimacing city blocks
With lock-legged steps;
And broken winds exhale columns of creaking
Epilogues from eyes without age . . .

No dozer, no-doze city and never-wink wailer,
Babbling through your Benzedrine and beer!

#2

Now disguised as a street lamp,
I am whiplashed/whiplashed into serpentine ecstasy
By lush scenarios
By concrete choruses
        And asphalt furies:
By the snaking quarrel of bi-lingual taxi-cabs—

Where the night turns yellow!
Where New York gets mel-looow!

—And perspiring tenements:

Toombs for pre-people returning home
From mystical voyages to be somebody;

By the hover-clusters of chuckling midgets
Who hurl diabolical ringshouts under thunder-tears
Of Gleeful gods: Apollo, Shango, John Henry & Bobo—
And rocket naughty clichés at bronze brickhouses,
Headhunters
Plush stallions,
Stark-denyers of indentities,
Penis-flingers
Cunt-lubricators,
Sweetboys
& Blood-borrowers:

eenie meenie mynie mo las night/night befo
spin yo bottom shoot yo shot keep her 'n creep her
let me blues ya fo I lose ya let me try ya
'fo I buy ya I got the jones 'nnn if you got
the bones dick haarrddd as Chinese Arithmetic

ya know I ain't tawkin bout yo momma wit hu good
o soul . . . uh uhhh! uh uhhh! uh uhhhhhhh!

#3

The neighborhood nextdoor is hallucinating:
Woman says she saw a BlackJesus riding in WhiteHog
Wearing a Green jumpsuit and holding two BrownFoxes;
A platinum barrel of death stares into the stomach
Of a short-order cook demanding the cashregister & life—*to go!*
A gentleman who wears low profiles tells his woman
That she makes love like his best buddy;

A Puerto Rican speaks Voodoo with an African accent;
A European speaks African with a Spanish accent;
A West Indian yawns in Yiddish and curses in Arabic;
An African speaks English in silence;
A slave revolt occurs under the cover of a blackout;
Color-crossed lovers hold hands in cross-eyed Central Park;
Subway trains are flying nonStop to South Africa;
Harlem has received the Nobel Prize for Peace;
Mountain climbers are trying to scale the City Debt;
The Indians are hijacking the Empire State Building;
This winter's snow turns out to be co-caine.

#4

Lucid lumrous eye
        New York;
Luminous fragments,
        Like New Year's Eve tin-foils,
        Collect into an epidemic of flesh-ignited candles
That refuse to go out—
Even when the temperament gods of Con-Edison are comatose;

Whir-City, heat forest
Of memorable fevers,
        Asphalt icon:

Jezzibel mesmerizer,
Sleep-exempt entrancer;
I rap-prance my congratulations on the achivement of your
excellent
        madness,
On the triumph of your pretty contradictions;
I tap-dance my salutes through your basement of shuttles and
barbituates;

I clop-clop along your rib-cage of cobblestones;
I pee-pee in the wee-wee hours of your doorways;
I mee-lee in your disco-drudgery;
I be-me in your awesome amber:

> *No dozer, no-doze city & never-wink wailer,*
> *Babbling through your Benzedrine and beer!*

Eugene B. Redmond (St. Louis)

¡Hey Yo / Yo Soy!

Hey!
  Yo! . . .
      Yo! . . . *Yo!* . . .
 Hey-ey! . . . *Yo! / Yo!* . . .
           Yo! . . . *Yo!* . . . *Yo!* . . .
               Yo! / Yo! . . . *Yo!* . . .
 Hey-ey! . . . *Yo! / Yo!* . . .
        Yo! . . . *Yo!* . . . *Yo!* . . .
      Yo! / Yo! . . . *Yo!* . . . *Yo!* . . .
          Hey-ey! Yo! . . .
           ¡Yo Soy
             Puertorriqueño, Bro! . . .

That's Right, . . . *Ése*
  That's What I Say, Jefe
      Que,
I, too, Am *PuroPutoUnico,*
      Uniqueó, Ése
  Just Like You, Like You
      Just
  Like You, Ése
      Que
  I Am Me,
      Que
  I Am You
     As You,
  Am Me—
      Que,
    Hey!
    Yo!
  Yo Soy
    Puertorriqueño. Bro!
        Que,
  It Is A *"We"* Thing—

:A Whole, Huge
Nosotro Trip
that governs this Ship,
el Planeta Earth,
that gives Us Birth—
in MultíColors
ofthe Universe!
And,
Everything That I Be
You Be, Too!
Tambien,
Se
Dice, Así
Ése

BeCause
BecauseBecause
BecauseBecause
BecauseWhy?! . . .
BecauseBecause
BecauseBecause
BeCauseWhy?! . . .
Because of Love
of A Love so deep
deep
that still it seeps
seeps
within Us deep
deep,
yet still
it seeps . . .

Que Mis Raices Son
de Ése, Ése
Nativo Taino
Indijino
de Paraiso,
bailando rítmo
rítmo Africano,
Que Fué
Violado
por un
Anti-Cholo
Españolo:
Therefore, Latino
Therefore,
Why

um rush the page

My Hair grows
—*So*, Bro! . . .

¿ComprendeVu

What I'm telling You?! . . .

Que Soy
a Modern *Latin*
from *el Barrio Manhattan!*

¡¿Y, Que?! . . .

This, *Thing*,
RACiSM!!!
is an Unnatural schism
that makes You
part of a SyStem
that puts yoU
in its prisoN
For almost
NO Reason

¡¿Y, Que?! . . .

That allows
For KiLLing
Your Own!

Ése!

That allows
For KiLLing
Your Own!

'Tis, It's the
SeaSon . . .
for a good Reason
To Show Cause,

For What Cause! (a)—
You would KiLL
KiLLKiLL!!!
Your Own Brother, *Ése!*

Ése allí,
y
Ése allí . . .
Ése allí,
y
Ése allí . . .

ComprendeMí!!!—

Ése allí,
y
Ése allí . . .
Ése allí,
y
Ése allí . . .

> *ComprendeMÌ!!! . . .*
>> *Ése allí,*
>>> *y*
>> *Ése allí . . .*

Jesús Papoleto Meléndez *(New York)*

Flying over America

i'm flying home
           flying, flying, flying, flying
      flying home

this ancient land was once
not unified but free to be
whatever the sun shone upon
not furrowed by industry
nor ribboned by concrete
but simply a life path
trod by bare and moccasined feet

now from coast to coast,
from great lakes to gulf
there is the mechanical roar of engines
the boom of bombs
the staccato stutter of hand guns
the quiet binary clicking of computer and
the tortured cry of nature writhing
twisted by modernity

i am an african encased in aviated metal
surrounded by the sad contentment
of civilized progress anxious to maintain
its hegemony of coercion
as we fly forward into the future
unmindful of the feces we leave behind

intermittently dozing i dream
of appreciating the simple silence
of a heavy metal epoch rusting to dust
of meditating in the amber
of a muted spangled banner song

this land we jet across was ancient once
and though i know we can never again
atavistically return home

into a nostalgic past, still i long
to see this soil be ancient once more

unmolested
by a social order so unrepentant
in its disdain
for the womb
of our earthly environment
that only its death
can justify the manifest destiny
of this nation's existence

only death
can possibly cover the debt &
repay the cost of creating
this hubristic nation state
which so wantonly & methodically murdered red,
so avariciously & cruelly enslaved black

if this is truly one nation under god
then surely their god must be a devil

Kalamu ya Salaam *(New Orleans)*

beauty is moving us forward

I'm a Hip Hop Cheerleader

I'm a hip hop cheerleader
carrying hand grenades and blood red pom poms
screaming from the sidelines of a stage I built
afraid to part down the middle
for feminine riddles
raining words of proverbs
of prophets who never get heard
because the microphone is just another phallic
    symbol
that allows jack to be nimble
jack too quick
leaving jill with a man who can't climb a hill
and a bucket of spit
she can't drink or find her reflection
inside   she hides

inside crooked eyes of amber
allows her life to be slandered
if hip hop is conscious
we must change the standard
my womb-mate's been slandered
i planned her arrival
of letters and lyrics never sent to those lovers
who claim that they know her
but still blow her off as flunky
not a microphone flunky
fiending for a quick fix
not fast cars & hoe tricks
her mouth matrix is taped
hooked on phonics escaped
left her language for rape
so she ate her words
and became an instant interlude
a cute break between the music
when she was an electric lady
a black flower rhyme scheme romantic
a breathe and release tantric with five tongues
and no one
understood why her flow was so fast
asked to slow down
hesitate—never last

to the finish I'm gonna win this
all the DJs gon' spin it
when you're a woman
sometimes all you have is a minute

I'm a hip hop cheerleader
I buy all your records
despite the misogyny
not looking for the blood in me
respond to me
I feel molested   hip hop fondled me
I know the conscious brothas follow me
hollow me with half breaths
real emcees don't half step
but I never slept
took my poems and made food
put my babies in school   taught me
to wait for no one
never turn my back from the sun of man
I know all my fly mommas understand
got the rifle on my back
with a mic in my hand
I'll be your tubman compass
so we can map out this land
I'll be the air that you breathe
I'll be your number one fan
I'll scream the HEYs
I'll tolerate all your hoes
I'm a hip hop cheerleader

there she go
there she goes

self love freed me
despite all your rhymes with bitches
I know you need me
complete thee believe me
I see you growing in me
looking out from my belly
your rhyme schemes are telling
sang those lullabies to nelly
walking close to my edge like melle
doing cartwheels and air splits
u stage diving into white chics
when I got your hair pick
your weapon of choice
I chose my voice

'cause I only gotta quarter left
on this microphone meter
I got on a short pleated skirt

I'm a hip hop cheerleader

there she go
there she goes . . .

Jessica Care Moore *(Atlanta)*

kill the dj

without my lyrical wizardry
your vinyl would be
a maze of melted misery
cuz you can't see the genius of my poetry
which allows me to
freestyle
corrupt and beguile
stretch rhymes a mile
long as the millennium
which soars from my cranium
drives you insane like some bum on the block
as I bodyrock
then wreck your shop
cuz you ain't hip-hop
you a thief
best get with W.I.C.
cuz you need the relief
plus a new set of teeth
busy beefin 'bout a bogus blunt
duckin and dodgin
sportin gold plated fronts
but them shits is fake
like the wax in your crate
listen up cous cuz you might get it straight
as I penetrate
your most spiritual place
dishin out a taste
like jesus feedin masses
blind as a bat
wearin pitch black glasses
so you can't see me
don't get near me
better fear me

or I'll
wax your wax
tax your scratch
better suck a cat
or pet a bottle of heinz
cuz it's primetime
you stop thinkin you the man
can't grab your dick cuz it's stitched to your hand
performing reverse revolutions
which equals zero solutions
to your
two-bit bullshit ass sample
you label skill
ill like the virus
silly as that rabbit
crack addicted habit of scratchin away
talkin 'bout how you was the bomb back in the day
with your
limp dick whack ass party time rhymes
committin crimes
claimin you king
can't dance
can't sing
can't even read
then got the nerve to tell me what the fuck I need
beats you break
like the subway trains
different lines
but them shits sound the same
so pack your crates
and take the glove off your hand
talkin 'bout you king of the artform
and still eatin motherfuckin SPAM

Reg E. Gaines *(Jersey City)*

Ms. Cousins' Rap
to my Project Victory I Students

Deep Youth, you've got the Victory
and You are the One

From the very start
i tried to do my part

got to teach the history
so it will be no mystery

each day live up to your best
and God will do the rest
this is about more
than a book and a test

too many rhymin
how to hurt and to kill
let this drop
with the hip-hop:
Chill, be still, and heal
it's not about how many die
it's all about how many RISE

and when you call any sister
out of her name
you got to face madd blame
you want respect for your sister,
    daughter, and mother?
then hey, Respect
the sisters, mothers,
daughters of others.

before i stop
    with the hip-hop
and before i decline
    with the righteous rhyme,
gonna drop this on ya one more time

Hey, Yo!
the positive way is the only
way to go.
wanna git down
    with da true Git Down?
then open da Eye. Realize.
the way Up is the only way Out
    No Doubt!

Linda Cousins (New York)

all up in there

singin   shoutin   joinin fingers   love chain
rockin and waivin hands back and forth
clappin & screamin   *hallelujah!*

standin up on the word when it gets good
fannin   shakin they head   pumpin they fist
dancin in aisles
message comin in lyrics
tongue quick
so much conviction sometimes
u think it's the voice of God itself!
(u will be known by the fruit u bear)
children runnin to and from the bathroom
till somebody had enough and holla
sit yo narrow ass down
with just a fixin of the eyes
poutin   sneakin   eatin candy
talkin too much   sleepin   turnin
lookin at everybody who come through the door
worryin about what she got on
know she know better than to wear pants in God's house!
watchin who puttin what in the plate
prayin witcha eyes open
tryna see who catchin the spirit, and if they fakin it
meetin   greetin   shakin hands and huggin at the benediction
goin home talkin in the car then talkin at the table
then talking again on the phone about everything you saw
amen

Derrin Maxwell *(New York)*

Doin'

Everything is real
and like the ups and downs of goin round
can take a hectic pace
so screaming horns must set in place
new found vibes for the drums to ride
and with the flute and vocals flowin in
Jah's *Love Child*
Music steps on in
ridin hard on heavy bass chords and piano strides
that seem to soar through the atmosphere out into space
bringing us love and peace from many a place!

The whole trip of it is
you get what you give
Do you feel the energy rising
Can you hear the sound of thunder clap
as lightning strikes the sky with love

The mysterious musical magical sounds of words
have always enchanted those who listened and heard
the message in the beat
the rhythm in they feet
dancin/prancin
deep down to the planet's core
every time you come up to breathe
you gotta go back down for a little bit more

As a work song
this will help you through your nine-to-five
it's a blues tune that'll make you glad you still alive
a love song with an impression you'll have to hum
you know it's gon be funky when we get done
My mind moves a million miles a minute
sometimes I don't know just where to begin it
because Rap was here before I was . . .
so watch it!

Atiba Kwabena (*New York*)

The Trash Talker

(half the game is in the talk)

i'm the man when
the rock is in my hand,
my skills in high demand.
rich white boys own the NBA; i own the park
i run these courts from 5:30 p.m. to after dark.
my killer cross-over and quick first step
got defenders calling for help
fake 'em out they shoes, leave 'em crying the blues
i dazzle the masses with no look passes.
the skills i'm possessin
leave niggas stressin and guessin
what move i'm making next
my game too complex.
better ask somebody who you checking.
if I did slow motion demonstrations
of my smooth penetrations
you'd still be confused by my swift hesitations.
i lead you right . . . oops . . . catch you sleeping, change
directions, then take you left.
it ain't nobody . . . that can hold me!
i got mad handles, a stupid J, and crazy ups.

i'm the illest, my skills the realest
but ain't we both missing somethin?
you don't have game,
and i don't have no competition

the spectators love me and know me
by many names like
The man, Mr. Real Deal, Mr. Clutch
Cash Money, Skillz, Downtown Brown,
Showtime . . . and the way i'm always creating something
from nothing, doing incredibly fantastic
amazingly-impossible-and-unbelievable things,
some even call me god
but you know who i am. so act like you know
and stand back and take notes
as i take this game to a whole notha level.
watch me watch me watch me
i'm almost completely in the zone.
i'm going   i'm going   i'm going   i'm gone

Howard Rambsy II (State College, PA)

Owed to Eminem

I'm the Slim Lady the real Slim Lady
the real Slim Lady just a little ole lady
uh-huh
uh-huh
I'm Slim Lady the real Slim Lady
all them other age ladies
just tryin to page me
but I'm Slim Lady the real Slim Lady
and I will
stand up
I will stand up

I assume that you fume while the
    dollar bills bloom
and you magnify scum while the
    critics stay mum
and you anguish and languish runnin
    straight to the bank
and you scheme and you team with
    false balls so you rank
at the top and you pop like the jury the
    victim
the judge

but the ghetto don't trip to the light
   stuff you flip
or the chain saw you skip
with
the rope and the knives and that bunk
   about tying who up like a punk in the
back of the trunk
or that dope about mothers and wives
   give you worse than a funeral hearse
fulla
hickies and hives
you fudge
where you come from or whether you
   mean it
the shit you can't make without
   sycophants see'n it
but nobody's dumb
enough to believe that you grieve
   because folks
can't conceive that you more than a
   moron
or why would you whore on
the hole in your sole?

At this stage of my rage
I'm a sage so I know how you blow
to the left then the right and you maim
every Columbine game about "No!
   Cuz he's white!"

But I am that I am
and I don't give a damn
and you mess with my jam
and I'll kill you
I will!

And if you insist listenin close for a dis
then you missin more than the gist in
   this
because
I gotcha pose by the nose

I hear how you laugh and cut corners
   in half
And I see you wigglin a line that's not
   flat
while you screwin around with more
   than all that

But I am that I am
and I don't give a damn
and you mess with my jam
and I'll kill you
I will!

Don't tell me you pissed or who's
    slashin whose wrists
or pretend about risks
to a blond millionaire
with a bodyguard crew that prey
behind shades and that pay
to get laid—What?
What's that about fair?

I'm not through with you!

I'm the bitch in the bedroom the
    faggot
you chump I'm the nigga for real so get
    ready to deal
I'm tired of wiggas that whine as they
    squeal
about bitches and faggots and little
    girls too!
I'm a Arab I'm a Muslim I'm a
    Orthodox Jew!

I'm the bitch come to take you
I'm the faggot to fake you
outta the closet
outta the closet
fulla the slime you deposit

for   fun

rhyme and run
you the number one
phony-ass gun

Oh! I am that I am
and I don't give a damn
but you mess with my jam
and I'll kill you
I will!

(Hey, Shady
you know what I'm sayin

I'm just playin!
You know I love you!)

Sincerely,

Slim Lady

June Jordan *(Berkeley)*

A Psychoalphadiscobetabioaquadoloop

All those
   Liquid love affairs,
Blind swimmers
   Trusting rumps.
We wiggled,
   Imagining water.
Wet, where was
   The One?
Never mind Atlantis
   And the promise
Of moving pictures,
   A lit candle
In the window
   Of our conscious minds.
Those who danced,
   Pretending to swim
Underwater,
   Did so out
Of pure allegiance.
   Some wore snorkels
Made with
   The waistbands
Of funky underwear,
   Others wet suits
With clothes pins
   Clamped to their noses,
Air-tight as
   Black Power handshakes.
Rump-by-rump,
   The strings attached
To our thangs were
   Reeled into The Deep.
Rhythmic as fins,
   Schools of P signs

Flapped and waved
    Like flags.
One nation
    Under a groove.
No one held their breath
    In the flashlit depth.
No one sank.

Thomas Sayers Ellis (Cleveland)

rapid transit

someone lights a saxophone
and the marvelous
breath of God
sweeps the subway

in my head I hear Baraka
return the symphonic burst
runnin color
all across the steps of history

callin tunes and changes
til nothin remains
what we want to believe

subway becomes
elevator
scattin til the floor drops out
the sax a giant key
tunin the player's hands

the suspended world
shakes itself and rolls over
pedals and machine parts
flashin 'til they sputter and catch

or spark and die
as Baraka leans back in
riffin the brass idiom

narratin our bestial
beginnins to mad
modernity and on through
the channels of space

inside sound
I cling to the axis

> vulnerable to speed
> but I must love the ride; otherwise
> the Word would not invade this body so

Nzadi Z. Keita (*Philly*)

hold it steady

on the one: the same
minimalist row
to hoe. a black man
cowskin sweats on the side
of a dirt road. screams.
his obsessive conk
goes back to an afro.
back again.

baby
baby
baby
    baby
    baby
    baby
        baby
        baby
        baby

this is an in-pocket work song.
hold it steady while I hit it.
(justonce)
do you reckon that's getting it?
(thenoncemore)
no machine quick tapping
just the sucking of that same
sweet plain beat.

on the one: strip
mining the syncretic
hole / the doors opening
like your nose.
what's my name?
you know my mama
didn't call me that.

say grace. then fry up this urban
fatback sweeter than butter.

psychotic
    black-eyed peas
on the side.
for
dessert you can have my cakes
& eat them too.

hold it steady
baby
baby
baby
hold it steady
(umph / thenoncemore)
hold it steady while i hit it
all the way
        home.
you take
the bottom.

Honorée Fanonne Jeffers (*Talladega, AL*)

Conversation with Duke Ellington and Louis (Pops) Armstrong

Dear Pops,
Dear Duke,
Let me introduce to you
a woman who plays
the clarinet and who
does mean a thing
'cause she's got that swing.

Her name's Doreen
of New Orleans
and can she swing!
Doo wop Doo wop Doo wop.
I tell you Duke, Merlin
must have jinxed
her clarinet 'cause
those folks,
stomping, screaming
and swaying
on Jackson Square
surely look entranced,
under a spell, as if

Marie Laveau
had left her tomb
to add some voodoo
to the swing . . .
Doo wop, Dor een!

Pops,
are you listening too?
Here's your woman-girl
not a Billie or a Bess,
but she's nonetheless
body-soul
of that man Mississippi.
Doo wop Dor een Doo wop!
Awesome, jazzy clarinetist
of New Orleans
blowing her magic wind
on Jackson Square.
She's blowing us . . . !
So good!

Carmen D. Lucca *(New York)*

For Lady and Prez
to Shirlena Harris

When Prez plays the blues
I hear Lady Day walking
out of the night club
dressing room
of Lester Young's saxophone

with tears
        in her veins
beneath an umbrella of rain
among her people
on dimly lit streets
of pain
dealers are hustling
        counterfeit rainbows

Theodore A. Harris *(Philly)*

breath

I

spinning ritual into fusion.

emancipated from treble clefs,
c-notes and quotes from men
i never met. de(a)f.

II

i am archie shepp and wyclef

jean combinant and gene harris
in my blood. one love.
there are no graveyards,
only ancient boulevards.

III

i am the dark eyes of sunken lullabies.

the child of "you don't knows,"
if i could's and promises
never broken, simply deferred.
i am my father's word.

IV

breath.

V

i am the depth of shadows.
the image upon brick walls,
the thump of basketballs,
the pound of black fists
the lisp of stereotypes. the night,
the day, and all that 365 circumstances
bring. i sing. cuz black folk do.

VI

i watch like the pavement does.

i am the grass struggling to grow
between the cracks. of hit 45″ singles
i am the backs, of hits of crack

i am the voice saying
this is mama's television—
gone. i am the pawn
broker, born of king and queen.

VII

and still i sing.

Daniel Gray-Kontar (Pittsburgh)

The Flow

Be-bop flows
extends and bends into
hip-hop
heads drop
feet stomp
it rocks
the spot
it'll groove ya ass
whether you like it
or not

You see that
hip-hop flow
is be-bop
in a lyrical rage
verbal assassins
taking center stage
heads crackin open
in the cipha
blunted reality
taking levels higher
and higher

It's that microphone check
1-2, 1-2
microphone check 1-2

Check the break beat
dancing feet
somersaulting in
the ring
like Miles got his thang
and Dizzy's got his swang
while Ella's scat-a-tat-tat

hits hard
like that
Boom Bap
Boof Baf
Dat Skat
I know you dig it
when I kick it, baby
'cause maybe just maybe
Miles' horn
will rock on and on
to the break of dawn
and coat the throats
of folks
like
Black Thought
and Q-Tip
creating verbal power
to devour
your soul
and all the while
freestyle
is a collective improvisation
as Coltrane blows staccato
and vibrato
into KRS' ear
like a whisper

It's the hipster
baddest baddest thing
we got
we got soul sonic forces
flowing layering rupturing
narrating orating innovating
skillz
and stylez
to be heard
and be fly
like Bird
Charlie
P-P-P-P-Parker
is so Digable
the planet rocks
and conscious cool
hard bops
not knocks
but inspires the funk
to revive and redesign
blended blue

like Guru
with riffs and shit
Yeah, it's jazz
re-blended
and extended
never never never
ending

Lynne d Johnson (New York)

Bebop Trumpet

for Arthur Brown

Ain't too many poets can quote a bebop riff
Catwalk a fence through Dizzy's moon-eyed smile
Sip *Bitches Brew* off the rim of Miles' blue/black lips
Ride a neon funk with Trane into a back alley night
and not give ah fuck 'bout destination
Ain't too many poets can do that
Find a *Love Supreme*
in the mouth of ah red-light night stalker pregnant with blues
Chase a *Yardbird* 'round ah sugar shack
Wake up the next morning an' be ah trumpet
spitting defiance in the eye of ah bloodshot sun
Be they own rhythm/song
Slow grind with ah barbedwire dream
Lick laughter from tears
Take they womens straight—no chaser
Speak to the world in mystic tongues
Look at death as a missing part of life's puzzle
Ain't too many poets can quote a bebop riff
Ain't too many poets can do that

Layding Lumumba Kaliba (New York)

conjugation of the verb: to blow

heyyyyyy yo!

you shoulda but
you wouldn't
wasn't like
you couldn't
if you wanted to

you woulda
an' you know I know!

you can only
write in phonics
you only
speak eubonics
readin books
is just moronic
'cause you told me so!

you can't spell
what you rap
think studyin's
a trap
an' the teachers'
full of crap
they don't know how it go!

it was later
steada now
when?
insteada how?
didn't do things
when you coulda
you began to blow!

tryin to look jiggy
ridin round the city
rappin to the pretties
'bout life and you don't know
chillin steada learnin
connin steada earnin
jivin and connivin
far as you could go!
messin with the cuties
doggin all the bootie
never did your duty
home, you sure was low

'cause you didn't know
your game is "to blow"

high enough to
fire a rocket
wind whistlin
in your pocket

don't know life
so you mock it
frontin like you know

poppin crackin
getting high
your best years
is cloudin by
did you ever
reach the sky?
man, just look at you!

now your wants
just hurt your feelins
and your needs
have got you stealin
and your ego
got you dealin
ain't nothin you can do!

you blew!
got
to
start
your life
brand new

'cause
the life
you had
you blew!

Fredrica Africa Payne (New York)

The Creed of a Graffiti Writer

for TCK, FSH, NVS, URN, WAS, 5MH, 2DX

We strike at night
the streets of New York
is our canvas
We hide in the shadows
when the pig patrol strolls by
the moon gives us our
only source of light
We are The Addicts of Aerosol

The Krylon Can Clan
The Rusto Patrol
We are the German tip spraying
backpack wearing
black book carrying
magnum pilot tagging
the wack toy buffers
We are The Brigade of Bombers
mounting on our midnight mission
of colorized madness
the color blending
spray paint and
mind melding maniacs
We are the ghetto Picassos
the modern day Matisses
the artistic Shakespeares
that tear white walls in half
We are The Street Canvas Killers
with one quick splat
of an ultra flat black
with silver outlines and
yellow highlights perfected
during 3 a.m. night skylines
We are the crews that redecorate
building walls with wildstyles
burning people's imagination
with motions of the can
the walls wailed words of life
through sight of krylon colors
on the streets of New York
We bomb city blocks
rocking throw-ups on top
of window sills
while standing on top of
garbage cans
We are the ones who set
Bronx-Brooklyn expeditions
in traditions of nomads
We go where no man's can
has sprayed on walls before
We are the underground tunnel turnstile
hoppers that bomb
posters with one light being our guide
Our names are found on
high rises and highways
bridges and building roofs
We are The Bandits of Burners
our plans are waterproof

shockproof and foolproof
We are The Tye Dye Tone
Tint Marauders that write
Graffiti Manifestos
on black walls with
a silver Uni, SG-7 and
white Pentel markers
We mark the many lands
and train stations
Our tags rag black books and cardboard
scratched on windows and train doors
stickers slapped over any motherfucker
you had beef with
only in self-defense
We are The Graffiti Gurus
that spray silver spots on blackness
that become stars on the walls of galaxies
We gaze at our glossy words
and lose ourselves in arrows and 3-D shadows
We are The 12oz Prophets
that write prophecies with
our hieroglyphics that help
humans understand us
It is simply the love
of seeing our name on the wall
It is the symbolic value
of feeling important in a world
we are lost in
It is the outlet that introduces
art into our way of thinking
We wear baggy jeans
hat to the back
and army fatigues
when we venture on our
trip of blending bombing wonderland
The street is our canvas
when art brushes and stencils
don't matter only liquitechs and spray paint
the toxic aroma that entered our bloodstream
on nights when we froze our fingertips
writing upside down with the can
when finishing a powerhouse
Feel the wrath of Graff
when society calls us
vandals and delinquents
That's why your child wants
to be just like us
We bomb your door to tell

you our name
It's a shame you erased our
high rise artistic motion trains:
the Far Rockaway-Lefferts A
the outside D, B, and Q in Brooklyn
the Coney Island F
the Canarsie-Broadway Junction L
the J, M, and the Z
over the Williamsburg Bridge
the N and the R in Astoria, Queens
the 1 and the 9 in Washington Heights
the 2 and the 5 in the Bronx
the New Lots 3
the Jerome 4
the Westchester 6
and the Flushing purple 7 train
Now we reign on your law
the Ink Scribe scribbles on your forehead
then pronounces you hip hoply dead
the 4th Son of Hip Hop
overshadowed by
technic table microphones
and Puma gray suede complexion tone
There is no Hip Hop without
Graffiti only Rap
So we wrap our hands
around cans becoming one
Our motions are studied
by plagiarist anthropologists
making money off our art
the sprits on clean canvas can
be hazardous to minds
when eyes can't understand
the buck wildstyle alphabet
sunrises call for travels
homeward bound
We are the ones that make
the *clikclakclikclakclikclakclikclak*
sound with the can on new land
when a tag could get our asses shot
We are the artistic poets
that perform magic with spray paint
and just call ourselves writers
Graffiti Writers

Steven Bonafide Rojas (New York)

Sonido Ink(quieto)*

Incamos a sonidos recreidos
entre páginas y plumas,
feathers spray painting walls.

We are the music of stories
rippling from pens
that send bassy vibrations
from floor to *tambor*,
refracting brass sensations
like grid-iron light,
sliding down strings
that cut the edges of night.

We rise over two-flats,
skyscrapers, liquor stores.
Our acrobatic musical scores
jump, dodge, skip in plurals
like *niños* playing hopscotch
in front of murals—
a graffiti of limbs. They are
satellites with their own
songs and prisms of flight.

We are caught
between cornfields
and prickly pears.
We swear
ink bleeds sounds
that last for centuries
waiting to be found.

Somos un sonido ink(quieto)
(inquieto, inquieto, inquieto).
Our own urban corridos
buscados y prohibidos
whisper from sewer caps,
steam rising to a snap
and hiss. We kiss anxious pitches,
flip the switches,

Never wait
for permission to wake our dead,

*Sonido Ink(quieto)—Restless Sound (Sonido Inquieto) with a play on the word "ink."

make sure they're fed,
bellies filled with *empanadas*
coaxing *carcajadas*,
bones cracking and cackling
in a hip ska, noisy Norteña,
a funky punk, punky funk
that refuses to be sunk
beneath any one's foot.

Our roots are restless,
clicking across kitchen floors,
pounding on doors to our own
streams of consciousness.
Somos gritos reclaiming our central axis *mitos*
que nos enseñan andar
truth our praxis
in a world that wants to spin
without us, lose us in the vortex
of inequity, passivity.
pero somos el central axis,
speaking truth, our praxis.

But we mix bilingual syllables
into bass and treble decibels,
drink *vasos de* ink
and bowls of sound
to feed the beat
that scorches the quiet of defeat.
We are boisterous and loud
so the clouds can hear us
shout jade and Mayan swirl
unplugged or turned up, electric,
brought to you digital or hi-fi.
Create and stay alive,
increible, nunca invisible,
increible, nunca invisible,
ink(quieto), ink(quieto), ink(quieto).

Brenda Cárdenas and Aidé Rodriguez (Chicago)

it was the music that made us

because I am   it's a race thing trip

I am asian   america
see who I am   look at me

fine black hair
almond shaped brown eyes
skin the color of peril
make me
the perpetual foreigner
what kind of FOB are you?
chinese or japanese
as if they were the only asians
vincent chin died
mistaken identity
cuz you know
all chinks look alike
but my armor is different
I'm the new FOB

                go back to your own country
what country?

I am hmong
               edward said
don't call me oriental
I am not a rug
for you to step on
because I am suppose to kow tow
on my knees
so my forehead touches the floor mat
              geisha
I mean
              china doll
I mean
              lotus blossom
I mean
              passive submissive exotic slant-eyed slut
I will not be   miss saigon
              soon yi
              yoko ono
              lucy liu
kissing ally mcbeal
don't make me your angel
charlie
I'm already one from the island
hey bond   james bond
I don't want to be your girl
cuz me only speak mee-nay-so-ta   yah
that's why I didn't go
to the university of caucasians lost among asians
to shoot the canon
with joy luck and woman warriors

keep your chin up, frank
and don't war with your writer sisters
aim for the blue green hazel violet plastic eyes
of kristi yamaguchi instead
that sister is blind
from the white picket fence teeth
of nancy kerrigan
and tell lisa ling
don't settle for a view
get a perspective
but not like connie chung
that will be our secret

america   railroads
america   laundry
america's chinese
america   home of the brave
america   sugar canes
america   concentration camps
america's japanese
america   land of the free
america   wonder bra and corsets
america   plastic surgery and liposuction
america's   demonization of women
don't lecture me about the savage practice of foot binding

from hollywood to bollywood
don't be a kung fu sellout
                    jackie chan
                    chow yun fat
where for art thou   jet li
if you must die
get the girl first
and don't be demasculinized

I show you   america
I am asian
because you won't let me
be an American

Chong Xiong (St. Paul)

Grasshopper

I turn my head and say, *Ah, grasshopper.*
I turn my head and say, *Ah, grasshopper,*
in imitation of the master who teaches

David Carradine that life is a series
of mountains to be destroyed
or resurrected in the imagination, or
a blade of grass atop which titters
a water drop that sticks
to the hind legs
of an insect
that flits
across grass as if across water.

Water-crawler, with legs so light,
body so weightless that it
lifts water to it, does not sit
on the oily surface,
glosses surface,
like a balloon
whose belly
is lighter than the air
around it. Translated, it goes
in and through and out; in and through
and up in a cloth bubble that takes us
around the world in a fraction of eighty days;

the Himalayas, the hemispheres below us
    like a chain of glass beads; the Indies East and West
        in the seismic tremor of lifting a hand to the breeze; in the
        ease with which a world is glossed. The huge wave of
    an arm across a distant horizon; the gesture *here is*
where it all begins.

But the fortieth day finds our man Jesus
in the desert, darkness settling him,
the light around him glowing,
refracting to show
the most

beautiful angel,
the great wings beating still,
the land spread before him, a new
world panorama. Yours
if you'll love me, the light
breathes.

We know the story: He eventually returns
on a donkey to the city that will kill him.
Martyrs always get it in the end,
but do grasshoppers?

I turn my head and say,
Ah, grasshopper.
I turn my head
and say, *Ah,*
grasshopper.

Danielle Legros Georges *(Boston)*

Grace

Eyes open in the womb. The struggle arrives to turn darkness into
light. Dangling on the wings of the Phoenix. The creative process
begins to turn ugly. Vandalizing and robbing graves of child prodigies
turning into serious discussions of Mass Murder and the therapeutic
value of Saturday morning shopping sprees. The betrayal of genius is
burning at the stake. The spider descends. The violence is always there.
The web embraces us all. More insidious than drugs. More pleasurable than
sex. Slightly entangled. Slightly confused. That possible criminal element
awakens you to the terror and loneliness of running into the silent
pain of someone else looking to you for answers. Glamorous and well
financed pools of blood profiling on neighborhood corners while
smiling at and tempting the boldest gangsta rap

The wealth we squandered on poor excuse and starving lines of poetry
inspired by the tenderness of your smile healed me, cleansed me of my
indifference to the Holy Scriptures should have told us something about
being children of God in all this Madness, against all these odds of too
intense and too delicate to be real lovers in real times. The wind, the
water, the waves so natural in our hands. Falling on notes and images
forever caressing the Full Moon and laughter too strong to be forgotten
on opening nights and wanting to be a big hit. Run . . . Run . . . Run . . . to
the birth, to the growth, to the experience of harmony so wise and peace-
ful desires to go back to the beginning and try to be good to yourself
and others . . . are searching too!

Umar Bin Hassan *(New York)*

The Low End

Bass was
36′ Lo chinos
and a sweatshirt
lamping on an aerosol wall
way passed 2:00 in the morning
you and I

it was the music that made us

so close to breaking ice
at thirty-three and a third

Bass was
bailing after buses
looking like extras from *Juice*
with empty backpacks
tinkling like high hats
screaming
Yo!
Yo!
at the driver not hearing
leaving us just hollering
('cause something made us want to)
running through cold semesters
without books
building our knowledge
the way the flows broke down
off album covers
and Mario Bauzá liner notes
sliding through the meaning
of *manteca*
taking flicks flicks
to document us
beaming
young and rugged
up
from the bottom
of forty-fever madness

as we do or die daily,
do or die,
we were brothers
you
and
I

Bass was
Hey, Chacho—
I call you son
because you
shine like one!
My brother
from another mother
cool
was born
and reborn
nightly;

sirens and saxophones
singing
into guarded East Side nights
'Cause if it wasn't for the music
there would've been no reason
we should have
a place called
home.
If it wasn't for the music
we would've never even came with:
I got love for you,
I love you,
man, *I love you*
or gave up those embraces
we called
"pounds."
If it wasn't for the music
we would've frozen up
in blue funk solitude
passing our last
hieroglyphic breaths
through Swisher Sweets.
It was
the beats.
It was
the music
that made us,
do or die daily,
do or die,
we were brothers,
you
and
I

Tomás Riley *(San Diego)*

rep/resent

word life / vs. verses where words urge murder / curses / criminal cultjams /
sub (liminal) sub (machine gun) / break beats / beat. break. /
gynocastrate w. BITCH razors / masturbate hate w. nickel plate triggerlingus /
nigger mortis tongues / ready. aim. (check 1 check 2) / double-barreled
djembe juba / fubu juju / cracklaced fufu / healers in drag w. heaters

   rep/resent w.
semiautomatic

BOOM (b bap)
boom (BAP   bap)
BOOM (b bap)
boom (BAP   bap)

liquor store bag men in / brown bags / nickel bags / body bags / stagolee
scions in voodoo skullies / bully bullets doggy style kindergarten bébés /
melee mouthed mic fiends / exhale pipe dreams on wax / life bootlegged for
timberlands / steel toe steppinfuckits / fetchin buckets of platinum
bullshit / for label pimps / 4 color pulp publications / for reps

rep/resent w.
semiautomatic
BOOM (b bap)
boom (BAP bap)
BOOM (b bap)
boom (BAP bap)

fatigued thinkers content to blend in / paramilitary gang bang slang / slung
through head phones / run trains on redboned war / scratchin off crabs /
catchin (gun) claps / clips loaded in tape decks / dicks loaded in harpoon
grooves / pluto bound sound bites / necks bled white / till heads are husks /
boombaps busk for bloodlust / adjust aim for wind (falls)

rep/resent w.
semiautomatic
BOOM (b bap)
boom (BAP   bap)
BOOM (b bap)
boom (BAP   bap)

mic stand auto rape / snuff love on audio tape / automated baaaaad niggers /
w. plantation specifications / radio station(ary) content / of
radio-friendly (fire) remixes / riddling helixes / w. pay style dirge jams /
murder-us flows in / battles kept real by / nielsen's mouth pieces / mouth
peaces but act wild / hide soul in crack vials / crack smiles behind gun
sights / say cheese

rep/resent w.
semiautomatic
BOOM (b bap)
boom (BAP   bap)
BOOM (b bap)
boom (BAP   bap)
                    BOOM

Douglas Kearney (Minneapolis)

2G (Another Millennium Poem)

Why we so worried 'bout 2G
while we still wallowin? like swine
n d xcrement of 1G's history.
D colorline still binds our brains
like rusty, dirt colored Antebellum chains.
Tryin' 2 get 2 d future b4 reconcilin' your past
is like puttin' on clean draws b4 washin' your ass.
A new coat of paint can hide old wood,
but it doesn't make it any stronger,
like age isn't d only parent 2 wisdom.
D mere reality of a Y2K bug is a trope
of man's nnate ability 2 fuck up a wet dream,
or d foolishness of creatin' an animal
2 b a biodegradable garbage can,
then turnin' around & makin' a ham sandwich from it.
Tryin' 2 kiss d sky w/marijuana is like
tryin' 2 call God w/BellSouth,
your modem is not transcendentally compliant.
Time's only value is how u use it,
& evolution means more than goin' 2 d moon
or d ability 2 cause mass destruction.
We have grown out but not up
4 we have nvested n everything but our souls,
puttin' more n2 d bank of man than d bank of God.
U can take d man out of d millennium,
but can u take d millennium out of d man?
Or, will he mpregnate 2G w/his
still stank, spoiled, pus filled sperm?
Oh yeah, happy new year.

C. Leigh McInnis (Jackson, MS)

enter(f*#@ckin)tained

You want to be entertained
You want to be entertained
With the bloodstains
That caused my words of pain
You want to be enter(f*#@ckin)tained?

Like promotional ads depicting weapons/you don't know how to shoot
Or like flyers and CD covers/showing cowards as criminals or punk-ass
    lovers
hiding under suspenders/too big to fit in closets

does the bitch you rhyme of/resemble what you in denial of

in need of spirituality/but perpetuating criminality/within a hip-hop
community

automatic negative verbal acrobatics/rap industry's traumatic

mental genocidal suicide/thru rap verbal homicide

I need poetry as shock therapy to revive me!

Evil you glamorize/we patronize self-suicide

Don't need no knife; gun; iron pipe; bat & chain

(like on the previous cover of a rap magazine)

When verbal cyanide emanates from the brain

Perpetratin a lifestyle you should not sustain

Cuz you just want to *enter(f*#@ckin)tain.*

That was for the punitive rappa n uh/the ho with a flo/but if you're not one

Then my eyes are distressed/cuz you *dress* like one

Da positive I caress/but gotta get this sh*t offa my chest.

Like *cum pouring out of an ass beaten black n blue*

I disdain how you like hearing Niggro words for shock value

Like a poem with dope words but a whack beat won't sell

But a whack rap with dope beats sells: real well.

Or like a female rappa who knows no other/way of selling work w/o her body

Over-sexy, repelling, smelling (but it's still selling)

Promotin punany and dickellect instead of intellect

Or a rapper who makes me not laugh/who knows not how to create the craft

Without boring terms like *nigga* and *gangsta*

Programmed into his and her language to each other

Your lips form into a mouth-flex/for your next/ego-trip skit

Like puppets, buttons easily pressed/an audience, missing the message

While you taint my lines with your cheer/from your reactionary ear/my
words are clear

With this poem you be *enter(f*#@ckin)tained* but cook your brain

With whack-rap killa-gangsta refrains/I maintain: if *some* of the content/of
our music

is any indication of a people/who were once saved

Then Nat Turner is turning/over in his grave.

Do you/listen to/the words/you dance to?

The same tired bullsh*t, why buy & support it?

Must our music become *sick* for some to like it?

Record labels/with names that're evil/obsessions with blood & death—that I
don't get

I balk/at your mafia guntalk/your mouth needs some salt

I'ma fill it with caulk/just B da youngstaz you are

not the prankstaz who walk/with that fake mobstaz talk.

You spend your last dollar on the latest CD/called *I KILL ME* on *Negative
Energy*

You make *(c) rap* artists' pockets phatter/your new slavemaster

Whose rhymes reveal sickness/hypocrisy in psychology/insanity of mentality

mental illness/and false reality/giving beatdowns like vigilantes

The people who died in the crush at City College
Shoulda gave us more knowledge
Who'd wanna be heard every day on Hot 97?
That sounds (1) boring, and (2) absurd
I ain't hung up on myself, like that's my word.
RAKIM/Lauryn Hill/Black Thought/Mos DEF/3rd Message
Doug-E Fresh/KRS/Bahamadia/Ursula Rucker/Dead Prez
Erykah/De La Soul/The Roots/The Grandmasters
Chuck D to Kid Capri/Kool Herc to Kool Mo Dee
Even Common Sense will tell you/Mo money, Mo cash is redundant
But it's okay/don't complain/U wanna be *enter(f*#@ckin)tained*.
Come with the real/can't conceal/what I feel
Even for the "arrogant" poet
Who entered a poetry slam but lost the contest
Then challenged the other to see who's the best
But what is this?!/New rule: I slam/you lose/We Duel?
What a bullsh*t epidemic poetic precedent!
Like a fanatic poetic president?
You actin like a baby/crazy without a bottle
now you 'bout to topple/just cuz you lost a battle
Think you the boss?! That slam you lost
was your friggin Middle Passage/to remind you, it's about the *message*
not your flow, your ego, nor the contest!
Think you hot/but you a poet who forgot
If actions speak louder than words/then yours do not.
Some spoken words gotcha goin absurd
By some who claim to be wordsmiths of the Word
I be the locksmith like the martial artist
Who knows the craft/unlockin the *fake* hold you have
Over your listener/with your fake wrath.
SLAMS don't bring reparations
SLAMS don't win liberation
SLAMS don't kill MUMIA's death penalty
SLAMS don't give legitimacy to poetry
Don't let SLAMS cause division among you & me
While we *entertain* them with our soliloquy
To the poet and the rapper/to bring this together
Know the ledge in the lyric/n keep the message in the music
Buy pozitiv rap
and *(#@X*)* a PHAT TRACK IF THE LYRICS ARE WHACK!

Nzinga Regtuinah Chavis (Jersey City)

it was the music that made us

Motherseed

I approach the canvas like a birth
An empty beginning on a blank page
A discovering of secrets revealed in me
Think of a color, any color
The color of the day, the moment
Lay it down
Brush it across the virgin space
As far as it will go
Staring at it, sometimes hours at a time
It becomes a meditation
Draws me into its world
Fantastic
Violent
More than I can see
And there,
In that little patch of life
In that amorphous initiation
A road of associations leads me
Into its labyrinth of imagery
The montage unfolds
Dream and metaphor surface into form
Gather momentum on a journey I cannot reverse
Lay the cadmium next to cerulean, pull it
Until it jumps out at me
Soft fade magenta into violet, accept it
Gently settling into me
Then
The final labor
Feverish push of form and meaning
Turbulent sky and funnel wind
Breathing and communion
Open mind and free space
A focusing that calls itself forth
Unstable earth and solid fire
That demands to be seen for itself, by itself
Boundaries in personal dimensions
On their own terms.

Sandra María Esteves (New York)

Wake Up, My Little Pretties

All 21st century artists maintaining below status quo levels of mass intelligence claiming to keep it real but it's remedial must find hiding for the veil is being lifted leaving only the gifted prophet MCs and poets to be authentic informants reporting in ghetto spirit hoods transmitting from interstellar galactic allies currently on standby to assist us through the earth changing shifts and martial law predators upon us. These caucus mountain wizards of fear can't hold me cause I'm so much more than I've been told BEHOLD and watch me poetically sabotage reptilian republic attempts to crush me while I metaphysically orchestrate the oldest human bone on the planet—come back activating watermelanin wild seed psychic attack like the spook who sat by the door. All ye sleeping giants AWAKE and settle the score igniting total memory recall defense against this waging war unplugging from the matrix seeking truth deep within grasshopper, let the connecting begin with our intergalactic freedom fighting ghetto gangster comrades ready on cue who don't flinch and show no love as martial law killer cops taste their own blood when organized thugs bang-bang against the beast. This is more than premonition, it's my female intuition to protect whenever the hairs on the back of my neck begin to stand. I've been clocking every step of your juvenile existence attempting to erase me makes me amplify my resistance, grab open mikes announcing RENEGADE REBEL! Taking acquisition to another level 'cause we ain't going nowhere and we won't submit to shit like New World Dis/O(r)der agents returning to desk duty switchamaroozie tricky moving court cases to Albany for cowboys of the hooded cloth with badges getting off on spilling family blood in the street—Fuck turn the other cheek! Better not sleep, but keep an open eye for Nat Turner resurrected live action crew coming to you multiplied laying in the cut masters of disguise like now you see me now you don't! I'm crafty: blinkity-blink-blink wiggle my nose make something happen nasty with a pen and a mike my gun plus a samurai ginsu tongue sprayin some savin some slaying ones who hate me 'cause my skin absorbs the sun—CLICK, the melanin gift ability to shape shift into Goddess from bitch a.k.a. superwitch wordslinger truth bringer message in the metaphor information bell ringer for the final hour (don't forget this country rose to power on plantation slave economy)—fast forward: bloody fingerprints leading to the prison industrial complex, yet simply put, Ain't shit changed but the scenery . . . So don't get stuck in the platinum poppy fields—Wake up, my little pretties, wake up!

Liza Jessie Peterson (New York)

nommo
how we come to speak

the first word was
incomplete

the next
though clearer

lacked balance

and was followed
by the third

who gave rise to
us

born of clay
water
fiber
drum

but before a generation
passed we children
of the third word
knew how to take
this gift of language
contort it crimson
and sew it to our teeth

how we mangle
this tongue that needs
constant translation
reiteration
clarification
purification
release

we require it to be
a constantly changing chameleon
a hypnotist, a con man, a cheat

with words we manufacture demons
who devour souls and erase memory
look at how often we honor speech
that can make us hate
that can cause us to deny
our mothers
our brothers
our self

we have articulated
a deadly weapon

that subverts knowledge
and betrays faith

so how now do we
scrape the slime from between our teeth
and rinse out the sourness of decay

how now do we
put our tongues back
in our mouths

again learn to listen
with more than ears

at once try to speak
with more than tongue

devorah major (San Francisco)

spaNglisH

Mami is part of that silent tribe that didn't bother to learn English
because she had my father and her children or any willing stranger
to translate for her. *En casa* she demanded that my brothers and
I speak Spanish and we did, but street life began choking our
Spanish early on. We had to negotiate ghetto streets with English
in our mouths to avoid any complications, like not being understood,
possibly being teased and getting into a fight.

The transitions from home to street and English to Spanish, had us
beat and break up both languages to the point where they meshed
into something all of its own—Spanglish. We could not be burdened
with what did not cart us between both worlds. Spanglish kept it
all together somehow—Mami and home and everything out there
en las calles triste, as she called them.

Lissette Norman (New York)

New Boogaloo

There's a disco ball
spinning starlight
on a new boogaloo

tell Sonia
that the bombs
are ready to drop
that we got *soneros*
ready to sing
to those flowers
that did not survive
Operation Green Thumb

tell Dwight
that the renaissance
he's been looking for
is ready to set up shop
that dreams
are starting to take
responsibility for themselves

tell Marcito
that painters are eating *piraguas*
sitting on milk crates
and kickin it with poets
who are bored
with keeping it real
so they tape words
to the floor
and let you decide

tell Rosalia
that the reverend Pedro
is on the rooftop
handing out passports
because the spaceship *casita*
is about to take off

> *oye, mamita*
> *no te apures*
> *que como like*
> *a Brook Avenue bombaso*
> *we gonna make you dance*
> *que como un cocotaso limpio*
> *we gonna make your head rock*

so tell Pachanga
that *sí no hablas español*
bienvenido
that *sí no hablas inglés*
bienvenido

por que you see
this shit is a 10
on a scale from 1 to 9

tell Domingo
that we gonna shoot it up
mainline
mainland
mainstream
underground
until we catch your vein
so take this sound
to the grave
and tell the whole
fucking block
that a *bambula*
building session
is about to begin

and it's gonna be like
two church boys
talking loud
on the train
praising the Lord
in espanglish hip-hop speak
pero que son
yo se que fui the Lord son
eso que—mira
you know what it is fam
we keep the Bible real kid
tu me entiende
pero que he wants me to learn
because he told me
to bring my notebook son
to all the sermons son
and I was like whoa
Cuando the reverend Pedro
was waiting for me
with a passport
and he told me
that this time
we gonna die knowing
how beautiful
we really
are

Willie Perdomo *(New York)*

Mi Negrito

he play *congas*
and *panderas*
he play ancestral tongues
through his hands: their mouth
        drums: their voice
      to *mi gente: hambre* for self
            sediento for message
             familyfightbackfindlovekeepkeepkeepingon
               neverforgetwhereyoucomefrom

he be *boricua*
finest *negrito* this side of san juan
he be *muy inteligente*
he got degrees
honoring legacy
got cinque, clemente, garifun and maroons
running strong through his veins

he so bad
he play da blues
in the *plenas* and the *bombas*
cuz
he be the rhythms
in a tone-deaf pace
the magic
in a wonder-less place
the blackness
in a lily-white space

he be son of oshun
brother to oya and yemaya
as warrior chango
he dance the dance
called *life*
        la vida
        la vida
he say
yo soy moreno
del barrio
yo toquo la musica afro-puertoriqueño

with hands: his *corazón*
      drums: his *alma*
he feeds ghana, nigeria and the congo
to *mi gente*

ready for sankofa
ready to fly
home

Anasuya Isaacs (New York)

News of the World

We must always return
to poems for news of the world
or perish for the lack

Strip it
block it with blood
the page is not enough
unless the sun rises in it

Old doctor Willi writes
crouched on a stoop
in Paterson, New Jersey.

I am torn by light

She cries into her own head.
The playing fields of death
are far from me. In Cambodia I carried
my mother's head in a sack
and ran three days and nights
through a rice field

Now I pick up vegetables
from old sacking and straighten
them on crates: tomatoes
burning plums, cabbages hard
as bone. I work in Manhattan.

The subway corrupts me
with scents the robed Muslims sell
with white magazines
with spittle and gum

I get lost underground

By Yankee Stadium
I stumble out

hands loaded down
fists clenched into balls

A man approaches
muck on his shirt
his head, a battering ram
he knows who I am

I stall:
the tracks flash
with a thousand suns.

Meena Alexander (New York)

Much of Your Poetry Is Beautiful

But the way you work
doesn't fit our needs or taste
I read the rejection note to
Another Wild Colored Woman Poet
Anna contemptuously
put her hands on her latin hips
and sagely speculated
I bet they don't eat pussy either—
Our raucous laughter finally drowned out
    those words
That would from time to time
float up from my past
Write, my ass!
Girl, get your Black self
into that kitchen and
help your mama.

Brenda Walcott (Boston)

Ginsberg

My man said *Howl*
Throw back your head & rage
At the moon,
At plaid wearing strangers,
At 400 lb. politicos smoking
Cunt-drenched cigars.
He said howl at the dying light,

At the waking child
& at the cracked-out, bruised-up,
pus-covered gay boys on the corner.
And when there's nothing else to howl at,
Do it again.
Open your mouth and howl at buses spewing exhaust,
For mothers mourning another loss,
For justice drooling behind her blindfold.
Howl because the world passes you by,
Because the dryer shorted you another sock.
Do it because the voice in your throat
Refuses to be repressed.
When they come to question why,
Howl at the stuffed inquisitors.
Howl because they never could—
Because their prejudice was only for themselves.
Howl because they never stopped to think they could.
And when there's nothing left,
When the larynx is raw and bleeding &
Can't support another gasped syllable,
Whisper
To the earth, her trees, her seemingly endless skies,
Whisper only love,
All will be satisfied.

Thomas C. Howell IV (Pittsburgh)

In Bed with James Tate

A paper clip of light falls
on the first poem titled
"Where Babies Come From."
I place the book aside because
Nightline is on with Harold
Bloom, who looks like a plate
of cold asparagus. The other
guest is Emily Dickinson,
whose breasts are poached
apples. Her nipples, stemless
cherries, galloping in wild
pentameters. She's belting, *I like
to see her lick my miles,*
accompanied by her band,
The Buzzing Flies. Ted Koppel
has an eloquent erection.

children of the word

He always shoots from the hip.
You find your way into
the bedroom reunited with your
loved ones like Captain Janeway
and her crew of Camel Lights.
Is it any good? you say, slipping
under the sheets like the rent
check sliding under the landlord's
door. I don't get the first poem.
Read it. I flip the channels
and find an infomercial selling
other James Tate books. *I like
this poem a lot,* you say and I say
what does this coconut line have
to do with conception? I would
start the poem here with the typhoon
and then end with Mama and Papa
standing on the shore. *No, No,
No,* you say *James Tate is saying
that babies come from anywhere
like the moon and maybe play
with an American flag.* But by now,
you're conversing with my foot
which is already half-asleep,
dreaming of little green men.

Regie Cabico (New York)

soulgroovin ditty #7

little green men play a samba in my mind
maddening little rhythm
it gets me every time
i dance the bossanova to appease them
the funky disco elves in my head
i find myself singing
just to please them
snatches of songs long forgotten
still they play incessantly
forever and ever
pestering me
forcing me to move my feet keeping time
i whip
i whirl
throw in the bump

do a little grind
they keep me dancing
twirling
prancing
body movin
funky groovin
the loco little disco elves
the people/party/happening elves
the soultrain/getdownboogie elves
that gyrate in my mind

Hannah Howard *(New York)*

Sundays

I went to the church and walked by niggas dealin
got in the church and watched single mothers give 10% of their income to the
upkeep of the church and pastoral homes in the suburbs while they reside
    in chic urban projects
where pastors rarely drive their
lexuses, benzes or town cars
I watched folks like me lose their inhibitions and praise the Lord,
    reminding me in the small
ways of my ancestors and their spiritual discourses.
I sat open-mouthed and watched homos sing and direct revenue generating
    mass choirs while
being castigated.
Chided.
CONDEMNED.
I laughed loudly catching the eyes of stern ushers.
Their looks forced me to concentrate on the "WORD" and the sounds of the
    Pastor's AMEN
CORNER as he made the connotation that all PHARAOHS were evil, satanic,
    based on the tales
of MOSES and the PHARAOH down in EGYPT LAND. making
me go home to ponder, chant, meditate, stand before the tree PRAY.
    Light candles Speak with
the CREATOR consult my astrology books touch my stones reread my
    favorite biblical passage
to figure out this madness
Then the answer came: WRITE A POEM.

Seitu J. Hart *(Bridgeport, CT)*

To Aretha Franklin from Sparkle

i wanna . . . wanna a blues poem

not because its blue

but cause it says so much shit . . .
causes so much shit to happen

like sugar cane farmers putting down their machetes
to lay down and cry for freedom!!

yeah . . . it stops women from suckling their babies to pick up
axes to kill to kill the enemy

i wanna a blues poem to tell me to dry my eyes
to give up this internal pain in my heart and put the strength of fire in my
    fists

yeah . . . i want Aretha to shout out
i wanna give you something you can feel

yeah . . . i wanna cover the waterfront with Billie Holiday in search of a
weapon to kill the enemy

i need a blues poem . . . that cries out! that shouts! that screams!

i want everybody to feel the hurt
that causes you   causes you to kill

the pain in my thighs tells my feet to march
with the people's army

i dont want my heart broke-up
i wanna sparkle with liberation
yeah aretha it would be so good to have freedom
to know what to do with all that feeling
no more sad shit
the thunder you . . . i feel is liberation
sing me a liberation blues poem
scream it!   from the bottom of your gut
so i can hear the beat
you know the slow thunder, that quiet motion
feeling that comes only when you really mean it

yeah, a real revolutionary blues poem
i wanna hear a southern guitar whine out the people's liberation
i wanna hear Bessie Smith cry out for liberation

yeah, Ma Rainey sing it to me pour it out
we need so much material things
oh lets don't dream
give it to me baby
man . . . woman show up with it now
i need something i can feel

the way aretha says it
you know
a real revolutionary blues poem
the kind that stops workers on the line
that tells everybody this shit ain't going to work never!
you know
a revolutionary blues
that kind what i mean,
one that calls for a funky revolution
where we the ones left to tell it all over the world

i need a real real funky blues poem

i won't be scared if the shit turns a red bright
to light up my life and bring out the woman in me
cause I'm hooked on liberation
the way the blues is hooked on Muddy Waters

i sure wanna do something everybody can feel

Amina Baraka (*Newark*)

Lumumba Blues

Did you hear about Lumumba?
Man, he sure had a hard time.
I say, did you hear tell about ole Lumumba?
That man sure had a hard time.
Take folks more than a little to forget that crime.

Well, he didn't want much,
Just like you and me.
No, he didn't want much,
The same as you and me.
He was speaking for his people.
He said, Set my people free.
(Don't you think we ought to be free?)

Poor ole Lumumba
Thought Freedom had a friend.
Poor Lumumba,
He thought Freedom had a friend.
Well, they blinded both his eyes
And lynched him in the end.

Lord, Lumumba! See what they did to you!
Poor black boy, I see what they did to you.
I can't help feeling they done that to me, too.

Freedom! Lumumba,
I hear you calling still.
Freedom! Oh, Freedom!
I hear you calling still.
I won't forget,
Don't think I ever will.

Raymond R. Patterson (New York)

All the shoes are shined and the cotton is picked

A long silence
and wonder
now comes and settles
on past deeds and tasks

hard lived lives and anger
linger and call for their place in this
ill-ridden wasteland
tell us who stand with newborns and futures
Now that all the shoes are shined
and the cotton is picked
what do you plan to do with us?

These institutions of corrections
are hidden camps of concentration
broken immunity grows weak
from those white flakes
and gas
and poison

Nine millimeter steel
lets us know
the plan
is death

Sharrif Simmons (Atlanta)

In this day and age
the motto

Protect and Serve

is a metaphor
for

spinal taps
armpit wounds

and death
by

asphyxiation!

Bruce George (New York)

The Trouble I've Seen

Dedicated to the memories of Albert Nuh
Washington, George Jackson, Young man-Child
Jonathan Jackson, Min. K.T., Don T. Taylor,
Merle Africa, Attica 32, Ajamu Nassar,
Mandingo, David Walker, Anita Mark Sheppard,
Derrick Smith, Calvin De Angelo Moore, Santana,
Larry Robeson, Willie Enoch, Shaka Sankofa, and
all casualties incurred behind the wall.

You've maced me and attacked me. Transferred me from private prison.
Oh, tape record this also, for I want the world to listen.
I've been forced to drink toxic water in order to survive.
While you bring in Black bodies by the boat load and call it a war on crime.
I know Brothers who were sentenced to 2 but ended up serving 10.
I'm aware of countless numbers of cats in these camps
who went to bed but never got up again.
Have you ever seen them enter with pride? Headstrong and sane
And they leave cut broken thinking a number is their name?

You ever seen a genius go crazy? A mastermind dismantled?
How about a man being shot up with more shit than a horse can handle?
I've seen grandfathers placed in cells with their own offspring
And I've seen a brother bleed and bleed 'til damn near no blood was left.
I heard him say hell *must* be better. I heard him pray for quick death.
I've seen Black men classified as C-numbers held over a quarter of a century.
And I've seen white men with triple murder leave the penitentiary.
Ever had to choose from what you need and what is necessary?
Ever been exploited by a prison commissary?
Heard of women turning tricks for sanitary tissue?
You ever been searched in a manner that truly dissed you?
Imagine four grown men forced in the same room.
What if the pig that beat you served you your food?
I've had property pissed on and given bogus charges.
I can't count the cats in coins, let alone beat uncensored
I've been awakened at three in the morning and told it's time to ride.
I've lost count of the times I heard them say guilty.
How many babies who haven't lived, but yet got the death penalty?
Did you know that Mumia was moved and placed in segregation
And given trumped up charges for refusing to cut his dreads?
Like magicians you drop drugs from thin air.
Murdered George (Jackson) in Quentin and claimed he was strapped in his
     hair.
How many "problem prisoners" were popped with ice picks?
From corn to shanks, you still farmers planting shit.
You keep me isolated and caged 24 hrs a day.
I've seen the effect of those who you claim to rehabilitate.
Now I know what you mean when you use the term correct.
For I've experienced your bad brutal ass, uncut, in the raw and undressed!

Fred Hampton Jr. *(Joliet, IL)*

Having Lost My Son, I Confront the Wreckage
after James Wright

During dark,
on the borderline between sea & soul
I walk yesterday's path, hunting everywhere,
seeking to explore every light
walking corridors that close around me
like the birth of a pearl.

Behind a star
its light on the chilled rubble
of my city-bred heart:
Frost, frost.

This is where he has gone
stillborn, under waves and smiling faces.

Bundled away under waves and smiling faces.

Beyond sick, I go on
clawing earth, making brick,
erecting monoliths. Here, on these altars
all the turns,
all the lost hopefuls.

This cold summer
Sun spills inhuman snow
the jewels of his tears burn my palms.

Living. He's living still.
I will not let him die!
I will not let his light escape
this beauteous ruin.

Wanda Coleman *(Marina Del Rey, CA)*

Bensonhurst

I am running down a street with a pistol and behind me is all of
the others and they are all me and in front of me is everyone else
and we will do what has to be done to the ones who deserve to
have it done to them and you know I am coming and you know
I have a gun and you know I will use it and you've always known
my name.

I am Joseph Fama.
I am holding this pistol and
I am running down the street and
If God is with me I will blow the fuck
out of that nigger.

I am Jack Wiler.
I am lying in my bed and
I am thinking why is it that I can know
Joseph Fama so well.
I am everyone in Bensonhurst.
I am everyone in Sewell.
I am everyone in Wenonah.
I am everyone in Sequatchie.
I am everyone in Jacksonville.
I am everyone in Jersey City Heights

I am everyone in Shaker Heights.
I am everyone in Germantown.
I am everyone in Belair.
I am everyone in Johannesburg.
I am young and I am angry.
I am white.
But you knew that I was coming and you knew I had a gun
and you knew that I would use it
so why are you surprised?
Haven't you had a beer with me?
Haven't you held my children?
Haven't you laughed with me?
Haven't you held my gun?
Touched its cold metal barrel.
Don't you know what it's for?

I am running down the street and it's a hot night in Bensonhurst
and all my pals are behind me and I'm gonna fuck up that nigger
and I have a gun and tonight that nigger's gonna die.

Jack Wiler (Jersey City)

For Michael Griffith, Murdered Dec. 21, 1986, Howard Beach, NY

Scrape
memory
from my brain
Outside,
it's 1986
Inside, I
count
strokes of history
A lump of tar
   in his throat
tire tracks
   obscuring fingertips
rags of blood
   hanging from limbs
I bury these images
every day
Sit here
greasing cartridges,
with my blood

Jeffrey Renard Allen (New York)

244

Lift Every Fist and Swing

Lift every fist and swing
till all their mouths cave in
cave in like crockery
breaking in liberty.

Let our pounding rise
swell up their devilish eyes,
let it resound with the glee
of waves in the sea.

Swing a blow, full of the horrors
that their hate has brought us;
swing one low, tear at the terror
that these rapists have taught us.

Facing their laser guns
dark shadows on the run
let us run on until
we fell a final kill.

Rohan B Preston *(Minneapolis)*

TV Dinner

Our intestines puke out images
that they can't digest.
The gut dictates our gray matter
repressing the daily regurgitation
in the pathetic lives
of the dead, the rich and famous.
CBS provides no subsistence
to the intestinal tract at large.
We cannot consume *Dynasty*
it is devoid of DNA.
The reruns have no nutrients
even when fed intravenously.
Even when our eyelids are
plastered to the screen.
Even when an IV transmits it
through our veins.
Even when a fiber strand is
tunneled down our throats.
Pour salt on the airwaves,
there is still no sense

in the propaganda of flagellation,
for the mutilation of the brain:
on the sacred celluloid ministry
of the no-hope-left insane.
Internal interface is available
at Crazy Eddie rates,
with every liposuction experiment
on our facial edifice.
There is no excremental relationship
between pure lies and unpure life.
The bloods in the hightops and
Perry Ellis sweats
cannot chew statistical apologies
for irrelevant classifieds.
The low-riding Ricans can't eat your
published rise in consumer price indexes
or the points of Dow and Jones.
even surfer boys cannot subsist for long
on box-top propaganda—
Even when you perform your propi
so manipulatively well,
even when you massage the G-spot
in our insatiable cerebrums,
even when you mouth us
with your divisive tongue:
The nigras take your property.
The illegals take your jobs.
The Arabs threaten your security.
The Japs superconduct your cars.
The Ruskies endanger your species
with their Nicaraguan pawns.
More catsup on my propaganda please.
This propi has no taste.
Can you fry it extra crispy?
Smother it with maple syrup?
Can you melt some Wisconsin cheese
on the peak of this piece?
Can you barbecue your words?
It might be more palatable
with a bit of Cajun dust
in a nouveau cuisine Americana
Clint Eastwood restaurant.
Pepper with your propi, ma'am?
Bleu cheese or vinaigrette?
Sauce it, cream it, sop it,
'til it's obscenely wet.

It still knows no substance.
It's missing something vital—
Like generic reality.
It can only placate the pissed off
for a little while
before the gut begins
to slap around.
Wounding Horatio Alger's philosophy;
bullying innocent bedtime ideas
shoving them to the precipice
emptying bystanders' pockets
of all their edibles.
Because the belly has no sense of etiquette
it is uncouth, untrained and rude.
It is society's most profound skeptic
it does not watch or worship
anchormen—our 20th century Lords.
It is wholly illiterate, although
brilliant in the brutal art
of regulating weightless rhetoric.
Some night the mind begins to growl—
assuming the character of the gut,
its acids churning internally
breaking things apart.
Discharging ancient unpleasantries,
like maybe imperial idiocies don't always work.
Perhaps the decline of this neo-Rome
ain't all our personal fault.
There are no caped crusaders in the
competition for a wage.
Despite our zealous overtime in the
lighthouse of blind faith,
we are only metaphysically convinced
we are eternally saved.
The second coming is still coming
after the same class is resurrected
to office again.
Turns out Ollie, heavenly Ollie,
is not the Messiah after all.
He cannot miraculously transform
TV Guide and Congressional hearings
into wine and Wonder Bread.

July 1988

Michael Warr (Chicago)

children of the word

Bluesman

i am
the clear unmuffled
voice of
the muzzled masses
struggling
for the air
of hope
the hope of
air—
the long sought
freedom
to breathe
without fear
of choking
feel my immortal
moans/my black heart
beating against
the ear's
drums of the deaf
dumb and blind pharaohs
of sunbelt capital
who refuse to see
the holy blood dripping
from righteous lips
that speak of
the change—
in things to come

i am
nation/song
with
field holler twist
and middle passage pain
chained to my wrist
(it never lets me forget
the things i know i
have to remember)

i am
voodoo chile
preacher/teacher
trying hard reach
rock and raise your
troubled mind with
a healing song sung

from the shady back
porch of history
i preach a gospel
soooooo gooooood
it'll make you wanna
jump scream shout
and solve the unsolved
mystery—the newfound
history of how we came
to be

i am
the word/sound
and furious magic power
of mojo powder
proclaiming the
midnight hour of
doom while stomping
a mudhole in the
stinking ass of oppression
and doing the doo
in the fleshy face
of genocidal politicos

and yeah
you
can call me
mean
and rough
and tough
and all
'cause
i am
BBBBAAAAAAADDDDDDD!
big daddy blues
hot poppa jazz
i turn water to wine
and wine into stone
beat an elephant's ass
with a black cat bone
tamed a wild wild mule
with the flick of a switch
say
i am
the almighty voice of the people
i am
the sweet soul of the nation

i am
the spirit/salt of the earth
i am
a people's poet
yeah
i say
i am
i am
i am
a BLLLLLLLUUUUUUUEEEEEESSSSSSSman!

Charlie Braxton *(Jackson, MS)*

We're Not Well Here

What are we coming to
a wild lost breed of dogs
foaming at the mouth
ready to bite anyone in our path
even ourselves
our souls have become infected sores
laying waste to a Spirit
that was once bright light
to show everyone the way
who are we now
that allow our children
to search through their own bowels for recognition
and laugh over the death of themselves
like it was only a cartoon
how have we tattered remnants of royalty
come to swallow this puke of our failures
and say we've eaten well
then watch our grandmothers raped
by their grandsons
leaving pieces of their hearts
along the streets
for roach-like cops to raid the neighborhood
and declare everyone a criminal
there is nothing sacred anymore
flowers don't bloom in Spring here
they are made in laboratories
love is a game you can buy hot on the street corner
hope is a cancerous tumor
festering inside our brains
and all the religious leaders of the world
make up excuses for masturbating

in the face of God
while governments make dying a lifestyle
This wretchedness
this wickedness
laced with cyanide dreams
of another planet
where no one laughs or sings or dances
but just waits like a stone
for an acid rain tide to wash them away
we are not well here
we all have been bitten by the dogs
they drag parts of our body
up and down the streets growling
and the world celebrates
with mandates and parades
with talk shows and rap records
and morsels of our brains are rolled
into spitballs
to blow in anybody's face
just because we've got nothing better to do
but if we survive this moment
this holocaust
this frantic searching
through the devil's soul
if we survive this
what will we become
will we still lock the doors
and walk the dog with a leash
or will we melt
into some unknown gas
that will last long enough
to start this whole world over again

Abiodun Oyewole (New York)

Nickel Wine and Deep Kisses

Cabrini Green Housing Project, Chicago, 1982

Hey, miz lady . . . bring your fine ass over here and talk to me . . .

I never assumed it a casual flirtation.
I knew you were as serious as the sidewalk
you stood on, from your studiously gaping gym shoes
to the Adidas symbol shaved carefully into the back
of your hair. I knew you hissed, *Hey, miz lady . . .*

exactly the way you mean to,
with promises of nickel wine and deep kisses
in a moonwashed Cabrini corner.
Even the industrious rumble of Division St. traffic
couldn't drown out the answer to my headache
screaming from the front of your jeans.

Sheathed in wool and oxford, briefcased and correct,
I scurried past your steamy threat
with just a bit of inherited shimmy,
and you saw it in me,
the bottom line I've tried for so long to hide.
Hey, I've done my bit for the underclass,
just don't intrude,
don't invade,
don't insist,
don't push me,
don't flick that switch,
don't make me mingle.

But behind midnight black shades,
your lizard-lidded eyes
cupped the cheeks of my ass and held on.
You were clearly not considering
the possibility of being turned down,
just wondering whether to turn me on
or turn me out.

Bad Cabrini baby, I've been warned about you.
In your eyes, I'd be less than nothing,
a willing receptacle for your accumulated heat.
I'd be your downtown woman,
and each time you sensed rebellion
you'd grab at my chest
through my oh-so-correct clothing
or appeal to my bragged-about liberal sensibilities.

You'd make me climb piss-slick stairs
to the box you lived in
and you'd pin me to a roach-eaten mattress,
tearing away at my nine-to-five with your teeth,
fucking away at my uptown bourgeois
at
ti
tude.
You'd play your role of underprivilege to the hilt,
wallowing in your furious clouds of reefer and wine,

daring me to once again
draw that socially acceptable line between us.

And I'd go on living my two lives,
playing Peter to your Jesus,
lying to my mother about the bright bruises
on my body,
denying your smell on my skin
three different times
to three different people.
And you'd always be waiting for me
at the entrance from one world to the other.

Hey, miz lady, come on back. Let's spend some time.
Harmless enough, so let loose my smile
and hurry away. You listen to my heels apologize.
Cause you know that your real meaning
will cling like brown to my skin all day:

Come back here, bitch.
I'll eat you alive.

Patricia Smith *(New York)*

The Coward

Last night
I stood in the cold dark
With my jeans pulled over my pajamas
And listened to my neighbor
Beat his wife
Only she's not his wife
They just live together

I couldn't move my arms
My breath fluttered in and out
I thought about the police
He would beat her worse after they left
He would come shouting and banging at my door

The police would call it a
Routine Domestic Quarrel
I wasn't so sure I could
Tell the difference
Between the sound of a killing

I held my breath and sneaked to the bathroom
So they wouldn't hear me
As if instead
They'd woken me with their lovemaking

After he was gone
She cried that she didn't understand
I wanted to go to her and hold her
But he slammed in again and it started all over

I guess I'm a coward
If I had been a man I wouldn't've been afraid
I would've beat on the wall
Yelled for them to shut up
So I could get some sleep
I crawled back under the covers
Put the pillow over my head
Went to sleep hoping nothing would happen

This morning his car was gone
I went to her door
I'm sure she's younger than she looks
Her mouth was cut
Her hand was shaking
I couldn't remember
What I wanted to say last night
We're both very reasonable and understanding
In the daylight

Kate Rushin *(Middletown, CT)*

Strip

A thin brown-haired girl pouts
high on stage. She cannot swing
her slight body round the new pole.
It runs floor to ceiling, piercing
the strip club like a shaft of light
the way the voice of God appears in movies.
Except this pole is plastic and God
would gurgle because it's full of liquid
like a lava-lamp. The words would have to sploosh
up through bubbles
like burps, one at a time like Jesus.

Is. Love. except the pole's sealed
and there is no place for love to go

so the bubbles just keep going up
and down and the girl
can't get her hands around it.
She says she misses the jungle-gym type bar
this bubble bar replaced.
She anticipates missing the smell
of its metals on her hands after work.

Training me, she instructs *Don't touch*
your thighs. Don't touch your knees.
Keep both feet on the floor at all times.
Don't do anything I do. She smiles
at the way everything is against some law.
I go on stage and the speakers spit
out the first lines of the song I picked:
I love myself/I want you to love me.
I dance for a man. He's fifty, at least,
his wife beside him. *But you're beautiful,*
she says like a mother comforting a taunted child,
like someone else's mother. Mine said, *There is nothing*
you can't talk your way out of.

The bar's dark and dollars scratch my skin.
When the next song starts I take off my bra,
my breasts covered, by Florida law,
with flesh brown tape. I wrap my arms, both legs
around the wide, bright pole,
spin slowly down to the floor.
Who else will pay for what he can't see?
Like God, I've always been invisible

Lyrae Van Clief-Stefanon *(Fairfax, VA)*

Sex

A lover nudges
the ghost
from my right breast, nipple
plucked like a blue
berry in quiet light.
I can't escape
what lurks
beneath skin, further back
than blood & bone, this sex
& another I can't
remember. Tonight
is the gatekeeper

of memory. I struggle
to be let in. Who
protects me? I dare
the ghost forward. Or is it
the God of Hard-Crossed
Hands, always watching? No.
Someone else
has been here, my flinched
face confesses. Who?
You?

Yona Harvey *(New Orleans)*

enemies

make you scream your own name they carry razors between their teeth
enemies smile a saber tooth smile they smell like nothing you've ever smelt
before
       enemies paste icons of martyrs on their sleeves
           enemies pass up beggars
on the street sing *we are the world we are the people* at the karyoke bar
they blow smoke in your face when they know you're trying to quit
    enemies are lovers

who enjoy watching you cry so they can comfort you   they lay their heads
   on your shoulders and
suck their thumbs pretending that you are their salvation

enemies speak with cotton mouths so you have to bend down to hear them
they wear flesh tone makeup they sit in beauty shops laughing

enemies steal your stuff and sell it on St. Marks and 2nd Avenue

enemies are short with furry tongues tall with shaved skulls
they open their mouths with their fists attached to their teeth
and bellow out the national hymn of the stoopids

enemies take it up the ole wahzoo they take it down the ole horn
     they take it on the brain and cackle at the moon

cops are the enemy
          enemies are next door neighbors
who strap combat boots on their 500 pound dog and play chase at 2 a.m.
in the morning   they cook burnt vomit they keep roaches as pets they
complain when the wrong mail is left in their box

enemies want to weaken the power of the word niggah so they use it over and
over and over again   enemies go to mass after an abortion they go to the
    mosque wrapped in cloth
from a clitorectomy   they say amen after rev. so-n-so
says all fornicators are goin to hell they gulp and say it's holy to do so
before wanting to dry fuck you

enemies talk in voices that are not their own
enemies have so many voices that they can't remember them all
they point they whisper they gossip they eat too much and throw up
they have talk shows dedicated to other enemies   enemies can't stop talking
enemies label their war tactics friendly fire   enemies pass you peace pipes
laced with cyanide
                    enemies don't die . . .

enemies swim across waters floating with the bloated carcasses of their
    enemies
enemies are light sleepers they never sleep they stay awake just to fuck
    with you

Tish Benson *(New York)*

American Poetry

Are there any american poets in here?
I wanna hear an american poem
Something american
A South Carolina slave shout a Alabama back woods church call and
    response

I wanna hear an american poem
an american poem
    about sharecroppers
on the side of the road of families in cardboard boxes
            not about kings
or majestic lands
    or how beautiful ugly can be
I wanna hear something american
something about ghettoes
of Italians
    of Germans
    of Jews
    of Black folk
about projects and lead poison
poverty and children in jail

I wanna hear a poem about picket lines
    a Joe Hill legend struggle for an eight hour day

hey hey you hey you yeah you
Where is all the american poetry
    about Harlem number runners
        and barbershop conversations
about colored faces on colored tv's
I wanna hear an american poem as american as a South Bronx burner bran-
    dished
on an abandoned building a breakbeat, backspin, a beatbox, a rap song in
Congo square
        Niggers beating on buckets on Broad St.
As american as the Zulu Nation and Latin Kings
i wanna hear an american poem
about a dead girl on Chadwick avenue with a bullet in her neck
from a colored cop doing his job
ordered by fascism and crack cocaine
    You know something made in the usa

Something american an Afro-Cuban Nuyorican Latin tinge beating Bomba y
    Plena
sprawling out of wide open tenement windows in the middle of winter on
    the verge of East Harlem or North Newark
Poems
of brown colonies
of Albizu being tortured for breathing Taino blood
screaming African tongues
and dialoguing in spanish
for being him PuertoRican self
and worst of all loving it
MY GOD
what happened to all the american poetry?
not poems about attics
or how your clothes fit
or fucking and stale slobber
nor your night befores and morning afters
i dont want to hear about your statues and their fantasies

theres no more american poetry
just death marches and stoic laughter
niggers being funny
no more american poets
I wont boost your morale
play your songs
make you feel comfortable
build your ego

I just wanna hear an american poem
something native
like the trail of tears
wounded knee small pox in blankets
An american poem with american images
like *welcome back kotter white shadow* or *different strokes*
about white gods who guide helpless darkies on the road to light

american
something that represents us
a colorful rainbow
a big bright fist
an uncorrected sentence
improper english
as american as cointelpro
peekskill, new york Robeson singing out the back of a truck
Nina Simone playing at the BlueNote w/ Baldwin next to her on a piano
    stool
and Amina and Amiri Baraka in the audience
air filled with smoke cognac and mississippi goddamn
capture that moment
right something abou that

an american masterpiece
an american poem
        something strictly american
like red summers, strange fruit, and the palmer raids

hey you you no you you and you yeah hey you
something american usa american usa american usa american usa
as american as the kkk

a poem about Emitt Till 'll do, the tallahatchie river
church bombings and child murders
about Alabama red dirt and boycotts in Montgomery
about families migrating north with dignity and shotguns

I wanna hear a poem
        a poem
about a beautiful blk boy
                see him
a beautiful blk boy colored into the night
his eyes the stars
his hands our will
about a beautiful blk boy
in the middle of a project
playing checkers with glass and stone

who beats buckets as drums
and plays the horn in his sleep
I wanna hear a poem about a beautiful brown girl
an incredibly beautiful brown girl
with an aged mahogany smile
and flower petals for lips
a beautiful brown girl
with a poem in her eyes
a poem in her eyes
   and a gun in her hand
sitting in a puddle of tears
in clinton's women facility
in the garden state
               in the land of the free
you know . . .
something american
something that represents me.

Ras Baraka (Newark)

So Many Books, So Little Time

for librarians & independent booksellers

Frequently during my mornings of pain & reflection
when I can't write
or articulate my thoughts
or locate the mindmusic needed
to complete the poems & essays
that are weeks plus days overdue
forcing me to stop, I say cease
answering my phone, eating right, running my miles,
reading my mail and making love.
(also, this is when my children do not seek me out
because I do not seek them out)
I escape north to the nearest library or used bookstore.
They are my retreats, my quiet energy/givers, my intellectual refuge.

For me it is not bluewater beaches, theme parks
or silent chapels hidden among forest greens.
Not multistored American malls, corporate book
supermarkets, mountain trails or Caribbean hideaways

My sanctuaries are liberated lighthouses of shelved books,
featuring forgotten poets, unread anthropologists &
playwrights; starring careful anthologists of art & photography,

upstart literary critics; introducing dissertations of tenure—
seeking assistant professors, self-published geniuses, remain-
dered first novelists; highlighting speed-written bestsellers,
wise historians & theologians, nobel & pulitzer prize winning
poets & fiction writers, overcertain political commentators,
small press wonderkinds & learned academics.
All are vitamins for my slow brain & sidetracked spirit in this
winter of creating.

I do not believe in smiling politicians, AMA doctors,
zebra-faced bankers, red-jacketed real estate or automobile
salespeople or singing preachers.

I believe in books,
it can be conveniently argued that knowledge,
not that which is condensed or computer packaged, but
pages of hard-fought words, dancing language
meticulously & contemplatively written by the likes of
        me & others,
shelved imperfectly at the levels of open hearts & minds
is preventive medicine strengthening me for the return to my
clear pages of incomplete ideas to be reworked, revised &
written as new worlds and words in all of their subjective con-
figurations to eventually be processed into books that will
hopefully be placed on the shelves of libraries &
bookstores to be found & browsed over by receptive
booklovers, readers & writers looking for a retreat,
looking for departure & home,
looking for open heart surgery without the knife.

Haki R. Madhubuti (*Chicago*)

How to Be a Street Poet

If you're going to be a street poet
make sure you have lots of friends
who drink fight steal or sell drugs.
They will always have problems
with the law, and you can write
poems about them.

Make sure one of them is a crackhead
cokehead dope fiend, they are sure to
take a really bad hit or a really good
hit and die, and then you can write a
poem about it.

Get a quiet, light-skinned girl from Yonkers
or Long Island to fall in love with you. Ask
her, occasionally, for her opinion on your
friends and your poetry. She will probably
say something naive. That's how you'll know
you're on the right track.

Meanwhile, get a loud, brown girl
from 'round the way to have your
baby, and then break up with her.
She will quite possibly stress you
whenever she can. Should the street
muse ever fail to keep its appointment
with you, you can call your baby
mama and ask her why she hasn't
let you see your child. She will
immediately go into single strong
independent brown mother woman
mode and GO OFF on that ass. This
will make you regret calling her, but
then you can write a poem about it.

Your child will grow up hating
you for being a part time dad—
good for happy meals and may-
be next times twenty-six week-
ends a year—instead of being a
live-in dad like the ones on TV.
You will forget her/his birthday
and sometimes her/his age, and
otherwise break her/his heart.
You'll be able to write poems
about that, too.

Keep odd hours, making sure to walk
into your parents' home menacingly
Sunday mornings, until you find sudden
travel bags filled with your underwear.
This will allow you to spend more time
at friends' houses on rooftops park benches
subways and in shelters where you can
further develop your street poet resumé
and, of course, write more street poems.

But that's okay because you can tell
your friends about all your street issues
as you sit in front of the corner store

with an almost-like-mom's dinner from
the caridad playing dominoes with your
friends who are still drinking fighting
stealing selling drugs unless they're in
jail, in which case they're still drinking
fighting stealing selling drugs, or dead.
When the store closes, ending the game,
you will make a final trip to the liquor
store next door to the corner store to buy
rum from an island you've never known
in order to feel like you belong there and
drag yourself to your solitary apartment
to pass out to wake up the next day with
a hangover and still another street poem.

John Rodriguez (New York)

The Adventures of Grandmaster Flash
(on the wheels of Poetry)

Grandmaster cuts faster
than any known, stone to the bone,
full grown, he's a one of a kind
and Flash is gonna rock your mind.

Deep down in the jungle where the tall grass grows
the Lion stepped on the monkey's toes,
the monkey said "Mr. Lion, can't you see?"
Grandmaster cuts faster.
In the room the women come and go
Talking of Michelangelo
but Grandmaster cuts faster
OUT OF THE CRADLE ENDLESSLY ROCKING.
In the room the women come and go
Talking of Michelangelo
but Grandmaster cuts faster
than any known, stone to the bone.

I AM A GENIUS CHILD, SHAKESPEARE IN HARLEM
with a jock spinning for me called DJ FLASH.
I AM A GENIUS CHILD, SHAKESPEARE IN HARLEM
down in the jungle where the tall grass grows.
I AM A GENIUS CHILD, SHAKESPEARE IN HARLEM
Talking of, Talking of DJ FLASH.
I AM A GENIUS CHILD, SHAKESPEARE IN HARLEM

ENDLESSLY-ENDLESSLY-ENDLESSLY ROCKING.
Now listen very closely and you will hear
of the midnight ride of DJ FLASH.
Now listen very closely and you will hear
DJ FLASH ENDLESSLY ROCKING.
Now listen very closely and you will hear
Talking of, Talking of DJ FLASH.
Now listen very closely and you will hear
Grandmaster cuts faster.

1-2-3-4-5-6-7 scratching like hell
and make it sound like heaven,
7-6-5-4-3-2-1 come on Flash
Come and get some.

Poems are bullshit unless they are trees
down in the jungle where the tall grass grows.
Poems are bullshit unless they are teeth
Talking of, Talking of DJ FLASH.
Poems are bullshit unless they are ROCKING
and Flash is gonna rock, Now listen

WHEN LILACS LAST IN THE DOORYARD BLOOM'D
the Lion stepped on the Monkey's toes
ENDLESSLY-ENDLESSLY-ENDLESSLY Talking
Talking of Michaelangelo.
WHEN LILACS LAST IN THE DOORYARD BLOOM'D
the Monkey said "Mr. Lion can't you see?"
Grandmaster cuts faster,
Now listen very closely and you will hear.

DJ Renegade (DC)

X

Everything we don't understand
        is explained
        in Art
        The Sun
    beats inside us
The Spirit courses in and out
    of us

A circling transbluesency
pumping Detroit Red inside, deep thru us
    like a Sea
         & who calls us bitter
          has bitten us
           & from that wound
            pours Malcolm
                Little
                by
                Little

Amiri Baraka *(Newark)*

The Tradition

Carry it on now.
Carry it on.

Carry it on now.
Carry it on.

Carry on the tradition.

There were Black People since the childhood of time
who carried it on.
In Ghana and Mali and Timbuktu
We carried it on.

Carried on the tradition.

We hid in the bush
when the slavemasters came
holding spears.
And when the moment was ripe,
leaped out and lanced the lifeblood
of would-be masters.

We carried it on.

On slave ships,
hurling ourselves into oceans.
Slitting the throats of our captors.

We took their whips.
And their ships.
Blood flowed in the Atlantic—
and it wasn't all ours.

We carried it on.

Fed Missy arsenic apple pies.
Stole the axes from the shed.
Went and chopped off master's head.

We ran. We fought.
We organized a railroad.
An underground.

We carried it on.

In newspapers. In meetings.
In arguments and streetfights.
We carried it on.

In tales told to children.
In chants and cantatas.
In poems and blues songs
and saxophone screams,
we carried it on.

On soapboxes and picket lines.
Welfare lines, unemployment lines.
Our lives on the line,
we carried it on.

On cold Missouri nights
Pitting shotguns against lynch mobs.
On burning Brooklyn streets.
Pitting rocks against rifles,
We carried it on.

Against water hoses and bulldogs.
Against nightsticks and bullets.
Against tanks and tear gas.
Needles and nooses.
Bombs and birth control.
We carried it on.

In Selma and San Juan.
Mozambique. Mississippi.

In Brazil and in Boston,
We carried it on.

Through the lies and the sell-outs.
The mistakes and the madness.
Through pain and hunger and frustration,
We carried it on.

Carried on the tradition.

Carried a strong tradition.

Carried a proud tradition.

Carried a Black tradition.

Carry it on.

Pass it down to the children.
Pass it down.
Carry it on.
Carry it on now.
Carry it on
TO FREEDOM!

Assata Shakur (Havana)

There It Is

My friend
they don't care
if you're an individualist
a leftist   a rightist
a shithead or a snake

They will try to exploit you
absorb you   confine you
disconnect you   isolate you
or kill you

and you will disappear into your own rage
into your own insanity
into your own poverty
into a word a phrase a slogan a cartoon
and then ashes

The ruling class will tell you that
there is no ruling class
as they organize their liberal supporters into
white supremacist lynch mobs
organize their children into
ku klux klan gangs
organize their police into
killer cops
organize their propaganda into
a device to ossify us with angel dust
pre-occupy us with western symbols in
african hair styles
inoculate us with hate
institutionalize us with ignorance
hypnotize us with a monotonous sound designed
to make us evade reality and stomp our lives away

And we are programmed to self-destruct
to fragment
to get buried under covert intelligence operations of
unintelligent committees impulsed toward death
And there it is

The enemies polishing their penises between
oil wells at the pentagon
the bulldozers leaping into demolition dances
the old folks dying of starvation
the informers wearing out shoes looking for crumbs
the lifeblood of the earth almost dead in
the greedy mouth of imperialism
And my friend
they don't care
if you're an individualist
a leftist   a rightist
a shithead or a snake

They will spray you with
a virus of legionnaire's disease
fill your nostrils with
the swine flu of their arrogance
stuff your body into a tampon of
toxic shock syndrome
try to pump all the resources of the world
into their own veins
and fly off into the wild blue yonder to
pollute another planet

And if we don't fight
if we don't resist
if we don't organize and unify and
get the power to control our own lives
Then we will wear
the exaggerated look of captivity
the stylized look of submission
the bizarre look of suicide
the dehumanized look of fear
and the decomposed look of repression
forever and ever and ever
And there it is

Jayne Cortez *(New York)*

CONTRIBUTORS

Abiyah is a recording artist, performance poet, clothing designer, activist, and mother. **Patricia A. Holt Abner,** a social worker for twenty years, was born and raised in North Philly. A graduate of Penn State, her work was selected by Sonia Sanchez for a special poetry edition of *Drumvoices Revue.* **Ayin Adams** grew up in Brooklyn, went to college in the Bronx, lived in Harlem and Queens, but now lives in Hawaii. Winner of the Audre Lorde and Pat Parker Poetry Award and nominated Poet of the Year by the International Society of Poets, she is the producer of a CD, *The Color of Her Tears.* **Jane Alberdeston-Carolín,** a Cave Canem fellow whose work has appeared in *Bilingual Review Press* and *Step into a World: Global Anthology of the New Black Literature,* is the author of *The Afrotaina Dreams.* **Meena Alexander,** who teaches at Hunter College (CUNY), is the author of many books, including *Manhattan Music, The Shock of Arrival: Reflections on Post Colonial Experience,* and *River and Bridge: Poems.* **Jeffrey Renard Allen,** who teaches at Queens College (CUNY), is the author of *Harbors and Spirits* and *Rails under My Back.* **Oktavi Allison,** whose work appears in *Fertile Ground, The Baltimore Review, Dark Eros,* and *Catch the Fire,* is a member of the Carolina African American Writer's Collective and the author of *Restoration* and *Amandla.* **Arthur Ade Amaker,** who teaches sixth grade Language Arts in the Chicago Public School system, is the co-editor of *Sons of Lovers.* Poet, cultural organizer, and radio host **Jolivette Anderson** is the author of *Past Lives, Still Living: Traveling the Pathways to Freedom,* and two CDs, *Love & Revolution Underground* and *At the End of a Rope in Mississippi.* **asha bandele,** who is an editor-at-large at *Essence* magazine, is the author of *Absence in the Palm of My Hands* and *The Prisoner's Wife.* Poet, activist, educator **Amina Baraka** is a member of Blue Ark, a poetry and jazz performance ensemble and author of *Poems for the Masses* and co-editor of *Confirmation* and *The Music.* Her work also appears in *In Defense of Mumia.* Poet, playwright, activist **Amiri Baraka,** a father of the Black Arts Movement, has been publishing for close to forty years. He is the author of over forty books, the most recent of which are *Transbluesency, Funk Lore, Eulogies,* and *The Fiction of LeRoi Jones/Amiri Baraka.* **Ras Baraka,** teacher, writer, activist, and politician, is coeditor of *In the Tradition: An Anthology of Young Black Writers.* **RoByn Baron** has a Bachelor's Fine Arts degree in writing, literature, and publishing from Emerson College, and runs a music booking and management company. The D Train Poet **Rich Bartee,** founder of Poettential Unltd, has been a producer and promoter of poets and poetry for the last thirty years. **Samiya A. Bashir,** former senior editor of *Black Issues Book Review,* and co-editor of *Role Call: A Generational Anthology of Black Literature & Art,* has published poems in *Other Countries Voices Rising, June Jordan's Poetry for the People,* and *Contemporary American Women Poets.* **Felice Belle,** host of the Friday Night Slam at the Nuyorican Poets Café, has appeared in *Drumvoices Revue.* **Tish Benson** is a poet and playwight whose work has appeared in *In the Tradition, Verses That Hurt,* and *Listen Up!* **Tara Betts** is a poet whose work has appeared in *Power Lines, Poetry Slam, Obsidian III,* and *Words on Fire,* a production at Chicago's Steppenwolf Theater. Poet and workshop instructor **Laura Boss,** publisher and editor of the literary journal *Lips,* is the author of several collections of poetry, including *On the Edge of the Hudson, Stripping,* and *Arms: New and Selected Poems.* Poet, filmmaker, scholar, and former editor of Dudley Randall's Broadside Press, **Melba Joyce Boyd** is the chair of the Africana Studies Department at Wayne State University and the author of *The Black Rose, Discarded Legacy,* and *The Black Unicorn: Dudley Randall and The Broadside Press* (film and critical biography). **Gwendolyn Brooks** was the first African-American to receive the Pulitzer Prize for poetry. Her literary career spanned six decades. Her many celebrated works include *A Street in Brownsville, Maud Martha: A Novel,* and *Blacks.* **John Watusi Branch** is founder and director of the Afrikan Poetry Theater; his several publications include *Kwanzaa* and *Journey to the Motherland.* **Charlie Braxton,** poet, music critic, and author of *Ascension from the Ashes,* has appeared in *In the Tradition, Trouble the Water, Step into a World,* and *Keeping Track.* **Kysha N. Brown,** co-editor of *Fertile Ground—Memories & Visions,* has appeared in several anthologies, including *Catch the Fire* and *360°—A Revolution of Black Poets.* **Shonda Buchanan,** publisher and editor of *Mother's Milk . . . The Holistic Lifestyle Ezine* (www.mothers-milk.com), has appeared in *Step into a World.* **Susana Cabañas,** author of *Poemario,* comes out of the Nuyorican activist movement as a teacher and poet who has also translated the work of Julio de Burgos. **Regie Cabico** is co-editor of *Poetry Nation.* His work appears in several anthologies, including *The Outlaw Bible of American Poetry* and *The World in Us: Gay & Lesbian Poets of the Next Wave.* **Valerie Caesar** has worked as an editorial intern at various publishing houses. She's studied at State University of New York at Stony Brook and is currently studying English and Pre Law at Cornell University. **Brenda Cárdenas**'s work has appeared in *Rattle, Learning by Heart, Under the Pomegranate Tree,* and *Prairie Schooner.* **Kenneth Carroll,** executive director of DC WritersCorps and author of *So What: For the White Dude Who Said This Ain't Poetry,* is a poet and playwright whose work appears in *In Search of Color Everywhere, Catch the Fire,* and *Spirit & Flame.* **Americo Casiano** is a Nuyorican jazz poet who has edited a literary magazine called *Sombra.* His work has appeared in *Nuyorican Poetry, The Next World, Aloud,* and *New Rain.* Poet and interdisciplinary artist **Adrian Castro,** whose work has appeared in several anthologies, including *Paper Dance* and *Step into a World,* is the author of *Cantos to Blood & Honey.* **Nzinga Regtuinah Chavis** is a performance poet and activist based in New Jersey. **James E. Cherry**'s work appears in *Crab Orchard Review, Obsidian II/III, Drumvoices Revue, African American Review, Callaloo,* and *BMa: The Sonia Sanchez Literary Journal.* **Jayne Cortez,** poet, filmmaker, and band leader of Firespitters, is the author of several volumes of poetry and CDs, the most recent of which is the collection *Somewhere in Advance of Nowhere.* She was the main organizer and film director of the Yari Yari Conference at New York University. **Clairesa Clay** is a poet, filmmaker, and teacher whose work appears in *In Defense of Mumia* and *Role Call.* **Ta'Lease Niche Cleveland,** an Andrew Mellon Fellow, was born in Inglewood, California, in 1976. **Taiyon J. Coleman,** a Cave Canem fellow, has studied with poet Rohan B Preston. A teacher of composition, literature, speech, and creative writing, her work has appeared in several publications, including *Drumvoices Revue.* **Wanda Coleman** is the author of numerous books, the most recent of which is *Mambo Hips,* a novel. **Jeneanne Collins,** originally from Milwaukee, Wisconsin, has lived in Baltimore, Maryland, for eight years where she spends her time writing and empowering youth. **Linda Cousins** is former publisher of the *Universal Black Writers* magazine and editor of several anthologies, including *Black and in Brooklyn.* **Teri Ellen Cross** is a Cave Canem fellow and producer with *Public Interest,* a National Public Radio syndicated talk radio show. **Michael Datcher** is the author of *Black Love, Raising Fences: A Black Man's Love Story, Tough Love: Cultural Criticisms & Familial Observations On the Life & Death of Tupac Shakur* and co-editor of *Tough Love.* **Hayes Davis,** a Cave Canem fellow and award-winning poet, teaches English at Georgetown Day High School in Washington, D.C. **Jarvis Q. DeBerry,** whose work appears in *Step into a World* and *Speak the Truth to the People,* is a member of the NOMMO Literary Society, a Cave Canem fellow, and an editorial writer at the *Times-Picayune* in New Orleans. Performance poet **Latasha Natasha Diggs** is currently a student at New York University. **R. Erica Doyle,** a Cave Canem fellow, is an M.F.A. candidate in poetry at the New School for Social Research in New York City. Her work has appeared in *Callaloo, Black Issues Book Review, Women in the Life,* and *Blithe House Quarterly.* **Carlos Raul Dufflar,** founder and artistic director of The Bread Is Rising Poetry Collective, is a poet and activist whose works include *El Barrio de Naomi, The Eye of the Flower, The Penthouse Class,* and *Haravek.* **Denise Duhamel** is a prolific poet whose most recent work includes *Queen for a Day: Selected and New Poems, The Star-Spangled Banner, Kinky,* and *Oyl* (with Maureen Seaton). **Cornelius Eady,** co-founder of Cave Canem, an African American Poetry Workshop/Retreat, is the author of seven volumes of poetry, the most recent of which is *Brutal Imagination.* **Thomas Sayers Ellis,** co-founder of the Dark Room Collective, teaches at Case Western Reserve University and in the Bennington Writing Seminars. He is the author of *The Good Junk, The Genuine Negro Hero,* and co-editor of *On the Verge.* **Empress,** whose given name is Atinuke Abayomi-Paul, is owner of Universal Soul Syndicate and is at work on opening a performance venue called 3rd Eye Stage. Poet and visual artist **Sandra María Esteves,** an original Nuyorican poet, is the author of *Yerba Buena, Undelivered Love Poems,* and *Blues Town Mocking Bird Mambo.* **Blair Ewing,** editor of the *Maryland Poetry Review* and associate editor of *Wordwrights* magazine, is the producer of the cable TV show *Poetry Jam* and the CD compilation *Word Up Baltimore* and the author of *Chainsaw Teddybear.* **José Angel Figueroa,** an original Nuyorican poet, teaches at Boricua College in New York City, and is the author of *East 110th*

Street. **James Flint** is a Pittsburgh-based poet. **Jaime Shaggy Flores,** poet, activist, and cultural worker, is the author of *Sancocho*. **Krista Franklin** was born in Ohio in 1970. Her work has appeared in *Nexus, QBR, The Black Book Review,* and *Footsteps* magazine. **Reg E. Gaines,** who wrote the libretto to the Broadway hit, *Bringin Da Noise Bringin the Funk,* is the author of *The Original Buckwheat,* as well as the CDs *Please Don't Take My Jordans* and *Sweeper Don't Sweep My Street.* **Carlos Omar Gardinet** is a poet and screenwriter currently at work on an adaption of Edwidge Danticat's novel *The Farming of Bones.* **Bruce George** is a poet, activist, and CEO of Nomenclature Records. He is a producer of the Def Poetry Jam. **Danielle Legros Georges** is the book review editor for *Obsidian III.* Her work appears in *The Beacon Best of 1999, The Butterfly's Way,* and *Step into a World.* **Maria Mazziotti Gillan,** director of the Poetry Center at Passaic Community College, in Paterson, New Jersey, and editor of *The Paterson Literary Review,* is the author of *Where I Come From: Selected and New Poems, Things My Mother Told Me,* and co-editor of *Unsettling America, Identity Lessons,* and *Growing Up Ethnic in America.* **Brian Gilmore,** poet and lawyer, is the author of *elvis presley is alive and well and living in harlem* and *jungle nights and soda fountain rags.* **Rha Goddess,** former member of the Zulu Nation, is a performance poet and producer of the spoken word CD, *Soulah Vibe.* **C. D. Grant,** a widely published poet and journalist, was the music editor for *Essence* magazine for five years. He is the author of the poetry collections, *Keeping Time* and *Images in a Shaded Light.* **Jackie Graves,** who is studying for a Masters of Fine Arts degree in creative writing, has appeared in *African Voices.* **Daniel Gray-Kontar,** co-founder of Cleveland's Black Poetic Society and founder of Evolutionary Writers Theater, is a poet and journalist. His work appears in *Spirit & Flame* and the CD compilation *Best of the National Poetry Slam,* vol. 1. **Marj Hahne,** performance poet, writer, educator, and creator of Patchwork Poets, a poetry workshop, is columnist of *museletter* for *Poetry.about.com* and author of *Finding What Hides.* **Kendra Hamilton** is a poet, essayist, and journalist whose work appears in *Callaloo, Brightleaf, Southern Cultures,* and *Shenandoah.* **Suheir Hammad** is the author of *Drops of This Story* and *Born Palestinian, Born Black.* **Fred Hampton, Jr.,** the son of legendary Black Panther Fred Hampton, who was gunned down by Chicago police on December 4, 1969, while he lay in bed with his pregnant girlfriend, is currently incarcerated at Joilet C.C. in Illinois for an arson he didn't commit. **Jewell M. Handy** is a teaching artist with Writers in the Schools, Teachers and Writers Collaborative, Theater and Dance Alliance, and Teach for America. **Duriel E. Harris,** earned a doctoral degree from the Program for Writers at UIC and is a poetry editor of *Obsidian III.* **Reginald Harris's** work has appeared in several literary journals, e-zines, and anthologies, including *The African American Review, Harvard Gay & Lesbian Review, Obsidian II, Men on Men 7,* and *Brown Sugar.* **Theodore A. Harris** is a poet, muralist, and collagist. His work is featured in the anthology *In Defense of Mumia* and in various journals, such as *Long Shot, Drum Voices Review,* and *Ratta Pallax.* **Venus Harris,** former dancer with Philadanco and Dance Theater of Harlem, is a performance poet who has performed her one-woman show in Berlin,

London, and Amsterdam. **Seitu J. Hart** is a poet and creative writing instructor from Bridgeport, Connecticut. **Yona Harvey**'s work has been anthologized in *Catch the Fire: A Cross Generational Anthology of Contemporary African American Poetry.* **Umar Bin Hassan** is an original member of The Last Poets. He is co-author, with Abiodun Oyewole, of *On a Mission: The Last Poets: Selected Poems and a History of The Last Poets.* **David Henderson,** poet and biographer, is the author of *Felix of the Silent Forest, The LowEast, Da Mayor of Harlem, 'Scuse Me While I Kiss the Sky: The Biography of Jimi Hendrix,* and *Neo-California.* **Safiya Henderson-Holmes** was an assistant professor in the Creative Writing Department of Syracuse University. She was a playwright as well as a poet, and the author of *Madness and a Bit of Hope* and *Daily Bread.* **Oneca Hitchman-Britton,** an English student at Packer Collegiate Institute in Brooklyn, New York, is co-editor of *Palm,* an alternative literary magazine. **Everett Hoagland,** author of *The City and Other Poems,* is a poet of the Black Arts Movement, who has been publishing consistently for the past thirty years. His work is featured in Dudley Randall's classic anthology, *The Black Poets.* **Andre O. Hoilette,** a former editor of *Nexus* magazine, is a Jamaican-born poet residing in the United States. His work has appeared in *Duct Tape Press* and *In Our Minds.* **Bob Holman,** a primary mover of the spoken word, is the author of *The Collect Call of the Wild* and co-editor of *Aloud: Voices from the Nuyorican Poets Cafe* and *The United States of Poetry.* **Hannah Howard,** who lives in Brooklyn, New York, cites Dr. Seuss, Shel Silverstein, Paul Laurence Dunbar, Pablo Neruda, Chester Himes, Ntozake Shange, and Maya Angelou as her primary influences. **Thomas C. Howell IV** was born and raised in Great Falls, Montana. He currently lives in Pittsburgh where he is at work on a doctorate degree in psychology. **Anasuya Isaacs** is a poet and playwright who was the poetry editor of *Authentic.* **Honorée Fanonne Jeffers,** who teaches at Talladega College, is a Cave Canem fellow and author of *The Gospel of Barbecue,* winner of the Wick Poetry First Book Series prize, selected by National Book Award winner Lucille Clifton. **Jemeni** is a performance poet who has performed in Toronto, Montreal, Ottawa, Detroit, New York, and New Jersey. **Tyehimba Jess** is the author of *when niggas love Revolution like they love the bulls.* **Jacqueline Johnson** is the author of *A Gathering of Mother Tongues* and *Stokely Carmichael: The Story of Black Power.* **Lynne d Johnson,** an editor and columnist at *BlackPlanet.com,* is also a performance poet and professor at the College of Mount Saint Vincent. **Gary Johnston,** publisher of Blind Beggar Press, is the co-editor of *New Rain.* Poet and playwright **Patricia Spears Jones** is the author of *The Weather That Kills.* **A. Van Jordan,** a Cave Canem fellow and the author of *Rise,* teaches in the undergraduate Writing Department at Warren Wilson College. Poet and activist **June Jordan** is the author of over thirty books of poetry and prose, the most recent of which is a memoir, *Soldier: A Poet's Childhood.* **Allison Joseph,** an editor of *Crab Orchard Review,* is the author of *In Every Seam, Soul Train,* and *What Keeps Us Here.* **Nwenna Kai,** co-founder of the Arts collective Ink & Image Productions, is an M.F.A. candidate in the Creative Writing Program at the School of the Art Institute of Chicago. **Gylan Kain,** an original member of The Last Poets, currently lives in the Netherlands. **Layding Lumumba Kaliba** is the poetry editor of *African Voices* literary magazine and the author of several volumes of poetry, including *Up on the Down Side, Still Outraged, The Moon Is My Witness,* and *African Spirits & Anthems*. Poet and political activist **Eliot Katz** is co-founder of the literary magazine *Longshot* and the author of *Space: And Other Poems, Unlocking the Exits* and co-editor of *Poems for the Nation.* **Douglas Kearney** was born in Brooklyn, New York, raised in Altadena, California, attended Howard University in Washington, D.C., and currently lives in Minneapolis. **Nzadi Z. Keita,** who teaches creative writing at Ursinus College and conducts writing workshops for the Geraldine R. Dodge Foundation, is the author of *Birthmarks*. **Atiba Kwabena** is director of the poetry and jazz ensemble Songhai Djeli. He has produced several audio tapes and CDs, and has been published in *New Rain*. **Michael C. Ladd,** the producer of several spoken word CDs, including *Easy Listening for Armageddon,* has appeared in *Aloud, In Defense of Mumia, Swing Low,* and frequently performs in Europe. **Jacqueline Jones LaMon** is a Cave Canem fellow and a member of the faculty at Antelope Valley College, Lancaster, California. **Quraysh Ali Lansana,** former poetry editor for *Black Issues Book Review,* is the author of *southside rain* and co-editor of *Role Call: A Generational Anthology of Social and Political Black Literature & Art.* Elder poet **Paul Laraque** is a Haitian exile from the Papa Doc regime. He has been consistently writing and publishing for the last forty years. **Staci Lightburn**'s work appears in *In Defense of Mumia* and *2000—Here's to Humanity.* **Lindamichellebaron** has a Ph.D. in Cross Categorical Studies from Columbia University's Teacher's College. As president of Harlin Jacque Publications, a publishing and consulting company, she developed the program Driving the Dream: Language-Driven Believing and Achieving. **Pedro López-Adorno,** a professor of Puerto Rican Studies and Latino Literature at Hunter College (City University of New York [CUNY]), is a poet, novelist, literary critic, and anthologist. *Rapto continuo* is the most recent of his ten publications. **esther Louise,** whose work has been anthologized in *New Rain,* among other publications, has studied under poet Quincy Troupe. **Candice Nicole Love** is a doctoral candidate in English at the University of North Carolina at Chapel Hill. Her work appears in *Essential Love.* **Carmen D. Lucca** has published consistently for twenty years. She was the first to translate a full volume of work by Julio de Burgos, *Roses in the Mirror.* Poet, activist, and professor **Haki R. Madhubuti,** publisher of Third World Press, is one of the major poets of the Black Arts Movement. His many volumes of work include *Claiming Earth, Heartlove,* and *Groundwork.* **Julia Maier** is a poet and graphic artist. She has recently edited, co-illustrated (with Elí Alvarado), and designed a children's book, *Maboití,* by Carmen D. Lucca. **devorah major** is the author of *Street Smarts, An Open Weave,* and *Traveling Women* (with Opal Palmer Adisa). **Mariposa,** whose given name is Maria Fernandez, is co-producer and co-host, with her fraternal twin, Maribel, of Sol in El Barrio, a weekly performance venue. Her work has appeared in *Drumvoices Revue* and *El Centro.* **Derrin Maxwell,** who has a degree in African Studies from the State University of New York at Stony Brook, has read his work at Cornell University, The New School for Social Research, and the University of New Haven. Philadelphia born **Deirdre May,** who lives and works in New York City, is currently at work on a children's book. **Shara McCallum,** who teaches at the University of Memphis, is a fiction editor of *Obsidian III* and the author of *The Water between Us.* Poet, critic, and literary organizer **C. Leigh McInnis,** who teaches at Jackson State University, is a prolific author whose many books include *Masters of Reality* and *The Lyrics of Prince.* **Ken McManus**'s work appears in *Lynx Eye, Urban Spaghetti,* and *In the Company of Rogues.* **Jesús Papoleto Meléndez,** one of the original Nuyorican poets, is the author of several volumes of poetry and plays, including *The Junkie Stole the Clock* and *Concertos on Market Street.* Poet and playwright **Nancy Mercado** is a professor at Boricua College in New York City, editor-in-chief of *Long Shot,* and the author of *It Concerns the Madness.* Performance poet **Tom Mitchelson,** who comes out of Gylain Kain's Holy Ghost Fallout Shelter, is the founding member of the Calabash Poets Workshop and New Renaissance Writers. His fiction has been dramatized on radio and published in several anthologies. A 2000 Hurston/Wright Foundation Fellow, **Kamilah Aisha Moon**'s work appears in *The Black Arts Quarterly of Stanford University, Obsidian III,* and *Bittersweet.* **Jessica Care Moore,** publisher of Moore Black Press, is the author of *The Words Don't Fit in My Mouth.* Poet, mentor, and haiku master **Lenard D. Moore,** founder and executive director of the Carolina African American Writers Collective, is the author of *The Open Eye, Forever Home,* and *Desert Storm.* **Malkia M'Buzi Moore,** poet and oral historian, is the author of *Sunstones* and *Mask;* she has also served as an editor of *New Rain.* **Tufara Waller Muhammad,** a student at Philander Smith College, is the host of *Sankofa Sessions,* a weekly radio show on KABF 88.3 Community Radio in Little Rock, Arkansas. **Jennifer Murphy**'s work appears in *Excess Compassion* magazine, *Inkwell Magazine,* and the recording *Leomoon.* **Lenina Nadal** is a poet, activist, and graduate of Hunter College (CUNY) whose work appears in *In Defense of Mumia.* **Kelly Elaine Navies** is a poet, teacher, and oral historian, currently at work on a doctorate in American history at the University of North Carolina at Chapel Hill. Her work appears in *June Jordan's Poetry for the People* and *Drumvoices Revue.* **Letta Neely** is the author of *Juba.* Her work appears in several anthologies, including *Catch the Fire.* **Zizwe Ngafua,** co-founder of the Calabash Poets Workshop and the short-lived Black Writers Union, was the author of many books, including *Blacks, Whites and the Blues*; *Nommo*; *Roots Run Deep*; and *Talkin' Chattahoochee.* **Ngoma,** a former member of Spirit House Movers and Serious Bizness, is a performance poet, multi-instrumentalist, singer–song writer, and producer of the spoken word CD, *Paradigm Shiftin' (ancient-future).* **Lissette Norman,** whose work has appeared in *Moving Beyond Boundaries,* lives and works in Staten Island, New York. **Chioma Okereke,** who was born in Benin, Nigeria, currently lives in London, England. **Sharon Olinka** is the author of *A Face Not My Own.* **Abiodun Oyewole** is an original member of The Last Poets. He is co-author, with Umar Bin Hassan, of *On a Mission: The Last Poets: Selected Poems and a History of The Last Poets.* **Ebony Page** has released a maxi-single, *my lil black book,* and has published in *Nature's Echoes Anthology, 2000 Edition.*

Gregory Pardlo, an associate editor of *Painted Bride Quarterly,* teaches at New York University and John Jay College. A Cave Canem fellow, he is currently completing an MFA at NYU as a *New York Times* Fellow in poetry. **Lucy Partlow** is a poet based in Baltimore, Maryland. **G. E. Patterson,** a Cave Canem fellow, is the author of *Tug.* **Raymond R. Patterson** was professor emeritus at City College (CUNY). He is the author of *26 Ways of Looking at a Black Man and Elemental Blues.* **Fredrica Africa Payne** was the founder and creative director of Lovetalk! Her poems and stories have appeared in various publications, including *The Black American, African Voices,* and *Essence.* **Lisa Pegram** is a poet, teacher, and vocalist whose work appears in the CD compilation that honors the late Dr. Betty Shabazz, *Strength of a Woman.* **Willie Perdomo,** whose work appears in several anthologies, including *In the Tradition, Aloud, In Defense of Mumia,* and *Step into a World,* is the author of *Where a Nickel Costs a Dime.* **Liza Jessie Peterson** is an actor, monologist, and performance poet. **Thien-bao Thuc Phi,** poet, activist, and hip-hop head, was born in Sai Gon, Vietnam, shortly before its fall. A Vietnamese American refugee, he was raised in Minneapolis's infamous Phillips neighborhood. **Pedro Pietri,** poet and playwright, is the author of *Puerto Rican Obituary, Traffic Violations, The Masses Are Asses,* and *Illusions of a Revolving Door.* **Pamela Plummer,** the 1998 recipient of the Hughes, Diop, Knight Award for Poetry from the Gwendolyn Brooks Center in Chicago, is a poet and social worker whose work has appeared in *Drumvoices Revue, Eyeball,* and *Warpland.* **Aarian Pope** is the author of *Painting Windows Big Enough to Climb Through* and appears on Koffee Brown's album, *Mars/Venus.* **Kevin Powell,** poet, journalist, curator, and lecturer, is the author of *In the Tradition, recognize, Keepin' It Real,* and *Step into a World.* **Rohan B Preston,** poet and theater critic, is the author of *Dreams in Soy Sauce* and co-editor of *Soulfires: Young Black Men on Love and Violence.* **Howard Rambsy II,** who has appeared in *The Richard Wright Newsletter* and *Step into a World,* is currently a graduate fellow in the American and African American Literature Program at Pennsylvania State University. **Dudley Randall** was the preeminent publisher of the Black Arts Movement with his Broadside Press out of Detroit. Randall was a librarian as well as a publisher and poet. His books include *More to Remember* and *After the Killing.* **Eugene B. Redmond,** poet, activist, and archivist, is the author of many books, including the seminal *Drumvoices* and *Eye in the Ceiling.* **Glenis Redmond,** author of *Backbone,* appears in *Obsidian II, Catch the Fire,* and *Poetry Slam.* **DJ Renegade,** poet, deejay, computer consultant, and Cave Canem fellow, is the author of *Shades of Blue.* **A. Wanjiku H. Reynolds** is the author of *Cognac & Collard Greens.* **Wendell Ricketts,** author of *Lesbian and Gay Men as Foster Parents,* earned an MFA in Creative Writing from the University of New Mexico. His poem, "Elegy for Matthew Shepard," was nominated for a Pushcart Prize. **Tomás Riley,** a member of San Diego's poetry and music collective, the Taco Shop Poets, is a professor of English and Chicano Studies. **Andrea Roberts** is a journalist, Black feminist, and Vassar graduate whose work has appeared in several publications, including *Poet on Watch, The Curbside Review,* and *The Gaither Reporter.* Performance poet **Aidé Rodriguez,** holds a B.A. in History and Sociology from the University of Michigan. **John Rodriguez** is a student at Lehman College (CUNY), in the Bronx, New York, where he teaches poetry to young people. **Luis J. Rodriguez,** founding publisher of Tia Chucha Press and co-founder of Tia Chucha's Café Cultural in Los Angeles, is the author of *Trochemoche, Always Running,* and *It Doesn't Have to Be This Way.* **Steven Bonafide Rojas** is a poet, photographer, and musician from the South Bronx and has a role in *Role Call.* Poet and activist **Kate Rushin,** author of the poem that gave the classic anthology *This Bridge Called My Back* its title, is also the author of the poetry collection, *The Black Back-Ups.* **Carl Hancock Rux** is the author of *Pagan Operetta* and the spoken word/music CD, *Rux Revue.* Black Arts poet and playwright **Kalamu ya Salaam,** co-founding publisher and editor of Runagate Press and the leader of the WordBand, a poetry performance ensemble, is co-editor of the anthologies, *Fertile Ground, Speak Truth to the People* and *360°—A Revolution of Black Poets.* He is also a founder of NOMMO Literary Society in New Orleans. **Kiini Ibura Salaam,** a member of the Red Clay Collective, has appeared in several publications, including *Essence, Anansi,* and *Dark Eros.* **Tijan M. Sallah** holds a Ph.D. in economics. The author of several books, including *Before the Earth,* his work has also appeared in *Step into a World.* **Benjamin Theolonius Sanders** is a performance poet based in Memphis. **Tanai Sanders,** whose work appears in *Quiet Storm: Voices of Young Black Poets,* is the poetry editor of *horizonMag.com.* **Michele Serros** is the author of *Chicana Falsa: And Other Stories of Death, Identity, & Oxnard* and *How to Be a Chicana Role Model.* **Kadija Sesay,** the director of the independent press, SAKS Publications, is co-editor of *IC3: The Penguin Book of New Black Writing in Britain.* **Assata Shakur,** also known as JoAnne Chesimard, is a former member of the Black Liberation Army who escaped from prison after being framed (and nearly killed) for allegedly killing a New Jersey state trooper. She has been forced to live in exile in Cuba for over twenty-five years. She tells her story in *Assata: An Autobiography.* **Jackie Sheeler** is the publisher of *poetz.com* and editor of a forthcoming anthology of poems written by and about the police. **Nichole L. Shields,** author of *One Less Road to Travel,* has appeared in *The Iowa Review, Nexus,* and *360°—A Revolution of Black Poets.* **Evie Shockley,** author of *The Gorgon Goddess,* has appeared in *Catch the Fire, Jane's Stories, Callaloo, Obsidian III, Blue Mesa Review,* and the *North American Review.* **Danny Shot,** an English teacher at A. Philip Randolph High School, is co-founder and publisher of *Long Shot* literary magazine, as well as Long Shot Productions, an independent press. Poet and musician **Sharrif Simmons** is the author of *Fast Cities & Objects That Burn.* **Beau Sia** is the author of *A Night without Armor II: The Revenge.* Poet and journalist **Patricia Smith** is the author of *Life According to Motown; Big Towns, Big Talk;* and *Close to Death.* **folade mondisa speaks,** a poet and painter who is currently an M.F.A. candidate in the Creative Writing Program at the School of the Art Institute of Chicago, has been published in *Nexus, Mad River Anthology, Milk* magazine, and *Shadetree.* **Lamont B. Steptoe,** poet, photographer, and Vietnam veteran, is a prolific author whose books include *America's Mourning/Morning, Mad Minute, Crimson River,* and *Uncle's South China Sea Blue Nightmare.*

Patrick Sylvain, a former member of the Dark Room Collective, has appeared in numerous publications, including *In the Tradition, Callaloo, The Butterfly's Way, Step into a World,* and *Keeping Track.* **George Edward Tait,** central to the post Black Arts Movement in New York City via his Afrikan Functional Theater, is the author of *At War* and *At Arms.* **Mariahadessa Ekere Tallie**'s work is featured in the anthologies *Catch the Fire!!!* and *Listen Up!* Poet and photographer **Cheryl Boyce Taylor** is the proud mother of Phife, from a Tribe Called Quest, and the author of *Raw Air* and *Night when Moon Follows.* **Mervyn Taylor** is the author of *An Island of His Own* and *The Goat.* **Sheree Renée Thomas,** publisher of *Anansi: Fiction of the African Diaspora* and editor of *Dark Matter,* is a poet and fiction writer whose work appears in *Drumvoices Revue, Obsidian III, Role Call,* and *Black Renaissance.* **Imani Tolliver**'s work appears in *Step into a World.* **Nancy D. Tolson,** a professor of Black children's literature at Illinois State University, is the author of *Tales of Africa.* **Edwin Torres** is an avant garde performance poet whose published work includes *Fractured Humorous,* a volume of poetry; *Onomalingua—Noise Songs and Poetry,* an e-book; and *Holy Kid,* a spoken word CD. **Askia M. Touré,** a major poet of the Black Arts Movement, is the author of *From the Pyramids to the Projects: Poems of Genocide and Resistance* and *Dawnsong!: The Epic Memory of Askia Touré.* **Tanya Tyler** is a performance poet and a producer of jazz poetry programs for WKCR FM at Columbia University. She's been published consistently in the *New Rain* series. Poet **Lyrae Van Clief-Stefanon,** a Cave Canem fellow, is featured in *Role Call, If the Drum Is a Woman,* and *Keeping Track,* and is currently at work on a biography. **Marco Villalobos** is a Chicano poet and journalist from Los Angeles transplanted in New York City illy style. You can peep another one of his joints in *Step into a World.* Poet and artist **Jamila Z. Wade,** a graduate of Spelman College, is in a master's program at Harvard Graduate School of Education. Her work has appeared in *Focus, Spelman's Literary Magazine,* and on *poetry.com.* **Brenda Walcott,** a member of Umbra, is a poet and playwright whose work appears in *In Defense of Mumia.* **Margaret Walker,** a preeminent poet, novelist, scholar, and political activist whose work, which spanned six decades, influenced generations. Her many works include *Jubilee, For My People, This Is My Century: New and Collected Poems,* and *On Being Female, Black, and Free: Essays by Margaret Walker, 1932–1996.* **Michael Warr,** former executive director of the Guild Complex, is the author of *We Are All the Black Boy.* Poet, playwright, and mentor **Afaa M. Weaver,** editor of *Obsidian III: Literature in the African Diaspora,* is a prolific poet whose books include *Multitudes: Poems Selected and New, Sandy Point,* and *The Ten Lights of God.* **Joe Weil,** a widely published poet and editor and director of the Poetswednesday series, is the author of several publications, including *A Portable Winter.* **Marvin K. White** is the author of the poetry collection *last rights.* **Jack Wiler,** a former editor of *Long Shot,* is the author of *I Have No Clue.* **Benin Williams** is a filmmaker, poet, essayist, and teacher who has earned an M.F.A. in film production from the School of Cinema-Television at the University of Southern California. **Karen Williams,** whose work has appeared in *Catch the Fire* and *Spirit & Flame,* is a Cave Canem fellow and a member of the Detroit Writer's Guild. **Kimmika L. H. Williams** is a professor in the Theater Department at Temple University. Her work has appeared in several publications, including *Erotique Noire, New Black Poetry, Say That the River Returns,* and *Concerned Poets on the Move.* **Treasure Williams,** daughter of legendary poet-archivist Eugene Redmond, is a poet, writer, and educator. Her work has appeared in *Obsidian III, Drumvoices Revue* (as guest regional editor for Memphis), as well as the recordings, *Drop the Axxe* and *Treasure.* **Ted Wilson** is a jazz poet dating back to the Black Arts Movement. His work has been anthologized in *Black Fire, In Defense of Mumia,* and *New Rain.* **Marvin X,** a major poet and playwright of the Black Arts Movement, is the author of *Love & War,* and founder of the Recovery Theater. **Chong Xiong,** a first-generation Hmong Asian American, is currently an English major at the University of Minnesota, Twin Cities, focusing on creative writing and the literature of American writers of color. New Orleans poet **Ahmos Zu-Bolton II,** currently a Visiting Writer in the Black Studies Program at the University of Missouri, Columbia, is a poet and playwright whose many books include *Ain't No Spring Chicken, Selected Poems.*

PERMISSIONS

ABOUT THE AUTHORS

TONY MEDINA is a poet, professor, and activist. He has taught at Long Island University's Brooklyn campus, Borough of Manhattan Community College, and New York University. The author of ten books, including *DeShawn Days, Love to Langston,* and *Role Call: A Generational Anthology of Social and Political Black Literature & Art,* his poetry, fiction, and essays appear in over twenty anthologies and two CD compilations. His anthology, *In Defense of Mumia* (edited with veteran activist S. E. Anderson) received the American Booksellers Association's first Firecracker Alternative Book Award in the category of poetry. Named by *Writer's Digest* as one of ten poets to watch in the new millennium, Medina was born in the South Bronx and currently lives in Harlem.

Poet-essayist **LOUIS REYES RIVERA** is a professor of Pan African, Caribbean, Puerto Rican, and African American history and literature who has taught at SUNY @ Stony Brook, Hunter College, Pratt Institute, College of New Rochelle, etc. The recipient of over 20 citations, including a 1986 Special Congressional Recognition Award for his work as an activist poet, Rivera is viewed by many as a living bridge between African and Latino Americans. His book, *Scattered Scripture,* earned him the Latin American Writers Institute's 1997 Poetry Prize and confirmed why he is called the Janitor of History. In addition to lectures and solos, he also works with jazz bands, including Ahmed Abdullah's Diaspora, the Sun Ra All-Star Project, and his own group of poets/musicians, The Jazzoets, regularly appearing at Sistas' Place in Brooklyn.

About Def Poetry Jam
DEF POETRY JAM is a multimedia poetry project launched by executive producers Bruce George, Danny Simmons, and Deborah Pointer, and sponsored by Russell Simmons. For more information about the Def Poetry Jam Project, visit their website www.defpoetryjam.com.